1.00

Studying God's Word

Book E

– Second Edition –

A Chronological Study

of the Old Testament from

Genesis to Ruth

Darrel A. Trulson

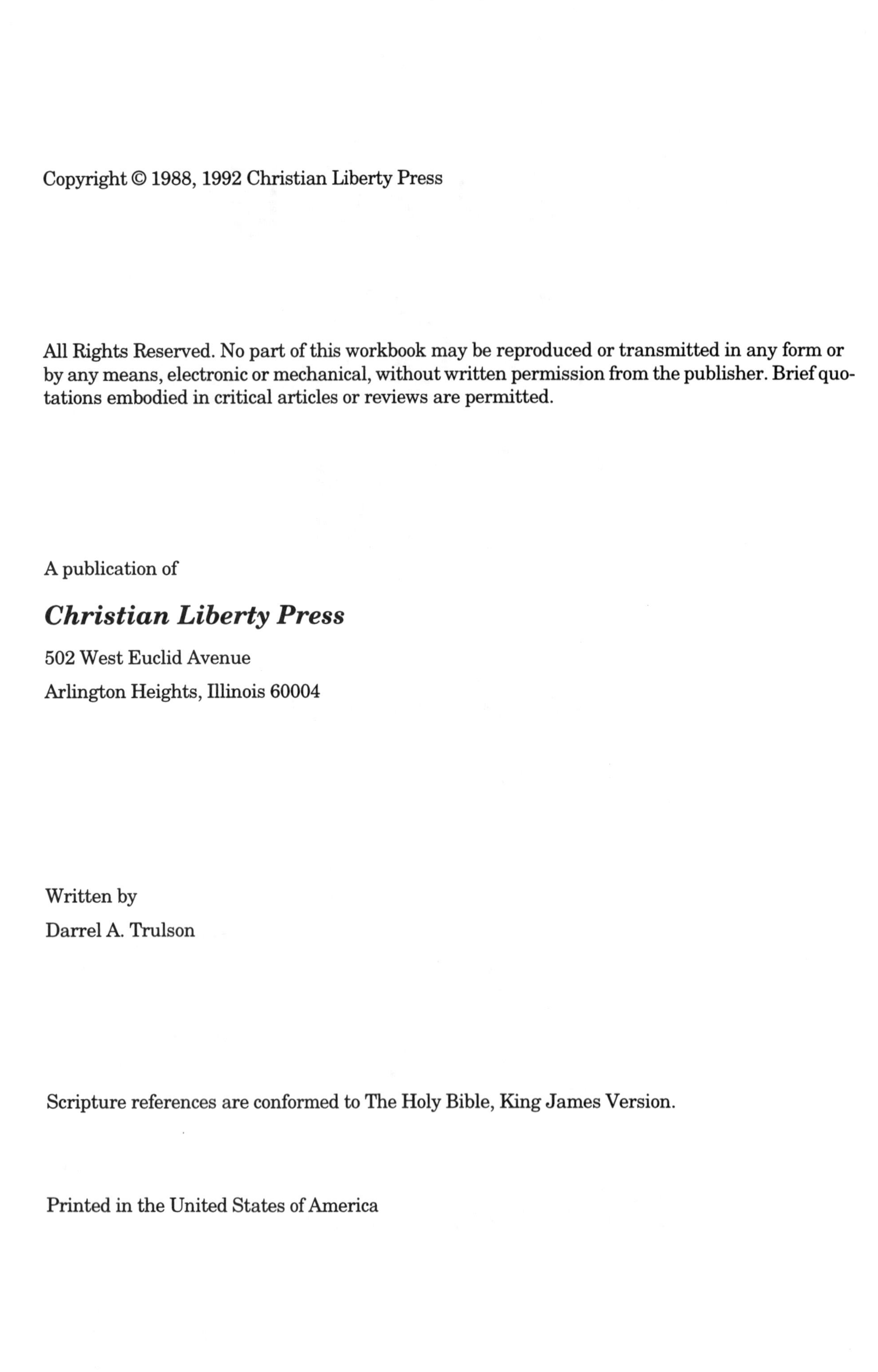

A publication of

Christian Liberty Press

502 West Euclid Avenue

Arlington Heights, Illinois 60004

Written by

Darrel A. Trulson

Scripture references are conformed to The Holy Bible, King James Version.

Printed in the United States of America

To my wife Debbie,

without whose vision

this dream never would

have become a reality.

Table of Contents

Table of Contents

Acknowledgments

When working on a project of this scope, there are inevitably many people to thank. As the *Studying God's Word* series grows and matures, I am continually brought to terms with my own inadequacies, not only as a writer but as a person. Were it not for the love, support, and encouragement of my friends and colleagues, these books would never be written. So to everyone who has not only stood with me, but also been an integral and necessary part of this project, I give you my deepest and warmest heart-felt thanks.

Many thanks to Mike McHugh for his invaluable friendship, direction, and guidance; Paul Lindstrom for his cooperation and understanding; Lois Tuck, Mabel Howard, and Scripture Press Publications for allowing me to use their illustrations; Steve Oleksy for his art work and creative talent; Terry Hall for his encouragement and guidance; Dave Cole, Eileen Vogel, Beth Roos, Sherri Carlton, Dave Smith, and Pat Taborsky, for their positive critique and comments during the editing, reviewing, and rewriting of this text.

Thanks to Dad and Mom, and to Don and Betty Dyson for their love and encouragement. Thank you for being there when the waters were both calm and rough.

A special thanks to the whole cast and crew of the CLASS Enrollment & Finance and Shipping & Receiving Departments, which would include Cheryl, Carla, Susan, Lina, Elizabeth, Sherri, Cherie, Nancy, Leila, Marie, Cindy, Jeff, Bob, Doug, Mike, Mac, Mike, and Al. Your patience and cooperation have been greatly appreciated. Thank you for doing your jobs so well that my job could be easier. Thank you for being the rack upon which I can hang my hats. More than ever, thank you for your support.

Many thanks to Peter Rubel, who sacrificially gave of his time, talent, and energy to make sure that this text was properly written and edited. Your contributions insured that the sum of this book would be greater than its parts. Your friendship, strength, and support are greatly appreciated.

Acknowledgments

I especially want to thank Eric Pfeiffelman, who along with many other responsibilities, took the time necessary to typeset and polish the final format for this book. Your dedication, commitment, and creative genius are greatly appreciated. Thank you for all your help and for the lunches at Jimmy's.

Since this is the second edition of *Studying God's Word Book E*, I especially want to thank all the families who purchased and used the first edition, thereby making this update possible. Back in 1988-1989 when this book was originally written, it was not only the first book that I had done, but also one of the first that Christian Liberty had produced and published. By God's grace the content was sound, but since Christian Liberty decided to re-typeset the book, I decided to rework and make changes to the lessons. Overall I would say that sixty percent of the book has been changed or is unique to the second edition. This is evidenced not only in the lessons, but also in the graphics and Supplemental Exercises. I am confident that the content and the visual appeal of this text is greatly enhanced. I sincerely hope that you enjoy this book as much as I enjoyed producing it.

Finally, I want to thank my wife Debbie, and my five children, Derek, Daniel, Joshua, Michael, and Lauren for their love, patience, and understanding. My love for you grows with each and every passing day. Thank you for being there by my side, helping me to maintain my perspective, and forgiving me when I fail.

Most of all, thank you to the Lord Jesus, through Whom everything is possible. God bless us all.

Preface

One of the primary goals of the *Studying God's Word* series is to encourage students to conform their thinking to the standard of God's revealed Word. When students begin to bring every one of their thoughts into captivity to God's Word, they begin to realize the joy of being conformed to the image of Jesus Christ.

In this series, a strong emphasis is placed on the need for young people to develop strong Christian character traits. Students are not only presented with important facts and truths from the Bible, they are also provided with a wealth of personal examples from the lives of God's people that illustrate the truths they need to comprehend.

In addition, this series utilizes a chronological approach to Bible study so young people can better understand the timing and order of the key events listed throughout Scripture. This approach permits students to gain an accurate understanding of the flow of events contained in the Bible.

It has often been said that "these are the times that try men's souls." Modern American culture is confronting God's people, both young and old alike, with many challenging trials and temptations. More than ever before, young people need to be equipped with the whole armor of God's Word so they can withstand the fiery darts of the wicked one. May the Lord use this Bible Study series to equip his children with the spiritual weapons that they need to fight the good fight of faith.

Michael J. McHugh
Curriculum Director

Dr. Paul D. Lindstrom
Superintendent of Schools

How to Use This Book

If you are like most people, you may forget to read the instructions or directions for something until you are half finished with it, and then discover you did something wrong. In order to understand this book and learn the most from it, **please read this section first!**

There are several types of learning tools woven into this book; each has a specific intention and purpose. The main body of the book consists of Bible lessons. These are taken exclusively from the first half of the Old Testament. Each lesson begins with a time line and the words "You Are Here," indicating the approximate historical location of the story taught in the lesson. The time line is presented in an effort to tie together the stories that take place within the Bible. A complete presentation of the time line is given in Appendix A. Within the time line, significant Biblical characters are given a date line which represents their life span. Numbers next to their names indicate the number of years they lived. The boxes within the time line represent specific individuals and the number of years they ruled over the Israelites.

There will be slight differences of opinion regarding the dates on the time line. Because of the nature of the Old Testament, it is often difficult to ascertain the exact date each event took place. For example, we know that Abraham lived around 2100 B.C., but we do not know exactly when. Please explain to your student that like any good Bible study book, the information is presented only as a guide and is not inspired. Only the Word of God is inspired.

Following the time line, the lesson will contain the goal, background text, and memory verse. The student is to read the background text before continuing with the lesson. It is up to the individual teacher to decide if the memory verse is to be learned for each lesson. All memory verses, lessons, and questions have been taken from the King James Version of the Bible, unless otherwise noted.

Each lesson will contain a few paragraphs in which the author suggests some principles from the text and applications for the student. This is followed by several questions covering the background reading, thought questions, and lesson review questions. Some lessons will have Supplemental Exercises for the student to do.

The Thought Questions are intended to be both difficult and challenging for the student. There may be times when they will not apply directly to your child; or you may find some questions to be inappropriate. In these instances, the question may be omitted. If the student feels more comfortable, he may answer the thought questions orally instead of writing his responses in the book. The purpose of these questions is not to embarrass anyone, but to encourage the reader to think about the truths of God's Word, and then to apply them directly to his life.

Additional sections of this book contain Map Studies, Unit Tests, Book Backgrounds, and other special information. The Map Studies attempt to point out the significant geographical locations in the Old Testament. Oftentimes, in order to have the proper Biblical understanding of a story, it is helpful to see where a place is located on a map.

Unit Tests should be taken without the help of this book, the Bible, or any outside source. Teachers should pretest their student before giving him the Unit Tests. It is recommended to review using similar, but not identical, questions to those in the tests. The purpose of this section is to help the teacher judge how much the student has learned. Please review those areas of your child's test answers in which you find weaknesses. Mastery of the material is important. The questions in the Unit Test will only cover the subject matter presented in that unit.

Each Old Testament book will have a background section which will explain the individual characteristics of each book. These are factual presentations of the unique material in each book. Although there are no questions in this section, they still need to be studied and understood. The Lesson Review questions cover information from the Book Backgrounds.

As you work through these lessons with your child, you will not only discover the joy there is in studying God's Word, but that your student will have many difficult questions which this book does not address or that you are not prepared to answer. As time permits, consult commentaries, Bible dictionaries, Bible encyclopedias, and other kinds of reference material at your disposal. The information gained from these sources will be invaluable to you as you address the difficult questions that arise.

The bibliography in the back of this book contains a listing of reference material that you should consider adding to your personal library. These tools will prove to be very beneficial as you pursue an understanding of the Holy Scriptures. "Study to show thyself approved unto God, a workman that needeth not to be ashamed, rightly dividing the Word of truth" (II Timothy 2:15).

Regrettably, time and space do not allow us to cover the whole Bible in this book. The Old Testament is presented in *Studying God's Word Book E* and *Studying God's Word Book F*. The Gospels and the life of Christ are reviewed in *Studying God's Word Book G*. The book of Acts is taught in *Studying God's Word Book H*. The rest of the New Testament will be covered in subsequent volumes of this series.

The goal and purpose of this book comes directly from Joshua 1:8: "This book of the Law shall not depart out of thy mouth; but thou shalt meditate therein day and night, that thou mayest observe to do according to all that is written therein: for then thou shalt make thy way prosperous, and then thou shalt have good success." It is the sincere hope of the author and all those at Christian Liberty who were involved in this project that God will use this book as a tool in the spiritual instruction and guidance of your child. May the Lord grant you wisdom and grace as you seek to raise your child in the truths and principles of His Word.

Let us not forget that our greatest testimony and witness is to our own children and family.

Introduction to the Chronological Method of Bible Study

Welcome to one of the most important discoveries you will ever make, the discovery of God's Word. Throughout your life, you will have the opportunity to study the Bible. Each time you do, the Holy Spirit will be there to guide and direct your thoughts to help you learn and grow in the Lord Jesus Christ. It is the hope and prayer of everyone involved in producing this book that through your study you will grow in the wisdom and understanding of God (Ephesians 1:17-19).

In order to make studying the Bible more interesting and beneficial, this book is written to follow the Old Testament in a Historical – Chronological pattern. We believe it is of utmost importance to the student that as he studies the Bible, he will understand how all the separate stories and books fit together. Imagine a large jigsaw puzzle of a beautiful mountain village. If you were to take a few pieces from different points and study them individually, could you understand what the complete picture was? Of course not. You need to see all the pieces in the correct pattern in order to understand the "big picture." The Bible is the same way. If all we do is read one story here and another one there, we will not understand the true meaning of God's Word. We have to look at the Bible completely and study it as one unit in order to understand God's "big picture."

Throughout this book, besides studying significant stories of the Old Testament, there will also be background information to each of the books as they appear in chronological order. This is available as helpful material so you can further understand the events that happen within the Bible itself.

At the end of this introduction, there is a complete listing of the Old Testament books in chronological order. Please study and memorize this chart so you can later complete the blanks when

a particular section is being reviewed. On the chart, the top line of blocks contain the eleven main books of the Old Testament, which include most of the stories and themes presented. Although the focus of our study will be in these eleven books, the other twenty-eight books will be mentioned and included to give you a true feeling for the flow of history that is recorded in the Bible.

The second row of boxes also represents the historical books of the Old Testament. These are not included in the first row because they do not chart the main flow of history, but rather provide details to what was taking place in the Old Testament at that time. For example, II Chronicles adds details to the events and stories presented in I and II Kings.

The third horizontal group of boxes includes Job, Psalms, Proverbs, Ecclesiastes, and the Song of Solomon. This group represents the poetic section of the Old Testament. Job is offset from the rest of the books of poetry because it was written much earlier, during the times of the Patriarchs.

The final block of boxes represents the minor prophets which were written during three basic time periods. The first group was written before the Babylonian captivity. The second group was written during the Babylonian captivity. The third group was written after the Babylonian captivity. The boxes for the minor prophets also indicate to which nation or group of people the book was originally written.

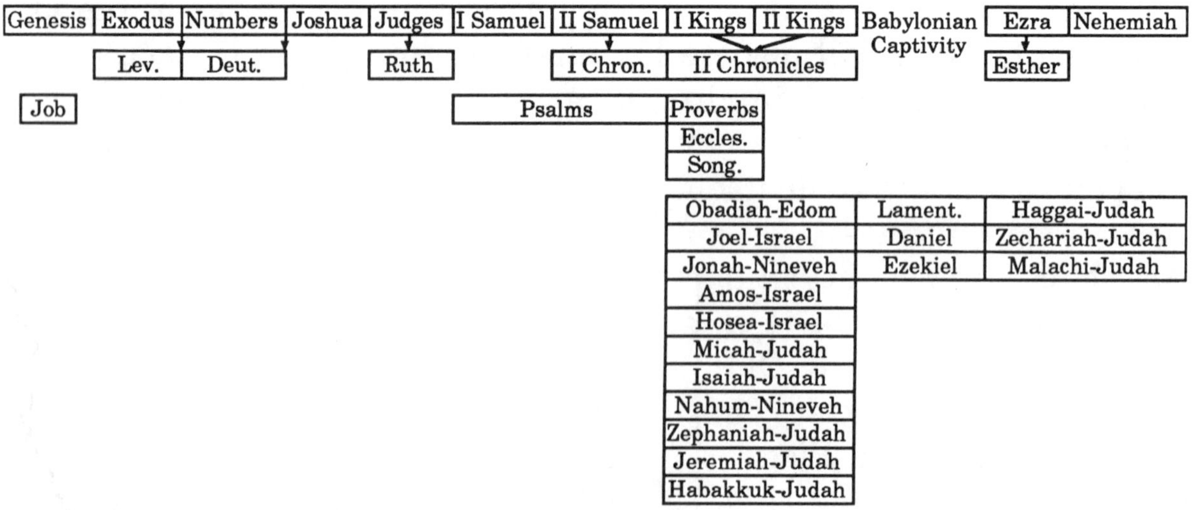

Genesis | Exodus | Numbers | Joshua | Judges | I Samuel | II Samuel | I Kings | II Kings | Babylonian Captivity | Ezra | Nehemiah

Lev. | Deut. | Ruth | I Chron. | II Chronicles | Esther

Job | Psalms | Proverbs | Eccles. | Song.

Obadiah-Edom	Lament.	Haggai-Judah
Joel-Israel	Daniel	Zechariah-Judah
Jonah-Nineveh	Ezekiel	Malachi-Judah
Amos-Israel		
Hosea-Israel		
Micah-Judah		
Isaiah-Judah		
Nahum-Nineveh		
Zephaniah-Judah		
Jeremiah-Judah		
Habakkuk-Judah		

The Creation
Lesson #1

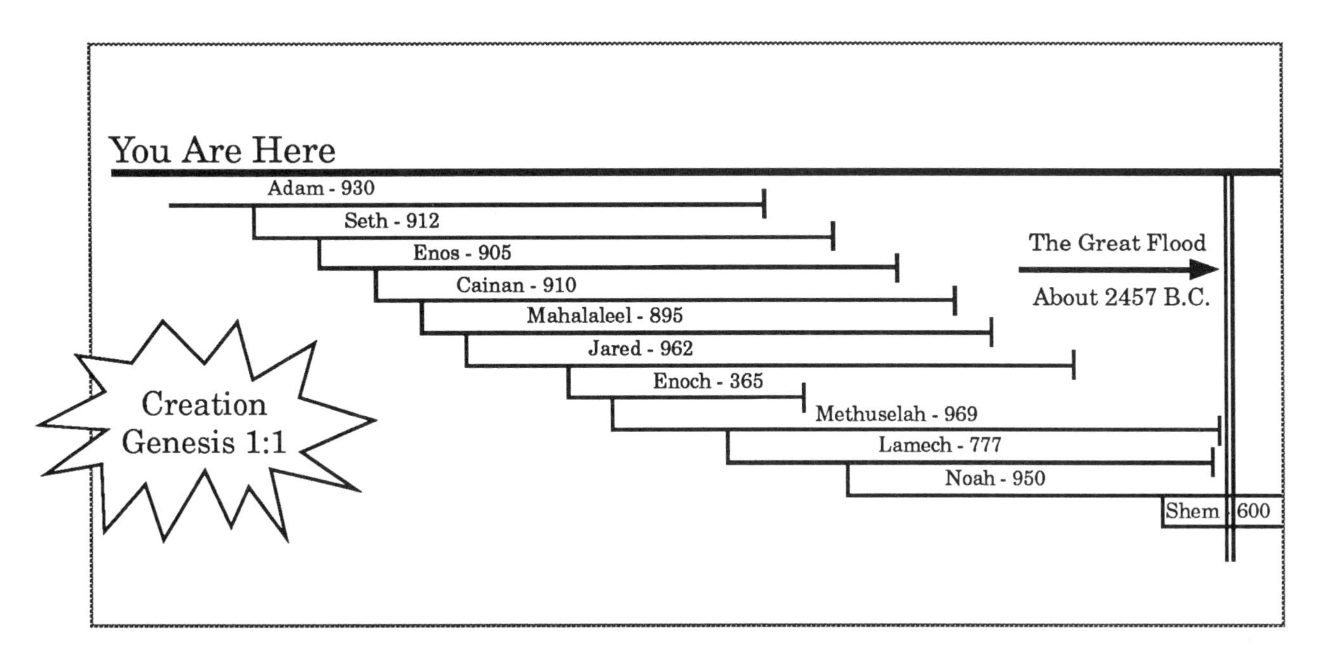

Lesson Goal: To understand that man was created in the image of God.

Background Text: Genesis 1-2

Memory Verse: In the beginning God created the heaven and the earth. Genesis 1:1

This is a very beautiful and great world in which we live. It extends much further than we can see, further indeed than we can even think. Have you ever examined the night sky and tried to count the stars, or walked along the beach and guessed how many grains of sand were under your feet? Have you ever sat under a shady tree and made pictures out of the big, fluffy clouds that drifted by? When we look at the world it seems big compared to our small bodies. However, that does not make us any less important to God.

We are special to God because Genesis 1:26 says, "Let us make man in our image, after our likeness." Do you know what "image" means in this verse? "Image" means that man was created in the likeness of God: to rule creation, to be intelligent, and to have a personality; but most importantly, man was created to have a soul. Man is different from the plants, animals, or any other created thing, because he has a soul. With our souls we can trust, worship, and glorify God.

Ephesians 1:4 explains that God chose us before the foundation of the world. It is amazing to think that God knew everything about us even before heaven and earth were created. God knew what we would like and dislike, what the color of our hair would be, where we would live, and everything else. Since God made us and knows all there is to know about us, we can have confidence that He will guide and protect us. With this understanding we should do all we can to please and glorify our all-knowing Lord.

When God created the universe, He did not labor at it, as we would in building a house. He simply spoke the word and it happened. There are many people today who do not believe in God. They teach that it took billions of years for plants, animals, and humans to evolve and become what they are today. This belief is wrong because the Bible does not teach this. Although we may not understand how it happened, we can believe through faith that our Lord is the creator of the universe and that we were made in His image.

Questions:

1. What did God make in each of the six days of creation?

   Day 1: (Genesis 1:3-5) ______________________________

   ____

   Day 2: (Genesis 1:6-8) ______________________________

   ____

   Day 3: (Genesis 1:9-13) ______________________________

   ____

   ____

   Day 4: (Genesis 1:14-19) ______________________________

   ____

   Day 5: (Genesis 1:20-22) ______________________________

   ____

   ____

   Day 6: (Genesis 1:24-27) ______________________________

   ____

   ____

2. What did God do on the seventh day? (Genesis 2:2-3) ______________

3. What went up from the earth? (Genesis 2:6) ______________

4. What was the name of the garden in which Adam and Eve lived? (Genesis 2:8) ______________

5. What two trees were in the midst of the garden? (Genesis 2:9) ______________

6. What were the names of the four rivers that flowed out of the garden? (Genesis 2:10-14) ______________

7. What was the first job God gave Adam to do? (Genesis 2:15) ______________

8. Of what tree was man not to eat? (Genesis 2:17) ______________

9. Why did God give Adam a helper? (Genesis 2:18-20) ______________

10. What did God take from Adam to make Eve? (Genesis 2:22) ______________

Thought Questions:

1. What does it mean to glorify God? ______________

2. What special talents and abilities do you have that you can use to glorify God? ______________________________

____

____

____

____

Supplemental Exercise: Find and circle the words listed in the word search puzzle. Words may be forward, backward, horizontal, vertical, or diagonal.

Adam	Creation	Eden	God	Rested	Tigris
Animals	Dust	Eve	Light	Rib	Tree Of Life
Birds	Earth	Garden	Plants		

```
A C G O D X D E T S E R W
N B E A G J M P B T U X Z
I A D F R H J Y R I B Q V
M U O S R D Z E O G R P M
A J H T R A E K L R P D O
L N D N S O A N Q I W U S
S E B A F T R U S S Y S N
Q D P L I G H T I E O T A
D E I P S L K D E J F D N
A F N B V C X V S K A S L
E N O I T A E R C M W I M
```

GENESIS 1:1

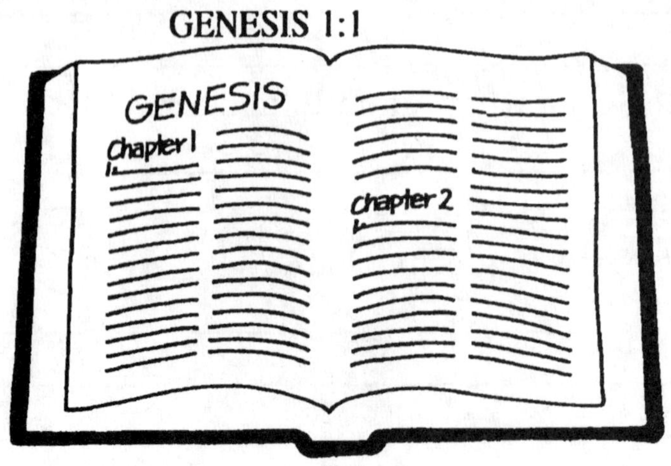

The Fall of Man
Lesson #2

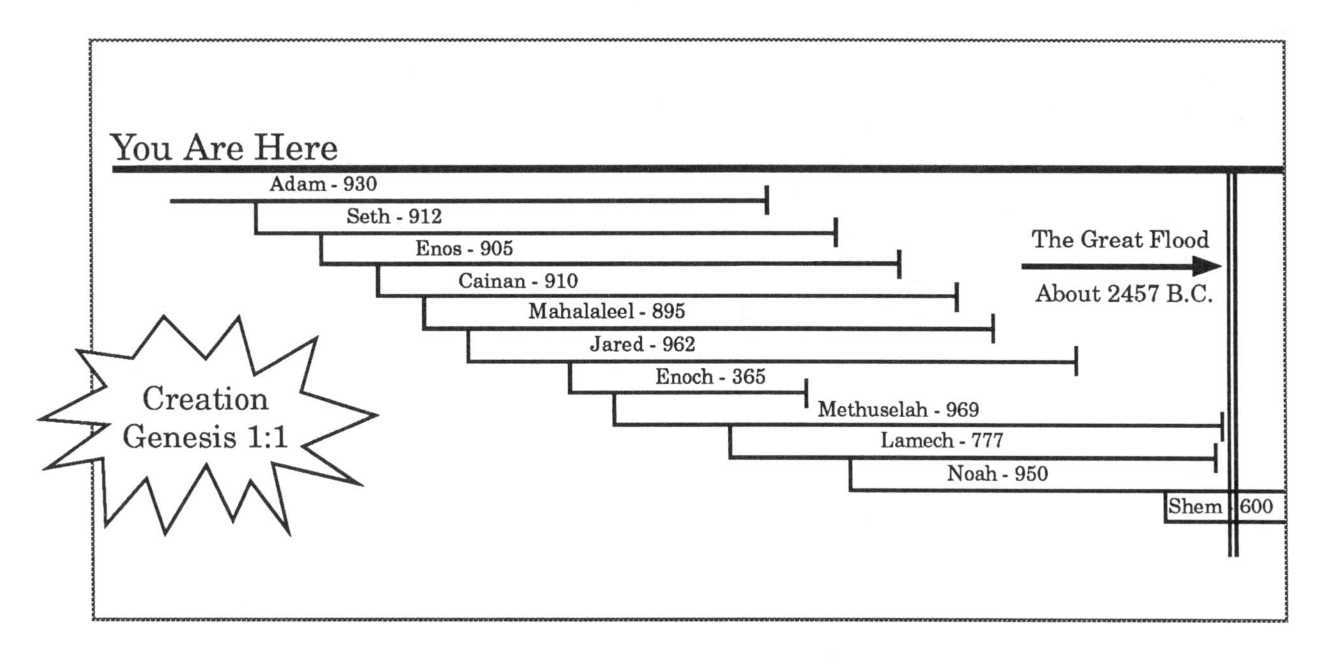

Lesson Goal: To gain a better understanding of God's forgiveness.

Background Text: Genesis 3

Memory Verse: Without shedding of blood, [there] is no remission. Hebrews 9:22

In our last lesson we discussed how God created us in His image by giving us souls. A terrible thing happened to Adam's soul. It turned away from God when Adam sinned. Before Adam sinned, his soul had perfect fellowship with God. That meant Adam could walk and talk with God similarly to the way you walk with your best friend or talk with your parents. However, when Adam sinned, he could no longer have fellowship with the Lord. That was because God hated sin and pronounced a sentence of death upon sinners.

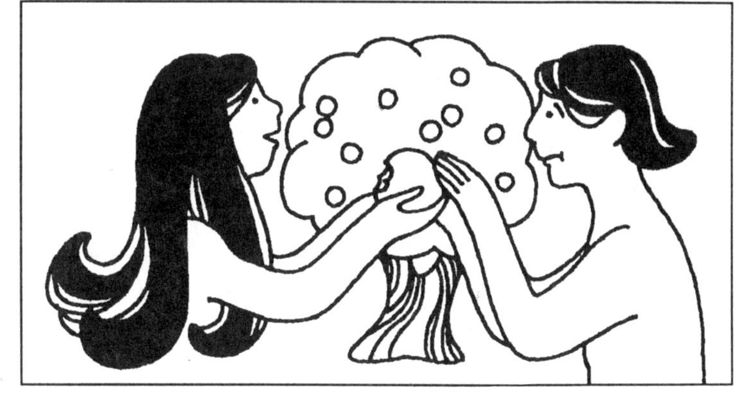

God hates sin in our lives, too. Every time we sin, it offends God because we

The Fall of Man

are not honoring and glorifying Him. Even though God hates sin, He still loves His children. For this reason He sent His Son, that by Christ's death and resurrection, we could have forgiveness (or remission) for our sins. When our sins are forgiven, then our souls can again have fellowship with God.

Before Jesus came and died on the cross, a way had to be made for man's sins to be forgiven, so he could have fellowship with God. We will learn later how the High Priest would sacrifice a lamb once a year, and spread its blood over the ark of the covenant as a means of atonement (or payment) for the sins of the people. The important principle to remember now is that sin cannot be forgiven unless blood is shed. After Adam and Eve sinned, God killed an animal and gave them the skin to cover their nakedness. God did this to show Adam and Eve that blood had to be shed to atone for their sins. This was a very necessary lesson for them to learn, because this pointed to the fact that one day God's Son would shed His blood as the final atonement for the sins of mankind (Hebrews 10:10-12).

Questions:

1. What was more subtle than any beast of the field? (Genesis 3:1)
   ____
2. What did the serpent say would be opened? (Genesis 3:5) ________
   ____
3. What did Adam and Eve make for themselves? (Genesis 3:7) _____
   ____
4. Who did the man say had given him from the tree to eat? (Genesis 3:12) ______________________________
5. What did God say the serpent would eat? (Genesis 3:14) ________
   ____

6. What would the seed of the woman bruise? (Genesis 3:15) ________

____

7. Who did God say would rule over the woman? (Genesis 3:16) _____

____

8. Why did Adam call his wife Eve? (Genesis 3:20) ________________

____

9. What did God make for Adam and Eve? (Genesis 3:21) _________

____

10. What did God place at the east end of the garden? (Genesis 3:24)

____

Thought Questions:

1. How has Satan tempted you to do wrong? ______________________

____

____

____

____

____

2. What does the temptation of Eve tell you about listening and obeying those who are in Godly authority over you? _______________

____

____

____

____

____

____

Lesson Review:

1. What did God create on the second day? (Lesson #1) ____________

____

2. What does it mean to be "created in God's image"? (Lesson #1) ____

____

____

____

3. What were we given because we were created in God's image? (Lesson #1) ______________________________

Cain and Abel
Lesson #3

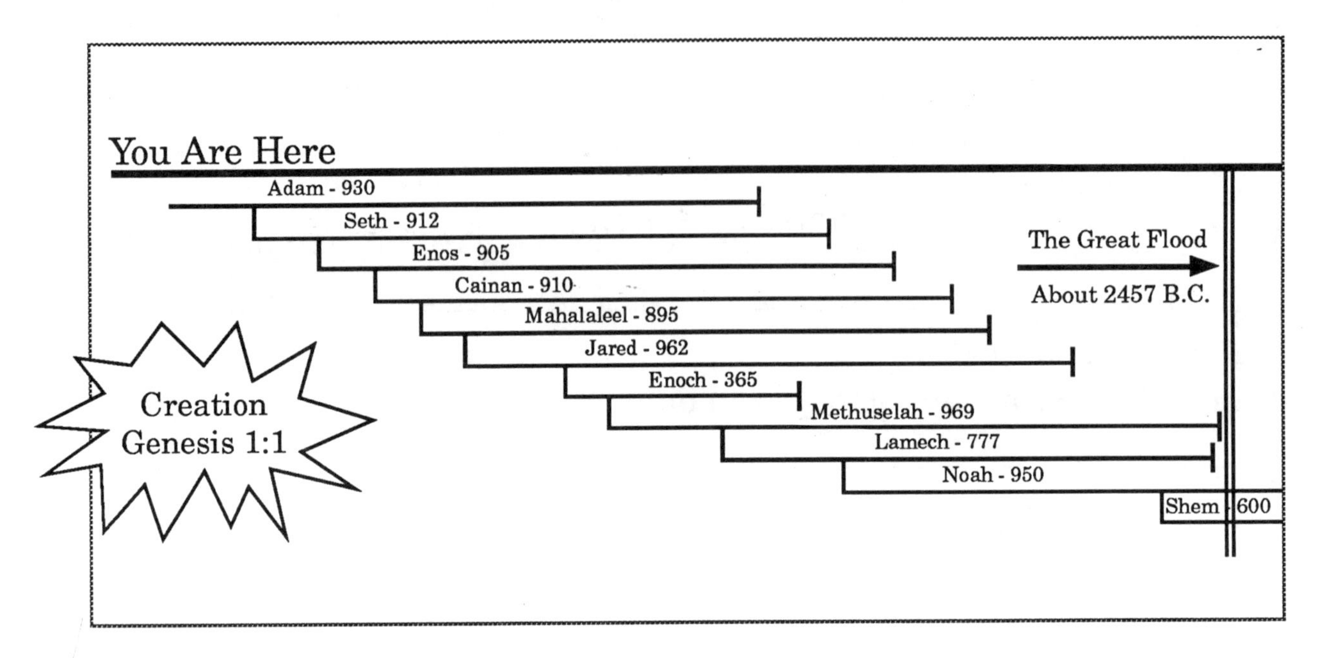

Lesson Goal: To understand that we please God by obeying Him and doing what He commands.

Background Text: Genesis 4

Memory Verse: Jesus saith unto him, I am the way, the truth, and the life: no man cometh unto the Father, but by me. John 14:6

Do you remember what we talked about in the last lesson? That is correct; it was atonement and forgiveness. In Genesis 4:4, we read that Abel made atonement for his sins by sacrificing one of his sheep. Cain tried to make atonement, but he did not give the sacrifice that God requested (Hebrews 11:4). Cain was a farmer, so he brought God some of his produce. God was not pleased with this and did not accept Cain's sacrifice. This made Cain very jealous toward Abel.

What did Cain do wrong? Was it not just as sincere of him to bring God his fruits and vegetables? It may have been so, but sincerity cannot save a person from his sins. Cain sinned because he tried to come to God in his own way. He did not trust God in faith but instead thought he could honor God by his own efforts. It is important to understand that obedience means that we respond to the wishes of those who are in authority, not by doing what we think should be the best thing to do. Our authority could be God, our parents, a policeman, or even a Sunday-school teacher.

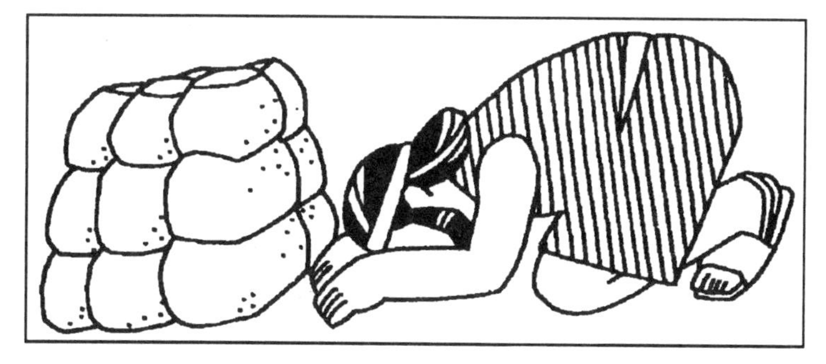

Even in our own day, there are people who believe the same way Cain did; they are called "humanists." A humanist believes that man can come to God by his own effort and that he does not have to do what the Bible teaches. Just as God was not pleased with Cain's sacrifice, God is not pleased with the humanist. It is not enough to simply believe in whatever we want, but we must believe in what God's Word teaches, and obey what it commands.

Questions:

1. Abel was a __Keeper__ of sheep, but Cain was a __tiller__ of the ground. (Genesis 4:2)
2. The Lord had __respect__ unto Abel and to his offering. (Genesis 4:4)
3. If thou doest well, shalt thou not be __accsepted__? And if thou doest not well, __sin__ lieth at the __door__. (Genesis 4:7)
4. Cain rose up against Abel his brother, and __slew__ him. (Genesis 4:8)
5. The __voice__ of thy brother's __blood__ crieth unto me from the ground. (Genesis 4:10)
6. Behold, thou hast driven me out this day from the __face__ of the __earth__; and from thy face shall I be hid. (Genesis 4:14)
7. Cain dwelt in the land of __nod__, on the east of __Eden__. (Genesis 4:16)
8. Jubal was the father of all such as handle the __flute__ and __harp__. (Genesis 4:21)
9. If Cain shall be avenged sevenfold, truly Lamech __seventy__ and sevenfold. (Genesis 4:24)
10. For God, said she, hath appointed me another __seed__ instead of __Abel__, whom Cain slew. (Genesis 4:25)

Cain and Abel

Thought Questions:

1. In what areas today do you see man's greatest rebellion and disobedience to God? wene one man kils another man.

2. In what areas has God shown you that you have not been obedient to Him? For barging into the girls room.

Lesson Review:

1. What did Adam and Eve learn when God gave them skins to cover themselves? (Lesson #2) not to sin.

2. What was the final "atonement" for our sins? (Lesson #2) Jesus diing on the cross.

3. How is man different from the plants, animals, or any other created thing? (Lesson #1) man has the abilaty to ride a horse.

Supplemental Exercise: Complete the crossword from Genesis 4:13-16.

Cain said, My 3-A is greater than I can bear. I shall be a fugitive and a 1-A in the earth. It shall come to 3-D, that every 2-D that finds me shall 7-A me. The Lord said, If anyone kills Cain, 1-D shall be 4-D on him sevenfold. And the Lord set a mark upon 5-A to protect him. Then Cain went out from the 9-A of the 8-A, and dwelt in the land of 6-D, on the east of Eden.

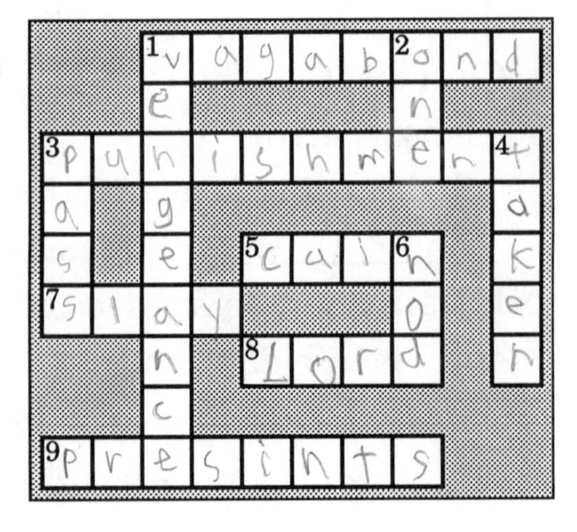

Genesis Background

Author of Genesis: Moses (Exodus 17:14; Deuteronomy 31:9, 31:24-26; Joshua 8:32; Mark 12:19).

Date of Writing: 1440-1400 B.C. Genesis was written during the forty years of wandering in the wilderness by the Israelites.

Purpose of Genesis: To detail the beginnings of the world, and to show God's plan and purpose for mankind.

Outline of Genesis:

I. Four Great Events (Genesis 1-11)
   A. Creation (Genesis 1-2)
      1. Chronological Account (1:1-2:3)
      2. Comparative Topical Account (2:4-26)
   B. Fall (Genesis 3-4)
      1. Origin of Sin in the World (Genesis 3)
      2. Outcome of Sin Ultimately (Genesis 4)
   C. Flood (Genesis 5-9)
      1. Events Before the Flood (Genesis 5-6)
      2. Events During the Flood (7:1-8:19)
      3. Events After the Flood (8:20-9:29)
   D. Babel (Genesis 10-11)
      1. Sons of Noah (Genesis 10)
      2. Scattering at Babel (11:1-9)
      3. Shem's Descendants to Abram (11:10-32)

II. Four Great Men (Genesis 12-50)
   A. Abraham (Genesis 12-25)
      1. Call from Haran to Canaan (Genesis 12-14)
      2. Covenant from God to Abram (15:1-18:22)
      3. Contrast of Abram with Lot (18:23-19:38)
      4. Coming of Isaac to Abraham (Genesis 20-21)
      5. Climax of Abraham's Faith (22:1-25:18)

B. Isaac (Genesis 25-26)

C. Jacob (Genesis 27-36)

1. Supplanter in Beer-sheba (27:1-41)
2. Servant in Padan-Aram (27:42-33:17)
3. Saint in Hebron (33:18-35:29)
4. Summary of Esau's Descendants (Genesis 36)

D. Joseph (Genesis 37-50)

1. Selling of Joseph into Slavery (Genesis 37)
2. Sin of Judah with Tamar (Genesis 38)
3. Suffering of Joseph in Prison (Genesis 39-41)
4. Saving of Jews by Joseph (Genesis 42-50)

<u>The Big Idea of Genesis</u>: Genesis can be divided into two major parts. The first part deals with four great events (creation, fall, flood, and Babel). The second part deals with four great men (Abraham, Isaac, Jacob, and Joseph). Throughout the book, the theme presented is God's covenant with His people. Adam sinned, so God provided a way of redemption. The world became corrupt, so God destroyed it; yet He saved Noah and his family. The Lord led Abraham into Canaan and promised him the land and many descendants, even though he was very old. His wife Sarah was also too old to have children, but then God blessed her with a son. Isaac and Jacob were taught to be faithful to God. Joseph saved his family and the Egyptian people from a terrible famine.

We can see by these stories that God had a plan and purpose for his followers. Although God's people sinned and did not always follow Him, God remained faithful to His promises and provided a way of redemption to those who trusted in Him.

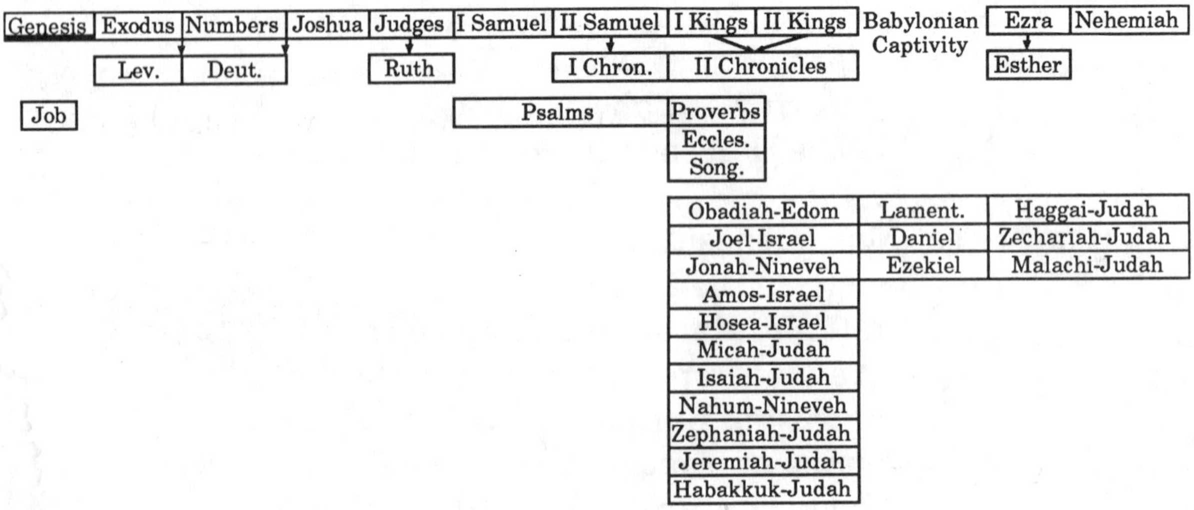

Genesis	Exodus	Numbers	Joshua	Judges	I Samuel	II Samuel	I Kings	II Kings	Babylonian Captivity	Ezra	Nehemiah
	Lev.	Deut.		Ruth		I Chron.	II Chronicles			Esther	

Job

Psalms | Proverbs | Eccles. | Song.

Obadiah-Edom	Lament.	Haggai-Judah
Joel-Israel	Daniel	Zechariah-Judah
Jonah-Nineveh	Ezekiel	Malachi-Judah
Amos-Israel		
Hosea-Israel		
Micah-Judah		
Isaiah-Judah		
Nahum-Nineveh		
Zephaniah-Judah		
Jeremiah-Judah		
Habakkuk-Judah		

Noah and the Flood
Lesson #4

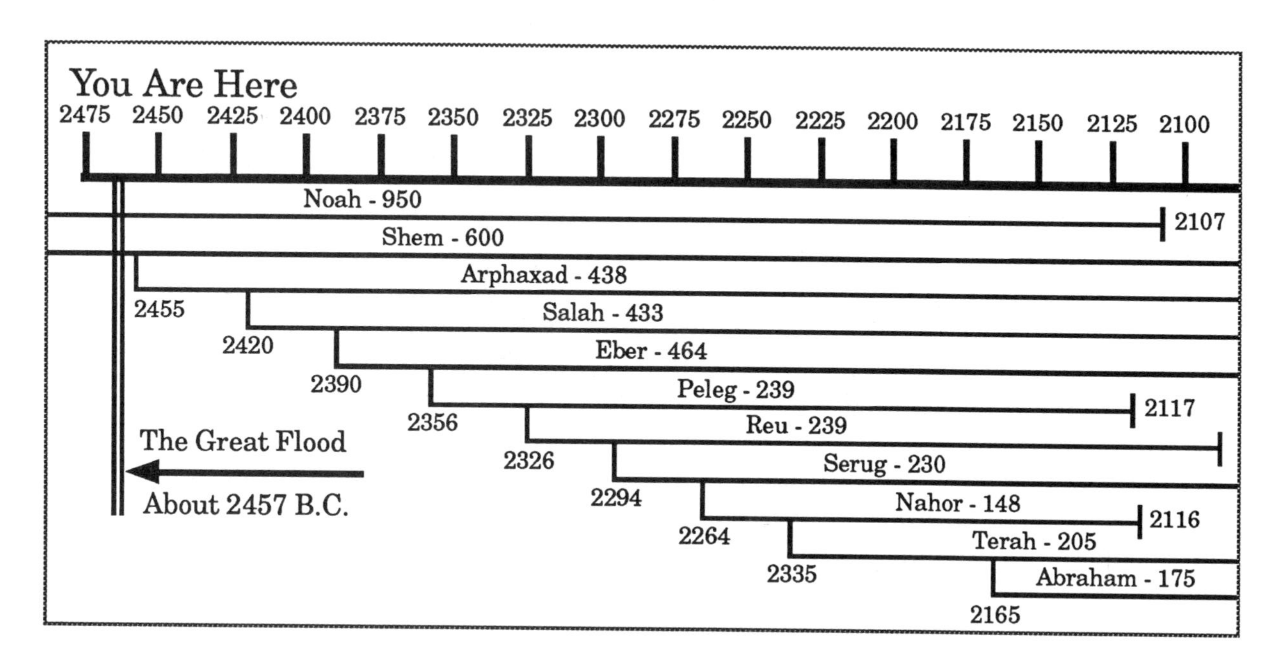

Lesson Goal: To understand the nature of God's covenant.

Background Text: Genesis 6-8

Memory Verse: But with thee will I establish my covenant; and thou shalt come into the ark, thou, and thy sons, and thy wife, and thy sons' wives with thee. Genesis 6:18

Have you ever made a promise to someone? I know I have. Often, I have told my children, "If you are good today, when I get home I promise I will buy you your favorite ice cream." I am sure all of us have made promises like this frequently. There is nothing wrong with making promises, as long as they are good ones and we keep them.

Did you know that God made a promise to Noah? The Bible calls this type of promise a "covenant." God promised that even though He would destroy the earth with a flood, Noah and his family would remain safe while in the ark. Noah had to have a lot of faith in

Noah and the Flood

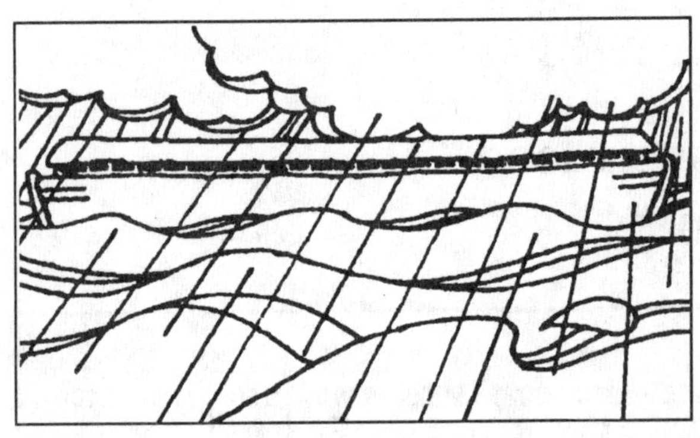

God to believe Him. It was this faith in God's covenant that brought Noah and his family safely through the flood (Hebrews 11:7).

Imagine what you would do if you were Noah. Let us say that God has just told you to build a big boat, far away from any large bodies of water. First you would need to cut down enough trees to provide all the wood and supplies necessary to build the ark. Then you would have to take hundreds of animals and load them onto the boat with you. Don't forget that you would need to have enough food and water for you and the animals to last over a year. What would you do? Well, God is not asking us to build arks today, but He is asking us to be obedient to His Word. This obedience means that we trust God's promises, and in this trusting not be afraid to let other people see and witness our faith.

The Chronology of the Flood

Rain fell for 40 days	7:12, 17	40
Water continued to rise for 110 days	7:24 (150-40=110)	110
Water decreased for 74 days	8:4-5	74
Forty days passed – the raven is sent	8:6	40
Seven days passed – first dove is sent	8:8,10	7
Seven days passed – second dove is sent	8:10	7
Seven days passed – third dove is sent	8:12	7
29 days passed between the sending of the last dove and the removal of the covering	7:11 & 8:13	29
57 days passed until the earth was dry and everyone left the ark	8:14	57
Total number of days spent in the ark		**371**

Questions: Match the correct answer with the proper question.

1. _d_ Noah found this in the eyes of the Lord. (Genesis 6:8)
2. _g_ The ark was made of this type of wood. (Genesis 6:14)
3. _j_ An agreement established between God and his people. (Genesis 6:18)
4. _f_ Number of pairs of clean animals brought into the ark. (Genesis 7:2)
5. _b_ Number of pairs of unclean animals brought into the ark. (Genesis 7:2)
6. _h_ Number of days the water prevailed upon the earth. (Genesis 7:24)
7. _i_ The mountains where the ark finally stopped. (Genesis 8:4)
8. _e_ The first type of bird Noah used to test to see if there was dry land. (Genesis 8:7)
9. _c_ The second type of bird Noah used to test to see if there was dry land. (Genesis 8:8)
10. _a_ Number of times Noah used the dove to test for dry land. (Genesis 8:8-12)

a. Three
b. Two
c. Dove
d. Grace
e. Raven
f. Seven
g. Gopher
h. One hundred and fifty
i. Ararat
j. Covenant

Thought Questions:

1. What do you think Noah's neighbors were saying to him when they watched him build the ark? you must be crazy.

2. What promises and/or covenants from God are the most meaningful to you in your life? Eternal life

Noah and the Flood

Lesson Review:

1. Who are the four great men emphasized in the book of Genesis? (Genesis Background) Abraham, Isaac, Jacob, and Joseph.

2. Why did God reject Cain's offering? (Lesson #3) He gave it with anger.

3. What did the High Priest do to atone for sins? (Lesson #2) He kild an animel.

Supplemental Exercise: Read Genesis 7:1-5 to find God's final instructions to Noah and complete the puzzle.

The Lord said to Noah, 3-A, and bring your family into the ark. Of every clean 9-D thou shalt take in by 8-D, the male and his 6-D. Of the beasts that are not 3-D, take in only two. Take the 6-A of the 10-A by sevens, to keep them 7-A upon the earth. In seven days I will 2-D it to rain upon the 5-D, forty days and 1-D nights; and every living creature that I have made will I destroy from off the 1-A of the 11-D. And 4-A did all that the Lord commanded him.

The Tower of Babel
Lesson #5

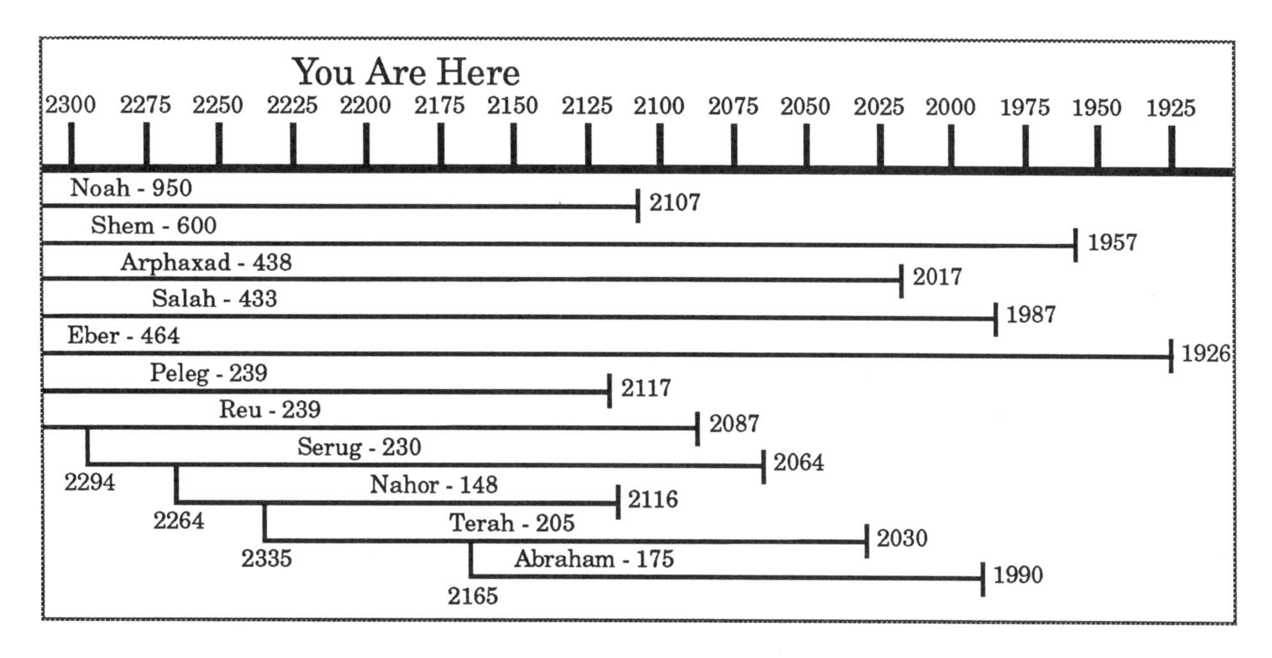

Lesson Goal: To understand that man will try to get to God his own way, instead of through the Lord Jesus Christ.

Background Text: Genesis 11:1-9

Memory Verse: Jesus said unto her, I am the resurrection, and the life: he that believeth in me, though he were dead, yet shall he live. John 11:25

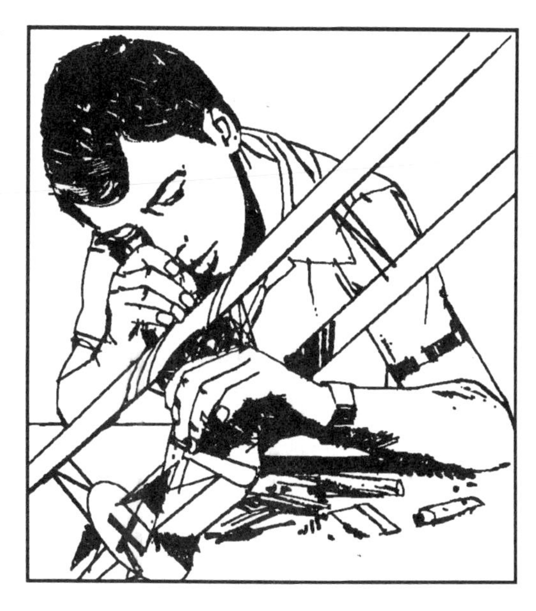

Have you ever taken wooden blocks or "Legos" and tried to stack them on top of one another to see how high of a tower you could build? If there were enough pieces, you could probably build a tower as tall as yourself.

Many years after the Flood of Noah, some people tried to build a tower, but they were not doing it to play or to have fun. These people were trying to govern their lives apart from God's authority. By building a tower to

The Tower of Babel

heaven, the people tried to get to the Lord by their own works. They refused to follow the way that God had given to them through faith and atonement for sins.

Even today there are people who think that by giving money to the church, doing good deeds, and being kind to a neighbor, they will be brought closer to God. These people try to build a tower of good works large enough to get them to heaven. The Bible teaches that the only way someone can know God is by trusting in the Lord Jesus Christ (Acts 16:30-31). Although good works are important to do as a Christian, they will not save someone from his sins. People who think they can get to God their own way will eventually discover their tower has been destroyed.

<u>Questions</u>: Multiple choice -- circle the correct answer for each question.

1. The whole world was of one what? (Genesis 11:1)
   *Language
   *Nationality
   *Race
   *Tribe

2. What did the people find in the land of Shinar? (Genesis 11:2)
   *Gold
   *A river
   *A plain
   *A tower

3. What did the people use for stone? (Genesis 11:3)
   *Big, heavy rocks
   *Bricks
   *Trees
   *Small, light rocks

4. What did the people use for mortar? (Genesis 11:3)
   *Cement
   *Mud
   *Sticks
   *Slime

5. Where did the people want the tower to reach? (Genesis 11:4)
   *To the next city
   *To heaven
   *To the top of the mountain
   *To the moon

6. Why did the people want to make a name for themselves? (Genesis 11:4)
   *They were tired of their old name
   *Lest they be scattered abroad upon the face of the whole earth
   *They were hiding from another group of people
   *They did not want to be associated with evil people

7. What did the Lord come down to see? (Genesis 11:5)
   *The city and tower which the children of men were building
   *The wickedness of the people
   *The ones who were truly following him
   *Noah's ark

8. Why did the Lord confound their language? (Genesis 11:7)
   *As a sign of his covenant with Noah
   *To punish them
   *So the people could learn to speak a second language
   *That they may not understand one another's speech

9. What did the people do after the Lord scattered them? (Genesis 11:8)
   *They left off (stopped) building the city
   *They learned to speak the same language again
   *They all learned one another's language
   *They divided into smaller groups and built more towers

The Tower of Babel

10. Why was the name of the place called Babel? (Genesis 11:9)
    *Because the people built a tower there
    *Because the people built a city there
    *Because the people were punished there
    *Because the Lord confounded the language of the earth

Thought Questions:

1. Why do you think people choose their own way rather than following God's way? ____________________

2. What would you tell a person if he asked you how he could follow God? ____________________

Lesson Review:

1. What are the four great events from the book of Genesis? (Genesis Background) ____________________

2. Why did Cain sin when he brought God his sacrifice? (Lesson #3)

3. Complete the empty boxes with the names of the books from the "Chronology of the Old Testament." (Genesis Background)

Genesis

Lev.

Judges

Job Background

Author of Job: It is difficult to determine who actually wrote the book of Job. Most conservative scholars say Moses, Elihu (a friend of Job), or Job himself.

Date of Writing: The book of Job was written during the time of the Patriarchs (Abraham, Isaac, and Jacob). We can determine this because Job 22:16 probably refers to the great Flood while there was no mention of Moses, the Israelites, or the Law within the book.

Purpose of Job: To deal with the problems of pain and misery by explaining why Godly people suffer trials and tribulations.

Outline of Job:

I. The Problem is Raised (Job 1-2) (Prose)

II. The Problem is Discussed (3:1-42:6) (Poetry)
- A. Discussion with Three Friends (Job 3-31)
  - 1. Introduction by Job (Job 3)
    - a. Discussion's First Round (Job 4-14)
      - (1) With Eliphaz (Job 4-7)
      - (2) With Bildad (Job 8-10)
      - (3) With Zophar (Job 11-14)
    - b. Discussion's Second Round (Job 15-21)
      - (1) With Eliphaz (Job 15-17)
      - (2) With Bildad (Job 18-19)
      - (3) With Zophar (Job 20-21)
    - c. Discussion's Third Round (Job 22-26)
      - (1) With Eliphaz (Job 22-24)
      - (2) With Bildad (Job 25-26)
  - 2. Conclusion by Job (Job 27-31)
- B. Discussion with Elihu (Job 32-37)
- C. Discussion with God (38:1-42:6)

III. The Problem is Solved (42:7-17) (Prose)

Job Background

The Big Idea of Job: This is the story of a man named Job. He was very righteous and wealthy; however, God allowed Satan to tempt him and bring him under great suffering. Throughout the book, Job dealt with people who gave him both good and bad advice to help him solve his problems. In the end, even though Job questioned God's justice, he remained faithful and God blessed him. This story dramatically illustrates several important principles for our lives. Life does not consist of the abundance of things that we own, but in a personal relationship with our Heavenly Father. Not all suffering is a direct result of sin, but is used to help people become stronger. And finally, unjust suffering does not negate God's justice or sovereignty.

Genesis | Exodus | Numbers | Joshua | Judges | I Samuel | II Samuel | I Kings | II Kings | Babylonian Captivity | Ezra | Nehemiah

Lev. | Deut. | Ruth | I Chron. | II Chronicles | Esther

Job

Psalms | Proverbs | Eccles. | Song.

Obadiah-Edom | Lament. | Haggai-Judah
Joel-Israel | Daniel | Zechariah-Judah
Jonah-Nineveh | Ezekiel | Malachi-Judah
Amos-Israel
Hosea-Israel
Micah-Judah
Isaiah-Judah
Nahum-Nineveh
Zephaniah-Judah
Jeremiah-Judah
Habakkuk-Judah

The Life of Job
Lesson #6

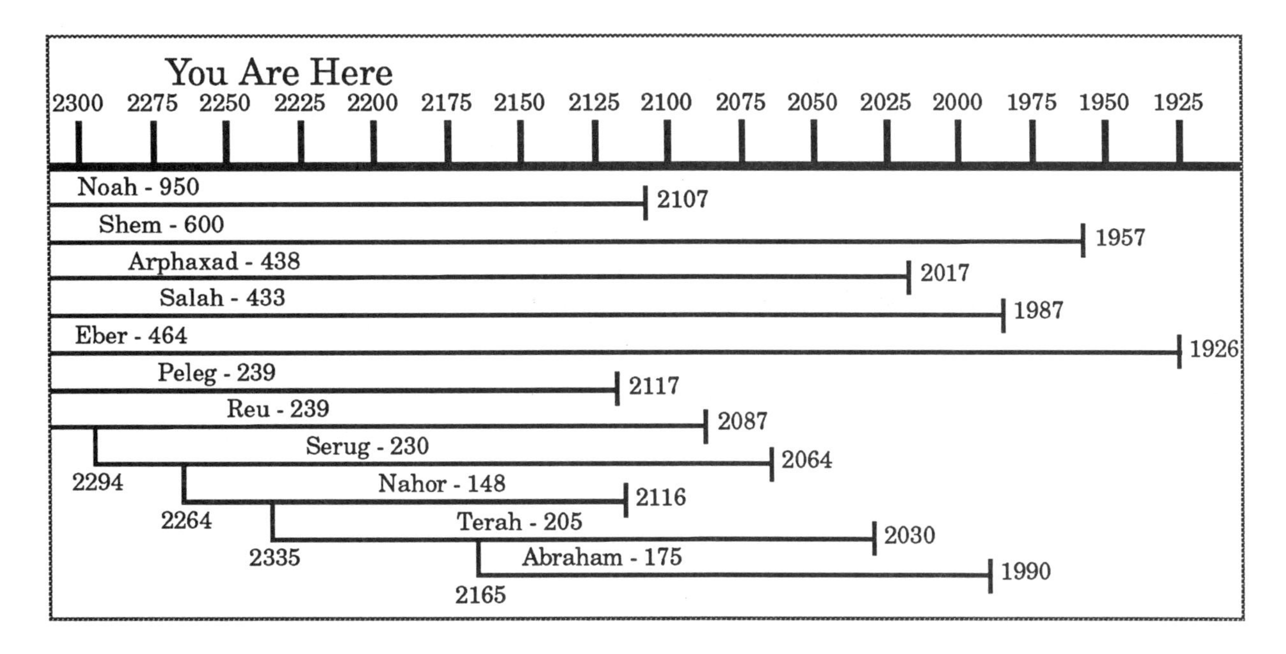

Lesson Goal: To understand that suffering can help the Christian become stronger.

Background Text: Job 1, 2, & 42

Memory Verse: And though after my skin worms destroy this body, yet in my flesh shall I see God. Job 19:26

The life of Job deals with a very important question. Why do Godly people suffer hardship and trials, even when they have done nothing wrong (Job 2:3)? We all have experienced hardship, perhaps a death of someone we love, or punishment for some wrong we did not commit. One question comes to mind during times like these: "Why did God allow this thing to happen to me?"

Job asked himself this same question, and he had the guidance of a few of his friends to help him answer it. At three different points, his friends argued with Job about the nature of suffering; however, they did not give him good advice. They all thought his suffering was the result of some sin in his life. Sometimes suffering is the result of sin, but that is not always the case (John 9:2-3; II Corinthians 12:7-10). Job chapter thirty-two explains that Elihu visited and gave the first

The Life of Job

bit of good advice to Job. He said that God does not have to give an account of His actions to man, and that God never acts unjustly. Finally, God appears and speaks to Job. The Lord explains that His judgment is not to be questioned, because He is in control of everything. Job then repents, and God rewards him with twice the blessings he had before his trial.

Even though Job lost all he possessed, and questioned God's working in his life, he continued to be faithful to the Lord. He realized in the end that Godly people sometimes suffer in order that their character may be purified. God's purpose was to strip away Job's self-righteousness and bring him to the place of complete dependence and trust in Him.

Questions:

1. Where did Job live? (Job 1:1) ______________________________
2. How many children did Job have in the beginning? (Job 1:2) ______

   ____
3. Job was the greatest among whom? (Job 1:3) __________________

   ____
4. What did Satan accuse God of making about Job? (Job 1:10) ______

   ____
5. What did Job do after he had heard that he had lost everything? (Job 1:20) ____

   ____
6. What did Job's wife tell him to do? (Job 2:9) _________________

   ____
7. What did Job's friends do for seven days and nights? (Job 2:13)

   ____
8. Why did Job's friends have to offer a sacrifice? (Job 42:8) ________

   ____

   ____

9. With what did God bless Job after the trial? (Job 42:12-13) ______

____

____

10. How long did Job live after his trial? (Job 42:16) ____________

Thought Questions:

1. When was the last time you suffered greatly, and what was your attitude toward God because of this suffering? ______________

____

____

____

____

2. If your attitude was negative, what can be done in your life to change your attitude to that of contentment? ______________

____

____

____

____

Lesson Review:

1. What was the purpose of the book of Job? (Job Background) ______

____

2. In what two styles does the outline of Job explain how the book was written? (Job Background) ______________________

____

3. What is the meaning of the word "covenant"? (Lesson #4) _______

____

____

Supplemental Exercise: Decode the symbols to understand the message. The key is in Appendix B.

____

. 42:2a

____

The Faith of Abraham
Lesson #7

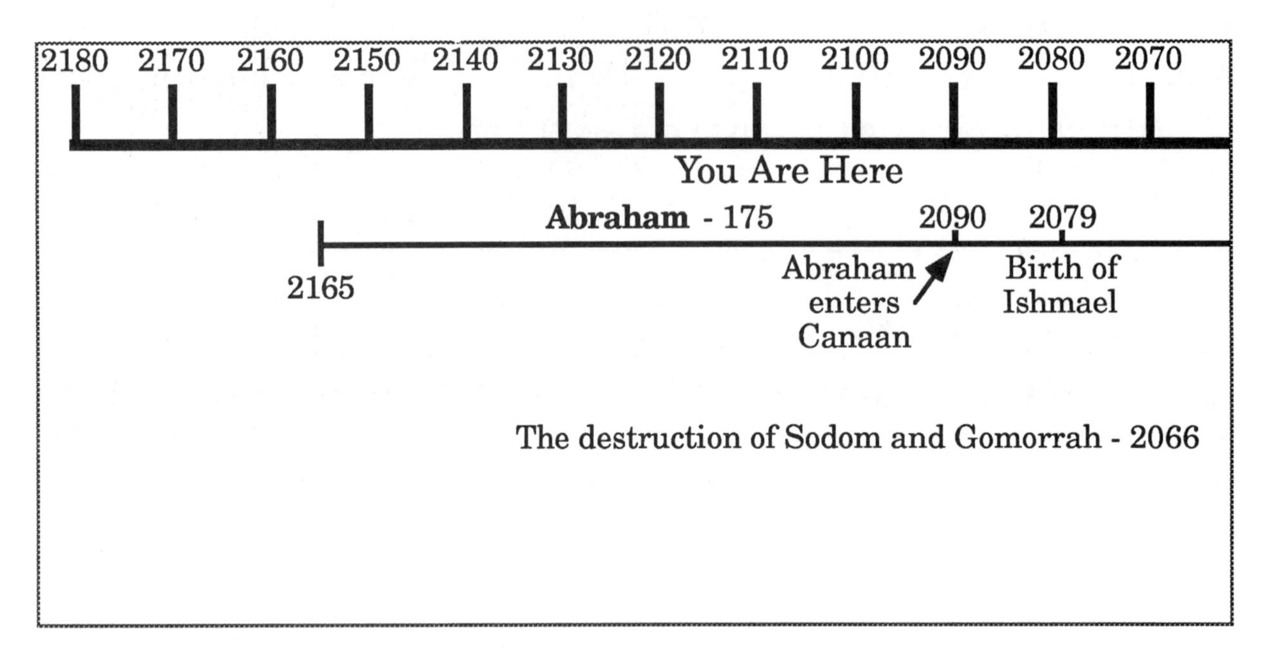

Lesson Goal: To understand what it means to have faith in God.

Background Text: Various parts of Genesis 12-22

Memory Verse: Know ye therefore that they which are of faith, the same are the children of Abraham. Galatians 3:7

In the life of Abraham, we find many wonderful examples of his faithfulness to God. Hebrews 11:8-19 summarizes Abraham's life by explaining that he lived by faith, dwelling in tents with Isaac and Jacob. Although Abraham had only one son by his wife Sarah, God promised that his family would have so many children that the number of them would be uncountable. Abraham waited patiently upon the Lord, as he was led from his home in Ur to the land God had prepared for him. Abraham died before he saw the fulfillment of God's promises. In spite of this, he still remained faithful to the Lord's guidance.

In our own spiritual lives, many times we do not know why God is working in our hearts the way He does. He may lead us, test us, teach us, and direct us into new opportunities or ask us to wait patiently upon Him. In all situations, we need to learn to trust the Lord and demonstrate our faith in Him.

Faith can be defined as the development of an unshakable confidence in God's Word, so that no matter what happens, we will still trust the Lord. This was the basis of Abraham's belief in God. He trusted the Lord even when it meant taking steps to sacrifice his own son Isaac (Genesis 22:10).

If you are going through a problem, or if you do not understand what God is doing in your life, remember that Abraham did not have all the answers either. He did not always know what God's plan and purpose were, but he remained faithful to the Lord's leading. We also need to live by faith and trust the Lord to guide us and take care of us, even when we are scared and troubled.

The Development of Abraham's Faith

Obedience of Faith (Genesis 12:1-9) Abraham's faith was strong enough to leave his father, land, and loved ones to follow God.

Sufficiency of Faith (Genesis 12:10) God was able to take care of Abraham in a time of need.

Weakness of Faith (Genesis 12:11-20) Abraham tells the Egyptians that Sarah was his sister.

Humility of Faith (Genesis 13) Abraham's faith is tested with Lot.

Boldness of Faith (Genesis 14:1-16) With 318 men, Abraham defeats four nations.

The Faith of Abraham

Gift of Faith (Genesis 14:17-20) Abraham gives a tithe to Melchizedek, the priest of God.

Dignity of Faith (Genesis 14:21-24) After Abraham's victory comes a test; he does not obligate himself to the King of Sodom.

Vision of Faith (Genesis 15) God Himself comes and gives Abraham a promise.

Impatience of Faith (Genesis 16) Abraham's faith is tested by his wife Sarah.

Walk of Faith (Genesis 17) Abraham circumcises all the males in his household in response to God's new command.

Loyalty of Faith (Genesis 18) Abraham uses his faith and asks God not to destroy anyone who is righteous in Sodom.

Lapse of Faith (Genesis 20) Abraham says Sarah is his sister.

Fulfillment of Faith (Genesis 21:1-8) Isaac is born to Abraham and Sarah.

Test of Faith (Genesis 22:1-19) God tests Abraham and asks him to sacrifice his own son.

Questions: From the list, "The Development of Abraham's Faith," read the text from two of the areas of Abraham's faith and answer these questions.

1. What did Abraham do to demonstrate his faith toward God? ______

2. Did Abraham become stronger or weaker in his faith? ______

3. What was God's response to Abraham's faith? ______

The Faith of Abraham

Thought Questions:

1. Throughout Abraham's life his faith varied from being stronger, to weaker, to stronger again. When has your faith in God been strongest, and what caused it to be that way? ____________________

2. When has your faith in God been weakest, and what caused it to be that way? ____________________

Lesson Review:

1. On what mountain did the ark finally rest? (Lesson #4) __________

2. When was the book of Genesis written? (Genesis Background) __________

3. What does a humanist believe? (Lesson #3) __________

Supplemental Exercise: Complete the puzzle and find the hidden phrase.

1. Abraham was asked to number these. (Genesis 15:5)
2. What did the Lord restrain Sarah from doing? (Genesis 16:2)
3. What was the name of Sarah's Egyptian maid? (Genesis 16:3)
4. What was the name of Abraham's first son? (Genesis 16:15)
5. Abraham was a __________ years old when God gave him a child. (Genesis 17:17)
6. God established a covenant with this person. (Genesis 17:19)
7. Abraham was to go to this land to sacrifice Isaac. (Genesis 22:2)

Abraham and Lot
Lesson #8

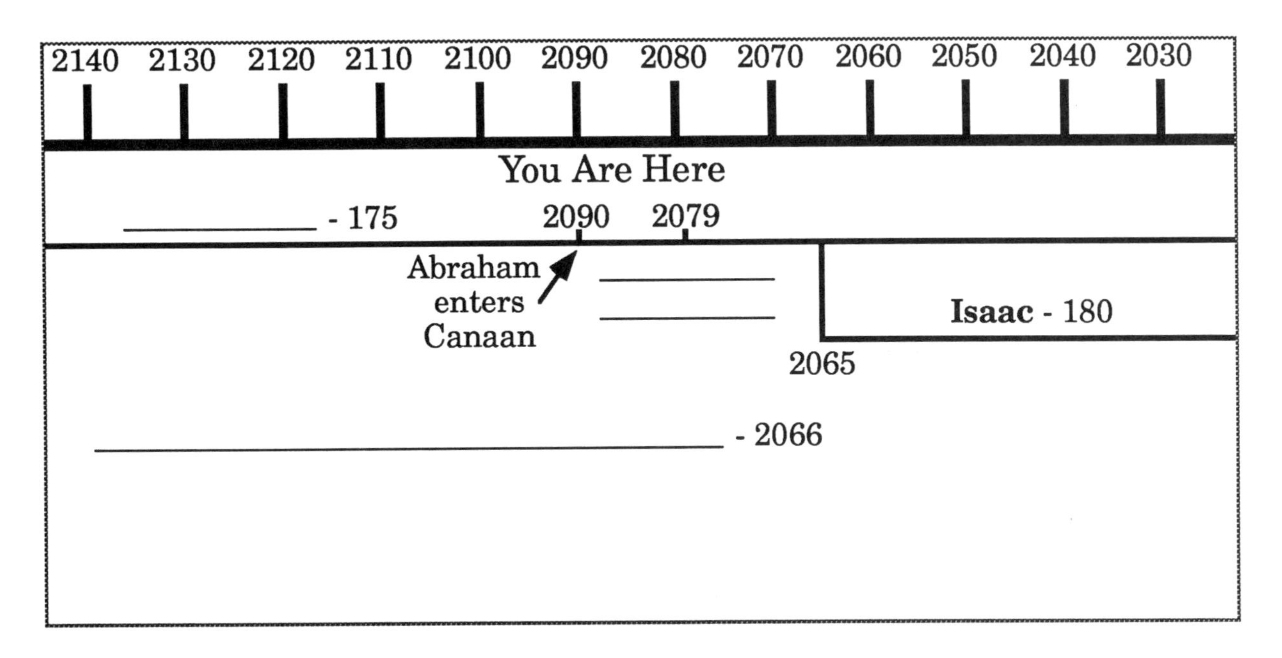

Lesson Goal: To understand the difference between selfishness and selflessness.

Background Text: Genesis 13, 14:11-16

Memory Verse: And be ye kind one to another, tenderhearted, forgiving one another, even as God for Christ's sake hath forgiven you. Ephesians 4:32

A series of books my children enjoy reading are called *The Happy Hollisters*. In these stories, there is a bad boy by the name of Joey Brill. Joey was very cruel and selfish, and he did all sorts of mean things to the other children. One time he made the Hollister's dog jump into the water where it was almost hit by a boat. Another time he tied tin cans to a cat's tail and laughed while the cat tried to run away from the noise. Do you know anyone who is mean and selfish like Joey Brill? I hope not – but if you do, how should you treat him if he behaves badly toward you?

Abraham and Lot's servants were quarreling with one another because there was not enough land and water for their animals to share. So, Abraham gave Lot the first choice of all the land for him to make his home. Lot chose very selfishly. He picked the best land for himself, even though it was close to some very evil and wicked cities. However, because Abraham trusted God, he was rewarded with more land and was promise many descendants.

Ephesians 4:32 reminds us to be kind, tenderhearted, and forgiving.

This would also apply to people who are not nice and kind to us. This was the type of attitude that Abraham had toward Lot. He was selfless in his dealing with Lot, because he trusted the Lord to take care of him. Lot, on the other hand, was only concerned with his own financial gain and well being.

Which person do we want to pattern our lives after – Abraham or Lot? If we want to be selfless like Abraham, it will mean that we must put other people's interests ahead of our own and trust the Lord to take care of us. If we want to be selfish like Lot, then we only need to think of ourselves and ignore the needs and wishes of those who are around us. I think we all know which individual God would want us to be like, but we need to make that decision for ourselves.

Questions:

1. In what was Abraham rich? (Genesis 13:2) ______________________

   ____

2. What did Lot have with him when he went with Abraham? (Genesis 13:5) ______________________________

   ____

3. Who was there strife between? (Genesis 13:7) ________________

   ____

4. Why did Lot choose to live in the plain of Jordan, near the city of Sodom? (Genesis 13:10) ___________________________

   ____

5. What did Lot choose for himself? (Genesis 13:11) ________________

____

6. How did God view the men of Sodom? (Genesis 13:13) ____________

____

7. What did God promise that He would give to Abraham? (Genesis 13:15) ______________________________________

8. God promised that Abraham's seed (descendants) would be as many as what? (Genesis 13:16) ______________________

____

9. In Hebron, what did Abraham build for the Lord? (Genesis 13:18)

____

10. How many servants did Abraham use to rescue Lot? (Genesis 14:14) ______________________________________

Thought Questions:

1. If you were Lot, how would you have responded to Abraham when he told you to choose the land? ______________________

____

____

____

____

2. If you were Abraham, would you have let Lot choose the best land for himself? Why? ______________________________

____

____

____

____

Lesson Review:

1. What does the Bible call the promise that God made with Noah? (Lesson #4) __________________________________

2. In the Old Testament, what had to be done in order for sins to be forgiven? (Lesson #2) ____________________________

____

____

3. On the time line at the beginning of this lesson, complete the blank spaces with the correct information.

Map Study #1

Now that we have studied several chapters from the book of Genesis, it is time we learn where these interesting places are located on a map. Map study is an important part of understanding the Old Testament. By studying maps, it helps us to learn and understand the lessons of the Bible. If we think of the Bible as a puzzle, learning all the places and cities from a map is just another piece of the puzzle that helps us to understand the "big picture" of God's Word.

Have you ever ridden in a car with people who were lost and did not know where they were going? What did they do to find their way? They could have stopped to ask directions, or maybe they looked at a map. Ask your dad, mom, or teacher to show you a map. Try to find where you live. Try to find where a friend or relative lives. Which roads would you take to drive from your house to the place where they live? Just as we need maps today to give us directions where we are going, we also need maps to give direction to understand the Bible.

On the following two maps, there are cities and places highlighted that are significant to the study of the Bible. Please review these maps before continuing with your lessons. Throughout this book you will be asked to refer to these maps, to add information and determine the location of certain places.

Questions: Use the maps on the next two pages to answer these questions.

1. Put an "A" next to the fourth river which was located in Eden. (Genesis 2:14)

2. Put a "B" next to the location where Noah's ark rested. (Genesis 8:4)

3. Put a "C" next to the city where Abraham first lived before moving to Canaan. (Genesis 11:31)

4. Put a "D" next to the city where Abraham's father died. (Genesis 11:32)

5. Put an "E" next to the location where Abraham built an altar to the Lord. (Genesis 12:8)

6. Put an "F" next to the city to where Lot moved after his quarrel with Abraham. (Genesis 13:12, 19:1)

7. Put a "G" next to the city where Sarah was buried. (Genesis 23:19)

8. Put an "H" next to the country where Abraham sent servants looking for a wife for Isaac. (Genesis 24:10)

9. Put an "I" next to the city where Isaac dwelt when there was a famine in the land. (Genesis 26:6)

10. Put a "J" next to the city where Jacob lived with Laban. (Genesis 29:4)

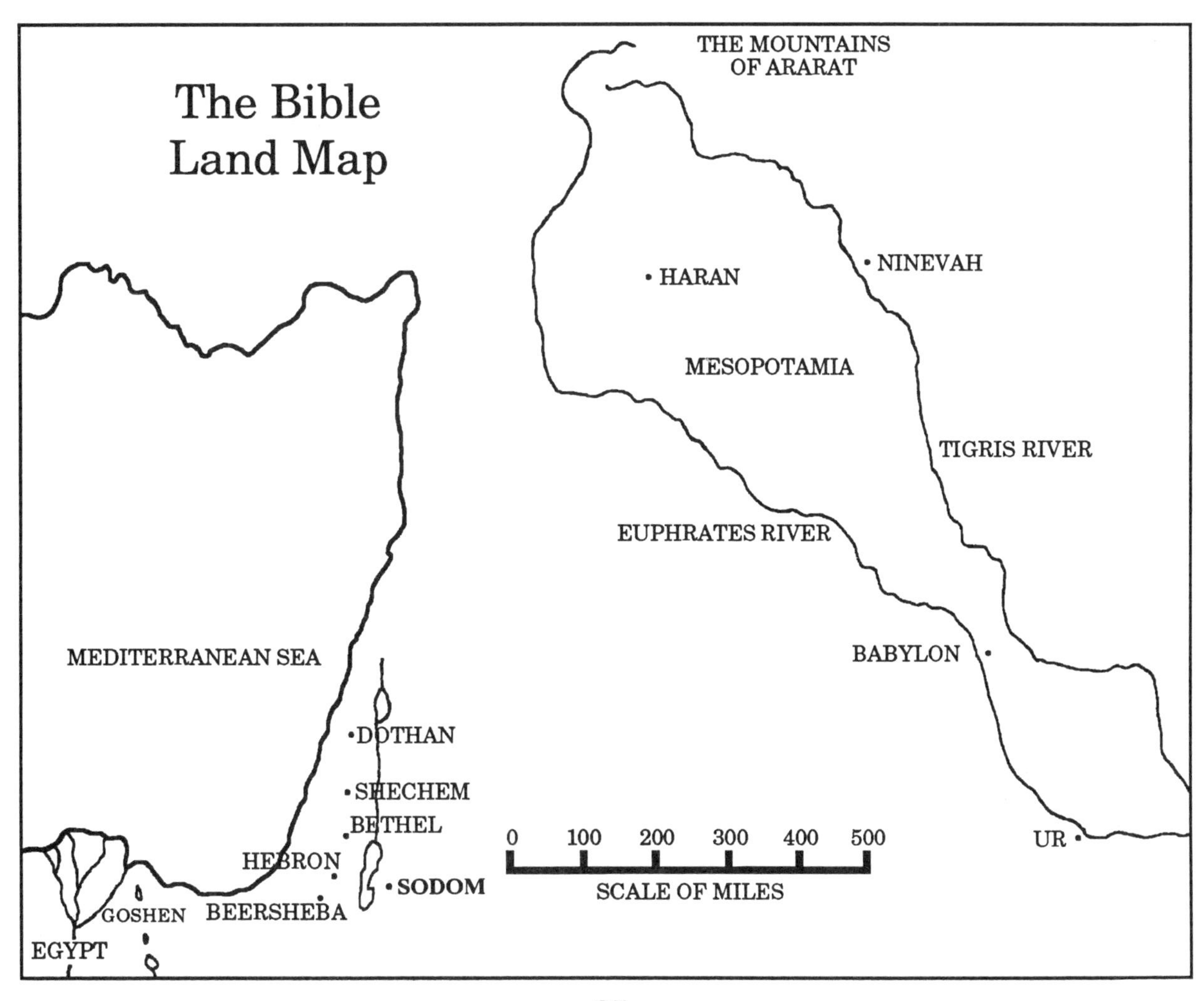

Map Study #1

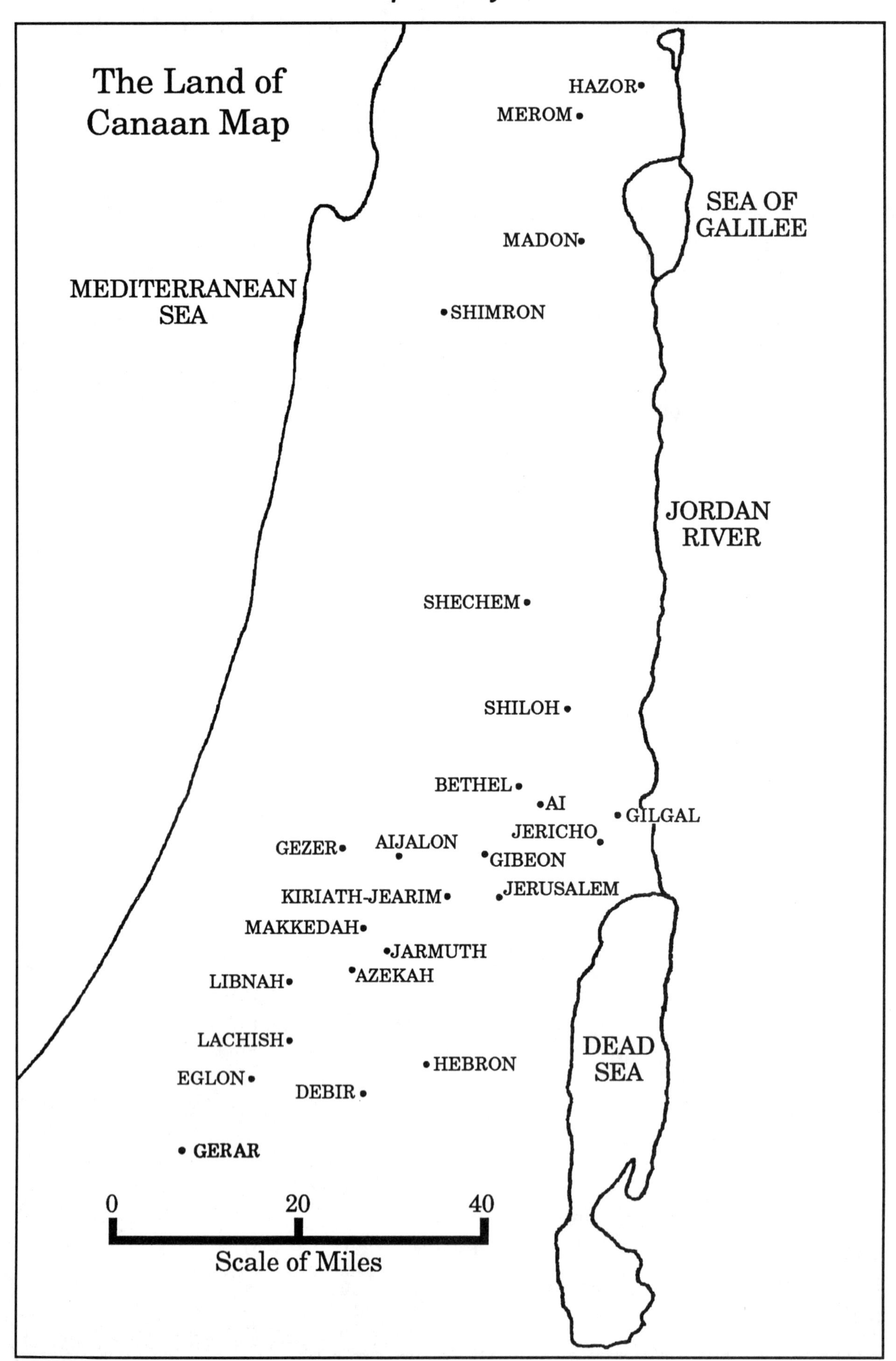

The Land of Canaan Map
MEDITERRANEAN SEA
SEA OF GALILEE
JORDAN RIVER
DEAD SEA
HAZOR
MEROM
MADON
SHIMRON
SHECHEM
SHILOH
BETHEL
AI
GILGAL
JERICHO
GEZER
AIJALON
GIBEON
KIRIATH-JEARIM
JERUSALEM
MAKKEDAH
JARMUTH
LIBNAH
AZEKAH
LACHISH
HEBRON
EGLON
DEBIR
GERAR
0
20
40
Scale of Miles

Lot's Failure
Lesson #9

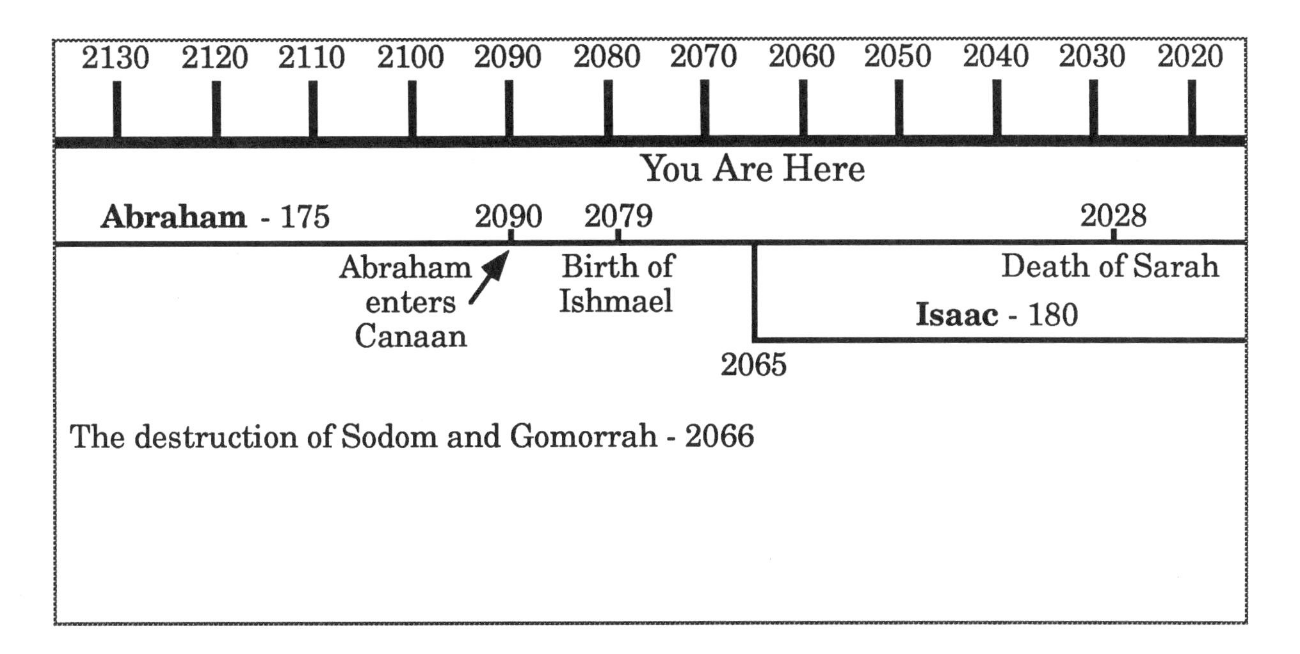

Lesson Goal: To understand the purpose of abiding by God's moral law.

Background Text: Genesis 19:1-30

Memory Verse: Let your light so shine before men, that they may see your good works, and glorify your Father, which is in heaven. Matthew 5:16

This lesson will take us into a further study of the life of Lot. Earlier, we were instructed that Lot was very selfish in his dealings with Abraham. Now we will see that Lot lacked the virtue in his life to stand up for his Godly convictions.

In the city of Sodom, which was an extremely wicked city, Lot was an important person. Genesis 19:1 tells us that Lot was sitting at the gate of the city. During that time,

only the most important people did that, so Lot was considered the same as a judge or politician. Now if Lot was so important, why was Sodom such an immoral city? The Bible does not specifically tell us, but Lot may have compromised his standards by not teaching God's absolutes in exchange for power and popularity. It could be that Lot did not allow his morality and understanding of God's laws to influence the decisions he made. Therefore, as the city of Sodom continued to become more and more evil, Lot refused to defend his moral convictions.

Today we have the same type of non-virtuous people who claim to be moral, but who are unwilling to influence society with Biblical absolutes. They do not believe it is correct to force their beliefs upon another person. Instead of basing their decisions upon God's Law, they operate according to society's idea of what is "good." That is not what the Bible teaches. God's Word instructs us that His laws are to be carried throughout the whole world. It does not matter if a person is Christian or non-Christian, rich or poor, black or white – everyone is commanded to abide by God's moral Law (Romans 1:20-32; II Timothy 3:1-5).

We tend to forget that God's Law was not only written to punish wickedness, but to also protect us from sin and danger. As a child, my parents had a law commanding me not to play near the street. They did not say this because they were mean or trying to punish me. This law was necessary to protect me from being hit by a car.

Lot was not an immoral person. In fact, II Peter 2:7-8 describes Lot as a righteous man, vexed by the sin of the wicked. However, Lot did not use his knowledge of God's absolutes to influence the people around him. He did not go to Sodom as a missionary, but in pursuit of wealth and material gain. Like many of us, Lot's righteous character was a mixed bag. He chose to live in the east (Sodom), where he sought his own good, but he welcomed and protected the angels when they came to warn him. We can learn a great lesson from this example by understanding that we have a responsibility to the people around us to explain the need for God's Law, and to warn them about the danger of sin.

Questions:

1. How many angels came to Sodom to see Lot? (Genesis 19:1) ______
2. What did Lot press upon the angels to do? (Genesis 19:2-3) ______
____
____
3. What did the angels do to the wicked men around Lot's house? (Genesis 19:11) ______________________________
____
4. Why did the angels say they would destroy this place? (Genesis 19:13) ______________________________
____
5. Where did the angels first tell Lot to go so he would not be consumed? (Genesis 19:17) ______________________
6. Why did Lot not want to go to the mountain? (Genesis 19:19) _____
____
7. How did God destroy Sodom and Gomorrah? (Genesis 19:24) _____
____
____
8. Why did Lot's wife become a pillar of salt? (Genesis 19:26) _______
____
9. What did Abraham see when he got up the next morning? (Genesis 19:27-28) ______________________________
____
____
10. Why did God save Lot from the destruction in Sodom? (Genesis 18:23-33, 19:29) ______________________________
____
____

Lot's Failure

Thought Questions:

1. From Lot's example, can you say that your life is virtuous? Why?

 ____

 ____

 ____

 ____

2. When was the last time you stood up for your convictions? What happened? ______________________________

 ____

 ____

 ____

 ____

Lesson Review:

1. What was the name of the city Abraham left to find the promised land? (Map Study #1) ______________________
2. What sea contains the location of the city of Sodom? (Map Study #1)

 ____

3. Why did the people build the tower of Babel? (Lesson #5) ________

 ____

 ____

Supplemental Exercise: Find and circle the words listed in the word search puzzle. Words may be forward, backward, horizontal, vertical, or diagonal.

```
A D E A B R A H A M
A F O D A G A T E Y
N E B O E R F O T I
G A I R R K A I Z O
E S U O E S C A P E
L T M G E A E O F K
S O D O M L D I M O
G U T O Z T W U A M
J D A U G H T E R S
```

ABRAHAM
ANGELS
BREAD
CITY
DAUGHTERS
DOOR
ESCAPE
FACE
FEAST
GATE
GOMORRAH
JUDGE
LOT
MOCKED
SALT
SMOKE
SODOM
WIFE
ZOAR

The Sacrifice of Isaac
Lesson #10

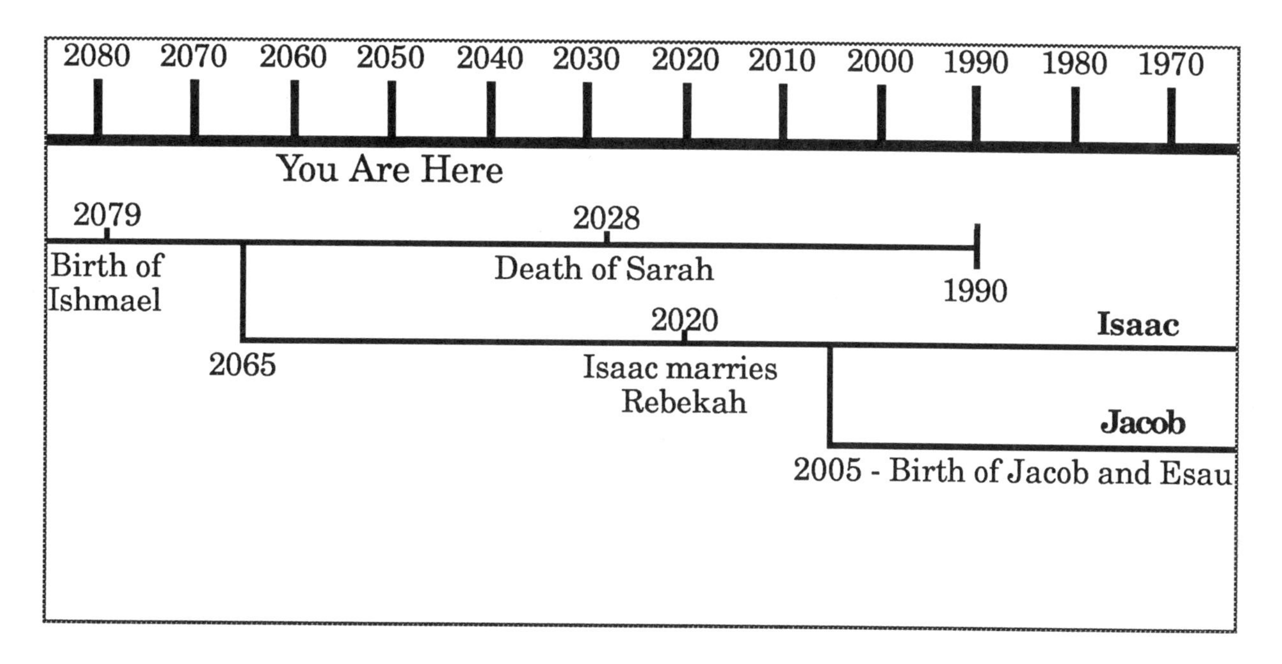

Lesson Goal: To understand the meaning of submission to authority.

Background Text: Genesis 22:1-19

Memory Verse: Trust in the Lord with all thine heart; and lean not unto thine own understanding. In all thy ways acknowledge him, and he shall direct thy paths. Proverbs 3:5-6

There may be times in our lives when someone in authority asks us to do something that we may not fully understand. Our parents may ask us to run an errand which in our minds seems unnecessary. Or maybe a church leader will request us to do a certain task, but we may not want to do it. What should be our response and attitude to situations like these?

First, let us look at Abraham and take an example from his life. God

The Sacrifice of Isaac

told Abraham to sacrifice his son Isaac as an offering. Abraham's response was simple. He did exactly what he was told. He did not hesitate in his response to God's commands, but went ahead and made preparations for the sacrifice. We should also have this type of response to God's Word. If the Holy Spirit is teaching us something through the Bible, we should do it. For example, if we find God's Word instructing us to be kind to our neighbor, we should be kind. This is an example of submission to Biblical authority.

In this lesson we also have another example of submission to authority, except this time we are allowed to question the authority. Isaac was not a young child when Abraham took him to be sacrificed. Rather, he was a teenager, probably around fifteen years old. Like many bright boys his age, he began to realize what was happening when Abraham brought him to the mountain, so he asked his father where the lamb was they were to sacrifice. Isaac was not being disobedient to his father; he was only questioning his father's motives and actions.

From this example we can see that it is proper to question authority, as long as we do it in an attitude of submissiveness and obedience. For instance, let us say your Sunday school teacher asked you to make a trip to the store to buy something, but you knew that someone else had already done the job. It would be proper to politely inform your teacher that someone else already made the trip. This way you are acting responsibly by giving him accurate information so he can make a correct decision. He can either tell you that he still needs you to go to the store, or that because of this new information, the trip is unnecessary. Once you have asked you question, and all the facts are known, you need to abide by whichever Godly decision is made.

After questioning his father's actions, Isaac humbly submitted, even to the point of death. He may not have understood exactly what his father was doing, but he did have complete trust and obedience in his father's decisions.

Questions:

1. Take now thy son, thine only son ________________, whom thou lovest, and get thee into the land of ____________. (Genesis 22:2)
2. On the ____________ day Abraham lifted up his ______________, and saw the place afar off. (Genesis 22:4)
3. Abraham took the _____________ of the burnt offering, and laid it upon ______________ his son. (Genesis 22:6)
4. Isaac asked, Behold the ___________ and the ____________: but where is the ____________ for a burnt offering? (Genesis 22:7)
5. God will provide Himself a ______________ for a ______________ offering: so they went both of them together. (Genesis 22:8)
6. And ________________ stretched forth his ____________, and took the ______________ to slay his son. (Genesis 22:10)
7. The ____________ of the Lord called unto him out of ____________, and said, ________________, ________________. (Genesis 22:11)
8. I know that thou ____________________ God, seeing thou hast not ________________ thy son. (Genesis 22:12)
9. Abraham lifted up his ___________, and looked, and behold behind him a ______________ caught in a ______________ by his horns. (Genesis 22:13)
10. I will multiply thy ___________ as the stars of the heaven, and as the ____________ which is upon the sea shore; and thy seed shall possess the ____________ of his ______________. (Genesis 22:17)

Thought Question:

1. Do you think Abraham really would have killed Isaac if God had not stopped him? Why? ____________________________________
2. What comparisons can you make between Abraham and Isaac, and God the Father and God the Son? ____________________________

The Sacrifice of Isaac

Lesson Review:

1. From Genesis 19:1, how do we know that Lot was an important person in Sodom? (Lesson #9) ____________________

____

2. Why was God's Law written? (Lesson #9) ____________________

____

3. Why were the herdmen of Abraham and Lot quarreling? (Lesson #7) ____________________

____

Map Review:

1. Fill in the blanks where the name of the city or object has been removed.

2. Circle the name of the city where Abraham and Lot quarreled.

3. Put an "X" on the spot where the city of Sodom most likely stood.

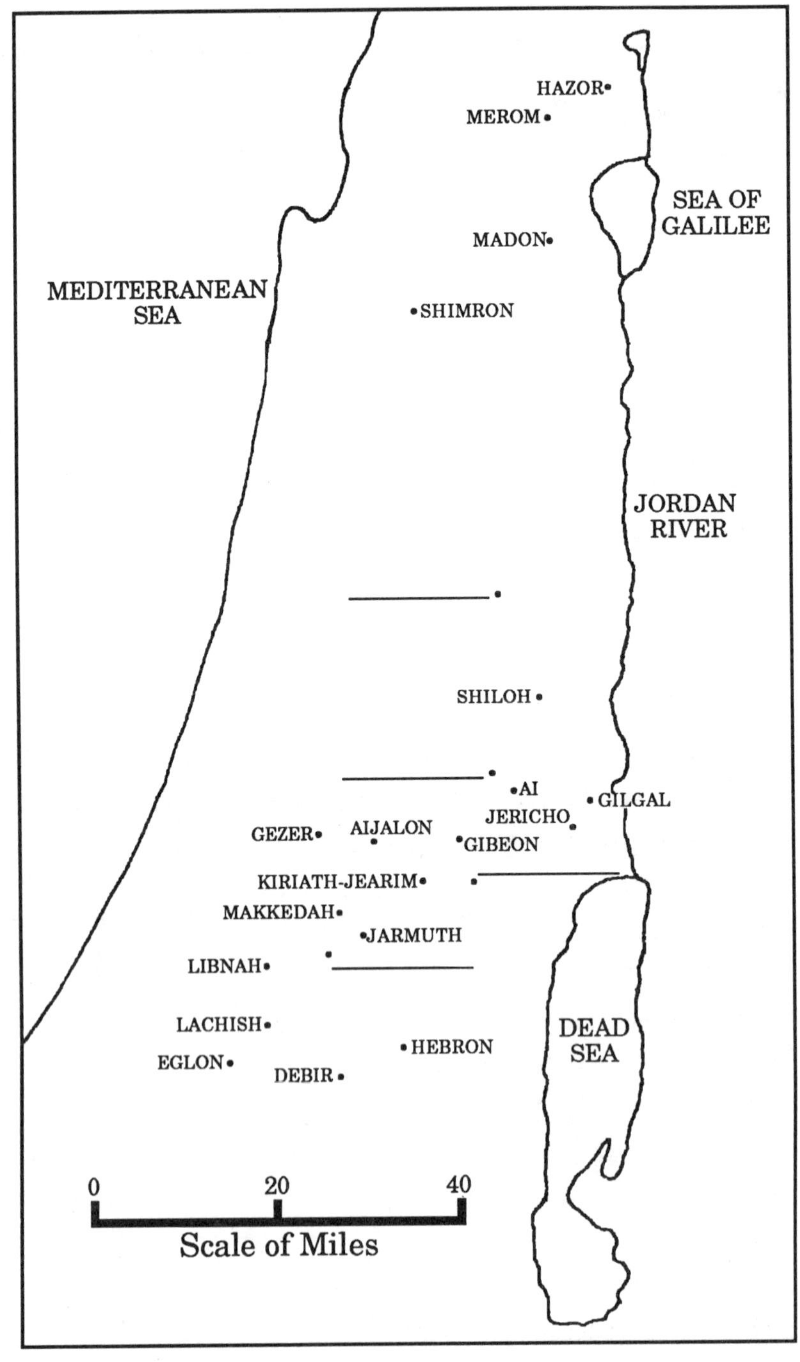

Jacob the Deceiver
Lesson #11

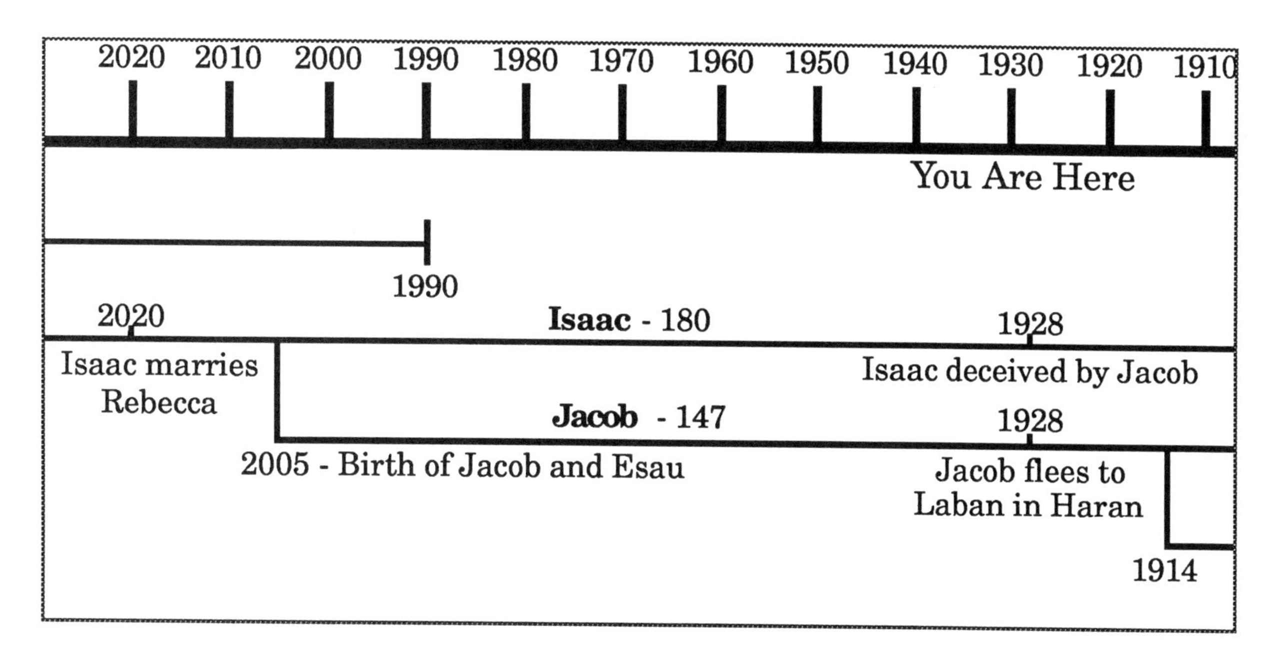

Lesson Goal: To understand the difference between tricks and deception.

Background Text: Genesis 27

Memory Verse: But I say unto you which hear, love your enemies, do good to them which hate you. Luke 6:27

I remember as a child visiting my uncle who would always have a new trick to show my brothers, sisters, and me. Once he had a quarter that he made disappear and then reappear in my ear. I was so impressed I wanted him to continue doing it until we had enough money to buy a bike. When I grew older, I learned that my uncle did not make the money come out of my ear, but was only showing me a trick.

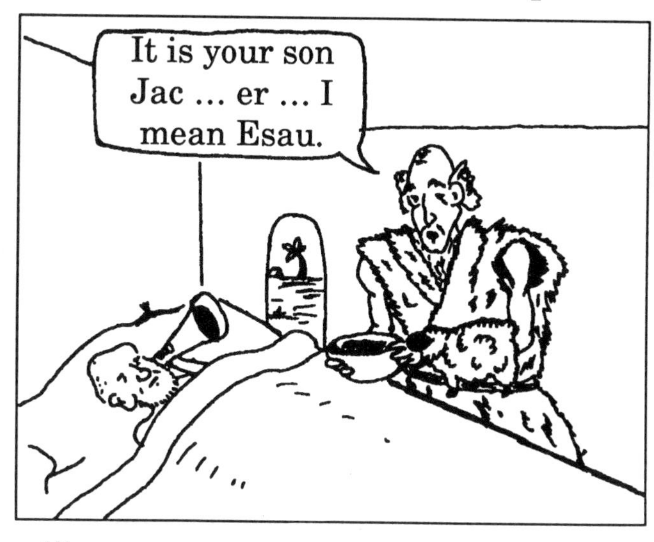

It is fun to play tricks or practical jokes on people, but

Jacob the Deceiver

we need to follow some guidelines to make sure the trick does not have bad results. First, we need to make certain that the trick will not hurt anyone. Then once the trick is done, the consequences must easily be changed back to what they were in the beginning. For example, you may throw water on someone, but make sure the water does not destroy anything that cannot be cleaned, fixed, or replaced. Third, ask permission to do the trick from someone who is in authority over you. For instance, if you want to play a trick on your brother, first ask your parents if they approve. Finally, ask yourself if God would be dishonored by the trick. If you feel that what you are planning does not glorify God, even if it passes the first three steps, do not do it.

Jacob had a bad habit of tricking people. He could be called a deceitful person because he did not always trust God, but relied upon his own tricks to get what he wanted. Later in his life, God blessed Jacob and established a covenant with him, but that was not until after Jacob had learned some important lessons.

Please keep in mind that Jacob was not a young man when he tricked his father, but around seventy-seven years old. Isaac at the time was about 137 years old.

<u>Questions</u>: Multiple choice -- circle the correct answer for each question.

1. When Isaac was old what could he not do? (Genesis 27:1)
   *Hear
   *See
   *Walk
   *Talk

2. What did Isaac want Esau to bring? (Genesis 27:3)
   *Beef
   *Pork
   *Goat
   *Venison

3. Who was Jacob asked to obey? (Genesis 27:6-8)
   *Isaac
   *Rebekah
   *Esau
   *God

4. What did Rebekah make for Isaac? (Genesis 27:14)
   *Dessert
   *A salad
   *Savory meat
   *A delicious dinner

5. How did Jacob say that he found the meat? (Genesis 27:20)
   *The Lord brought it to him
   *He was a good hunter
   *He was a good shot
   *His mother had prepared the meal

6. How did Isaac check to see if his son was Esau? (Genesis 27:21-23)
   *He did not check at all
   *Felt his skin
   *Listened to his voice
   *Ate the food

7. What did Isaac's blessing to Jacob include? (Genesis 27:28-29)
   *He would defeat all his enemies
   *He would rule the world
   *Nations would bow down to him
   *The earth would be his footstool

8. From where did Esau come after Jacob left Isaac? (Genesis 27:30)
   *Fishing
   *Cooking the food
   *Hunting
   *Changing his clothes

9. Why did Esau hate Jacob? (Genesis 27:41)
   *Because Esau sold his birthright
   *Because Rebecca loved Jacob more than himself
   *Because he was the first born
   *Because of the blessing his father gave Jacob

10. To where did Rebekah tell Jacob to flee? (Genesis 27:43)
   *To Egypt
   *To her uncle in Ur
   *To the land of Canaan
   *To her brother in Haran

Thought Questions:

1. Why is it wrong to deceive people? ______________________________
____
____
____
____
____

2. Explain a time when you played a trick upon someone and it had a bad result. How did you repair the damage and apologize to the person? ______________________________
____
____
____
____
____

Lesson Review:

1. How did Isaac respond to his father's authority when they went to make the sacrifice? (Lesson #10) ______________________
____

2. What type of promise did God establish with Noah? (Lesson #4)
____
____

3. What did God create on the sixth day? (Lesson #1) ____________
____
____

Genealogy

Have you ever made a family tree? A family tree is a listing of your relatives and how they are related to you. Many bookstores have beautiful layouts that you can purchase which will help you list and organize your family tree. Genealogies, which are the same as family trees, are important because they help us to gain a sense of our family history and background. Later in this book you will be asked to make a family tree for yourself, but right now we want to look at the genealogy of a very special family in the Bible.

The following page contains a genealogy from Adam to the sons of Joseph. This family was important because it established the Jewish race and was the family line through which Christ Jesus was born. Most of the stories in the Old Testament center around the Jews, so it is important to understand their history and family significance.

The names and descendants for this genealogy are taken from several places in the Bible (Genesis 10, 11:10-32; Matthew 1:1-17; Luke 3:23-38). It is important to understand that the word "begot," which is used in the Biblical genealogies, may not mean an immediate descendant, but of the same family line. For example, Enoch may not be the direct son of Jared, but his grandson or great grandson. For our understanding of Scripture, it is not necessary to know what the relationship between Enoch and Jared was, but simply that Enoch was a descendant from the line of Jared.

The bottom half of the genealogy contains the descendants of Abraham and his father Terah. Pay close attention to this area. The descendants tended to marry within the same family, so the line can become quite confusing. After careful study you will be able to understand the family line from Terah to Jacob and his twelve sons.

Genealogy

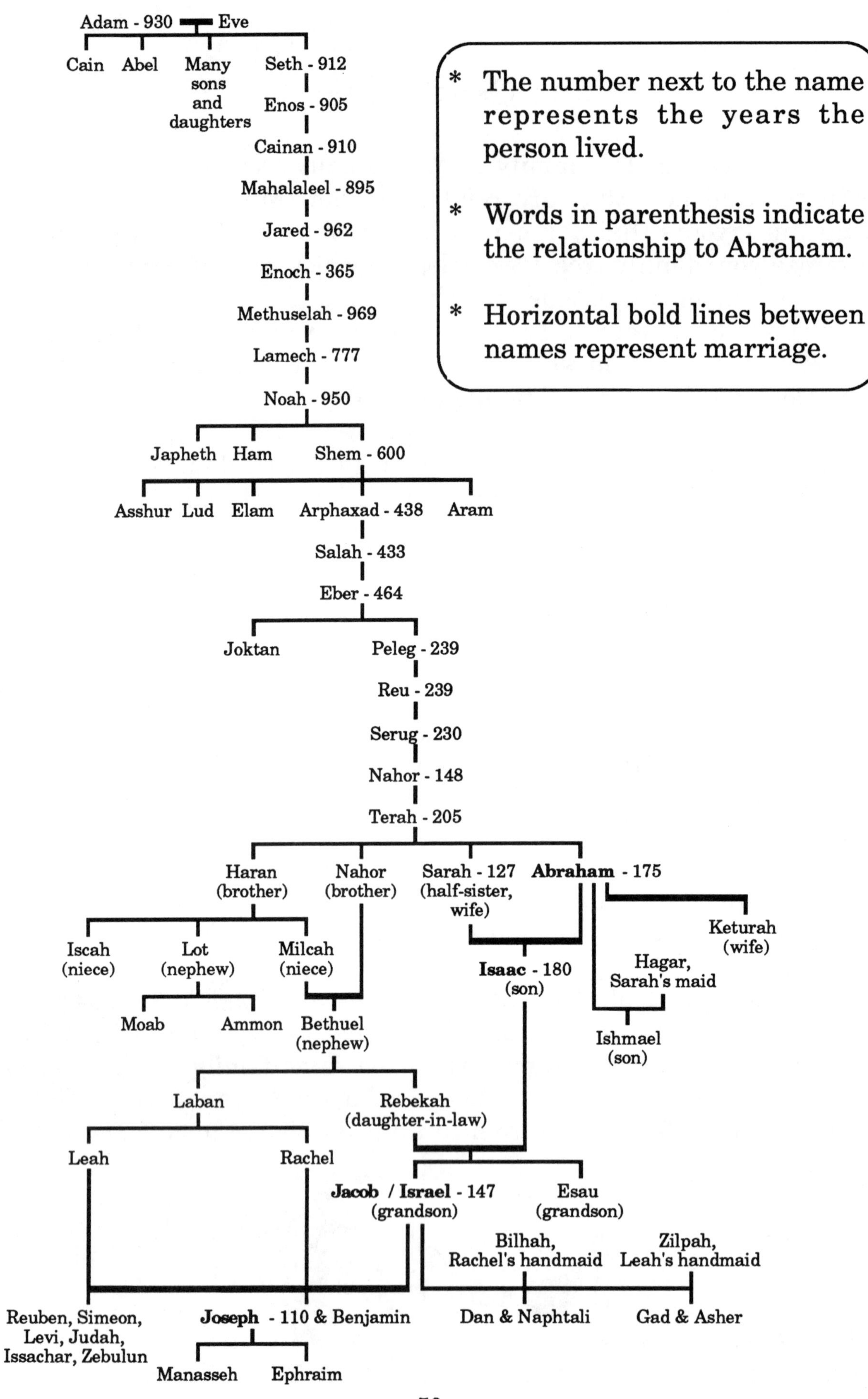

* The number next to the name represents the years the person lived.

* Words in parenthesis indicate the relationship to Abraham.

* Horizontal bold lines between names represent marriage.

The Trials of Joseph
Lesson #12

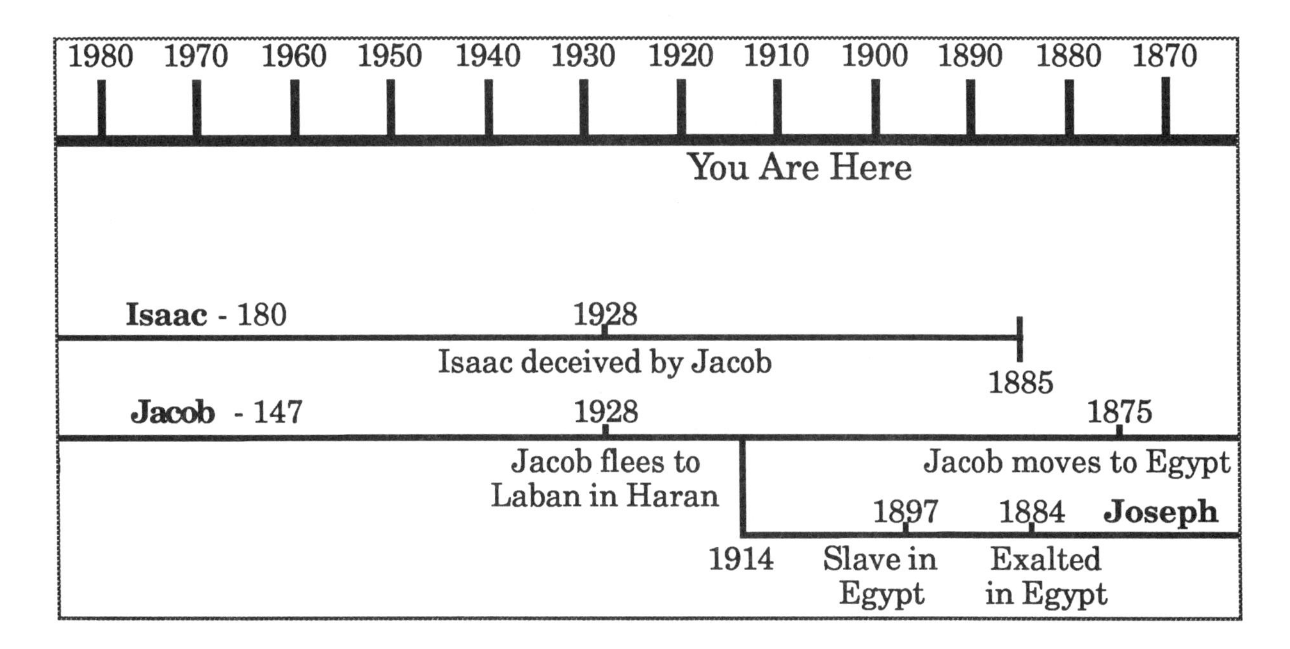

Lesson Goal: To understand that God has complete sovereignty over our lives.

Background Text: Genesis 37 & 40

Memory Verse: And we know that all things work together for good to them that love God, to them who are the called according to his purpose. Romans 8:28

Do you know what the word "sovereign" means, especially when we talk about it within the context of God's sovereignty? Sovereign means that God is in control of everything, and nothing happens in the universe that God does not already know. Joseph, who was mistreated by his brothers and sold into slavery as a teenager, came to understand what God's sovereignty meant. Throughout his life, whether as a

slave, a prisoner, or even as second in command over all of Egypt, Joseph trusted that God was in control, guiding and directing his actions (Genesis 50:20).

As we grow older, we will face trials and difficulties which may seem impossible to overcome. These trials do not have to be something to fear, because God is sovereign over everything. We cannot control the events that happen in and around our lives, but we can control how we respond to them. As our memory verse says, even our trials and problems will eventually be good if we love God and remain faithful to His will.

Questions: Who said this?

1. I loved Joseph more than all my other sons. (Genesis 37:3) ______
   ______
2. I suggested that rather than killing Joseph, we should throw him into a pit. (Genesis 37:22) ______
3. We were traveling to Egypt with camels when we bought Joseph from his brothers. (Genesis 37:25) ______
4. I dreamed that my father and brothers would bow down to me. (Genesis 37:6-9) ______
5. I mourned for many days after they told me Joseph had died. (Genesis 37:34) ______

6. I bought Joseph from the Midianites. (Genesis 37:36) ____________
7. I had a dream about wine and grapes. (Genesis 40:9-10) ___________
8. I had a dream about bread and a basket on my head. (Genesis 40:17) ____________
9. I was the captain of the guard and an officer in Pharaoh's army. (Genesis 37:36) ____________
10. I was angry with two of my servants and threw them into prison. (Genesis 40:2) ____________

Thought Questions:

1. What can you do to make certain you grow closer to God through your trials and problems? ____________

2. Think about what you would do if you were separated from your family as Joseph was. Could you continue to trust God as he did? Why? ____________

Lesson Review:

1. List several ways that Abraham's faith was developed? (Lesson #7)

2. How many pairs of clean animals did Noah bring on the ark? (Lesson #4) ____________
3. What is the purpose of the book of Genesis? (Genesis Background)

The Temptation of Joseph
Lesson #13

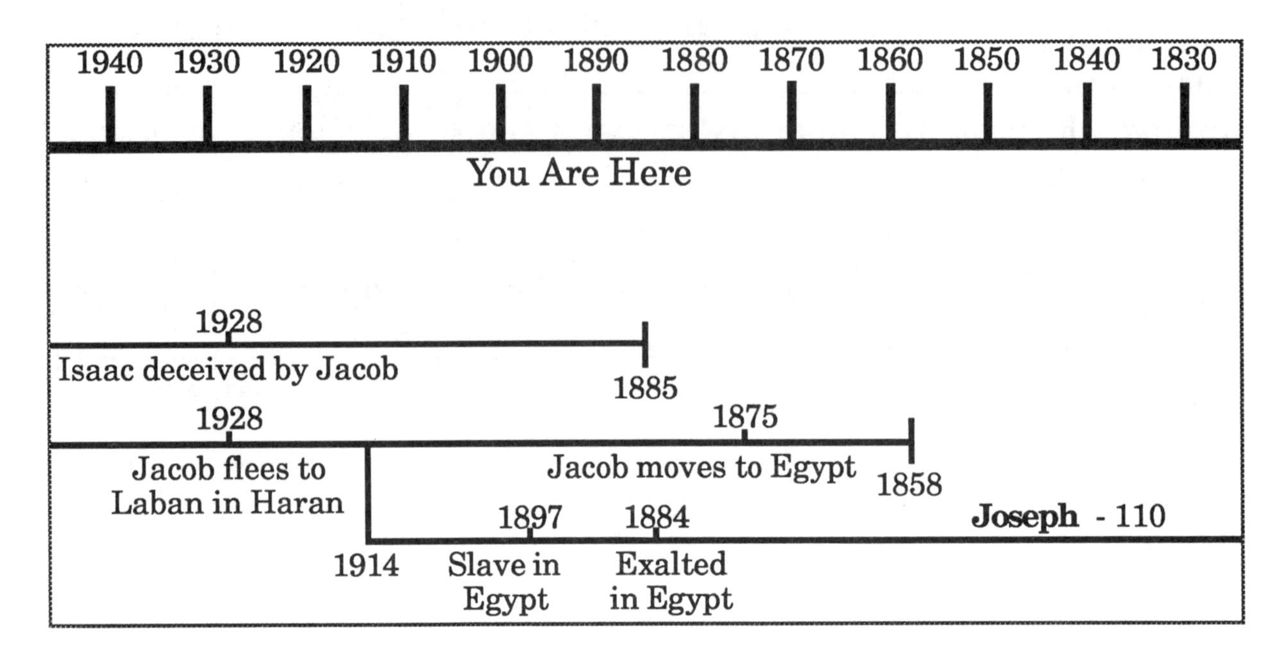

Lesson Goal: To understand nature of temptation and how we can avoid sinning.

Background Text: Genesis 39

Memory Verse: Submit yourselves therefore to God. Resist the devil, and he will flee from you. James 4:7

What is temptation? There are many different ways we can define this term, but the one I like best is "prompting to do something that we should not do." Satan will use our evil desires to tempt us to sin and break God's moral Law (James 1:14). It is Satan's desire that we sin because he wants us to turn away from God. It is important to realize that temptation is not sin. However, we sin when we do the thing that we were tempted to do.

When Eve was tempted by Satan in the garden to eat the fruit from the tree of knowledge of good and evil, she did not sin until she ate the fruit. On the other hand, Joseph did not sin when he was tempted by Potiphar's wife because he resisted the temptation. Whenever we are tempted to do something that is wrong, we make the decision to sin or not to sin. If we are to serve God and honor Him, we must not submit to the temptation and fall into sin.

The Bible lists three different ways we can respond to temptation in order to prevent us from sinning. First of all, we can simply remove the object of the temptation from our life. If we are tempted to read a magazine that we should not look at, we can remove it, destroy it, or get rid of it, so it is no longer there to bother us. Next, we can resist temptation. James 4:7 says, "Submit yourselves therefore to God. Resist the devil, and he will flee from you." There may be times when it is impossible to remove the temptation, so we must stand firm and resist it. The best way to resist it is to draw near to God. Praying, reading the Bible, and thinking of good things are ways of standing up against temptation and drawing near to God (Philippians 4:8). Finally, we can run from the temptation (II Timothy 2:22). This is what Joseph eventually had to do with Potiphar's wife. Had Joseph remained, he might have fallen into sin by submitting to this wicked woman. So instead, he simply ran away from the temptation so it could not reach him.

Resisting temptation is very difficult, but we should not forget I Corinthians 10:13 which says, "....God is faithful, who will not suffer you to be tempted above that ye are able; but will with the temptation also make a way to escape, that ye may be able to bear it." Then, even when we do sin, we need to humbly repent and try not to give in to the temptation the next time it happens.

Questions:

1. Joseph was brought down to ____________; and __________________, bought him of the hands of the ____________________. (Genesis 39:1)

The Temptation of Joseph

2. The Lord made all that Joseph did to _______________ in his hand. (Genesis 39:3)
3. And he made Joseph ________________ over his ____________, and all that he had he put into his ______________. (Genesis 39:4)
4. Joseph said, How then can I do this great _________________, and _________ against God? (Genesis 39:9)
5. It came to pass about this time, that ______________ went into the ______________ to do his ________________; and there was none of the ______________ of the house there within. (Genesis 39:11)
6. And she caught him by his garment, saying, ___________ with me: and he left his _________________ in her hand, and ___________, and got him out. (Genesis 39:12)
7. Potiphar's wife lied by saying, He has brought in a ____________ unto us to mock us; he came in unto me to _________ with me, and I cried out with a loud ______________. (Genesis 39:14)
8. Joseph's master took him, and put him into _____________, a place where the __________ prisoners were ___________. (Genesis 39:20)
9. The Lord was with _____________, and showed him ____________, and gave him _____________ in the sight of the ______________ of the prison. (Genesis 39:21)
10. The keeper of the prison committed to Joseph's hand all the ______________ that were in the ______________. (Genesis 39:22)

Thought Questions:

1. Is there an area in your life in which you are often tempted? What is it? ____
____
____
____
____

2. From what you have learned in this lesson, what can you do to fight the temptation? ______________________________________
____
____
____
____

Lesson Review:

1. How old was Joseph when his brothers sold him? (Lesson #12 - Time line) ______
2. What are the four tests to use before playing a trick on someone? (Lesson #11) ______
3. Is it disobedient to humbly question human authority when asked to do something? Explain your answer. (Lesson #10) ______

Supplemental Exercise: From the Genealogy, complete the dotted lines with the correct information.

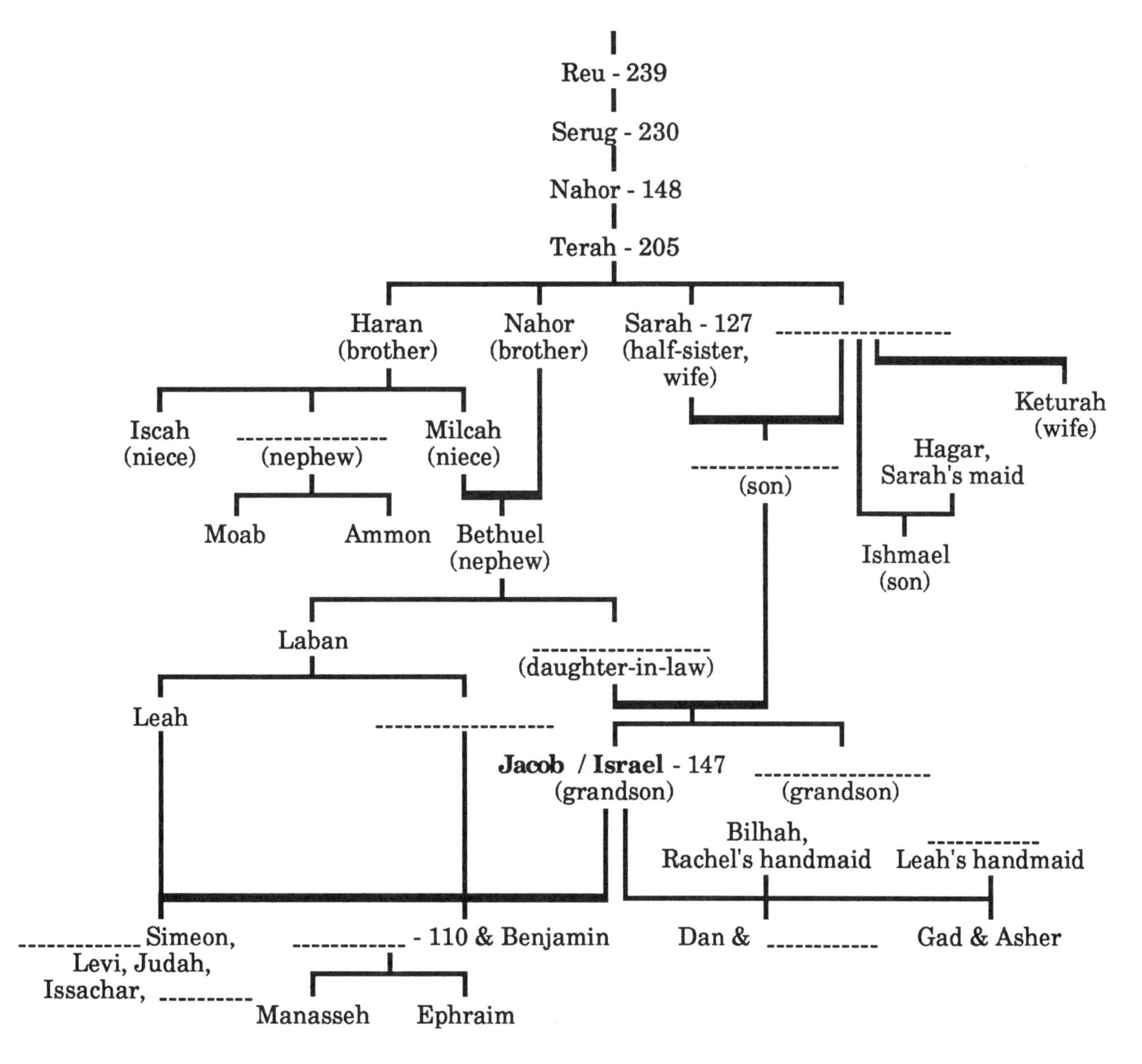

The Triumph of Joseph
Lesson #14

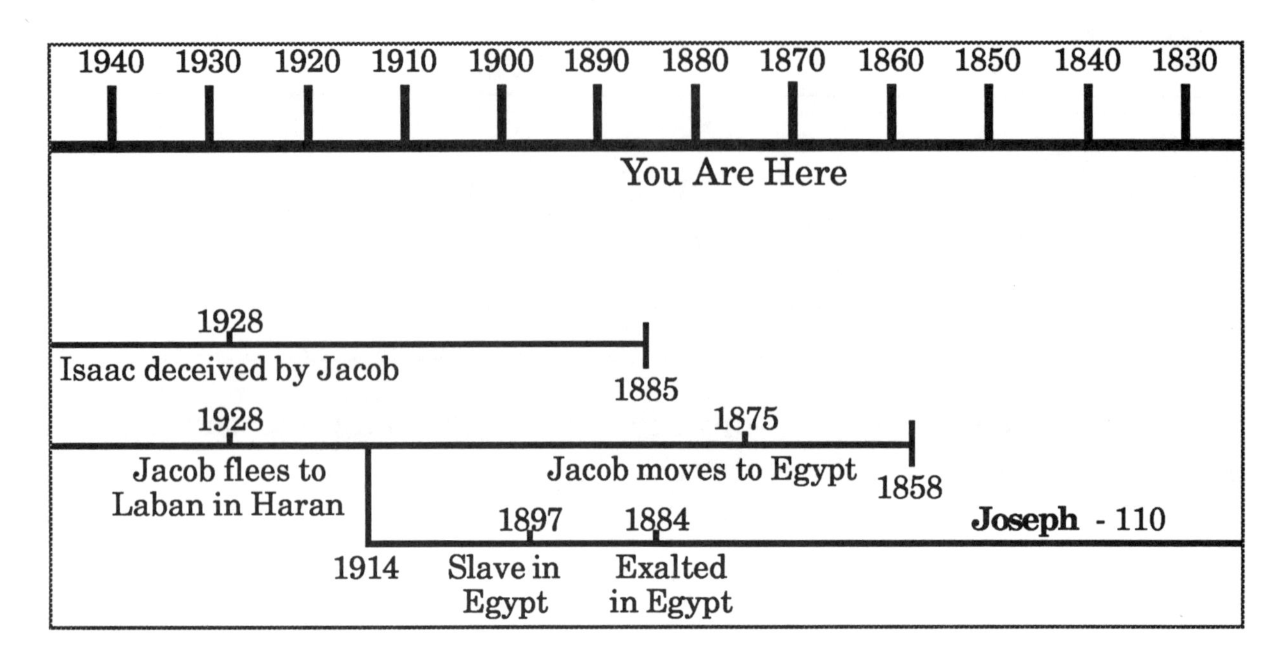

Lesson Goal: To understand that we need to allow God to shape us into His own design.

Background Text: Genesis 41

Memory Verse: Only fear the Lord, and serve him in truth with all your heart: for consider how great things he hath done for you. I Samuel 12:24

In the last lesson, we studied temptation and what steps we can take to avoid sin. Joseph was our example of running away from temptation when it becomes very strong. Since Joseph was faithful to God and did not sin, the Lord richly honored and blessed him. Through God's direction, Joseph was able to help the nation of Egypt have enough food to last through seven years of famine. God was able to use Joseph and bless him this way because Joseph had allowed God to teach him and direct his life.

Have you ever worked with clay to make pots, jars, or perhaps even a flower vase for your mother? To make a pot, you need to have a lump of soft, moist clay that you throw on a wheel which is quickly spinning in front of you. Then, as the clay and wheel are spinning, you take your hands and begin shaping the clay into the form of a pot. You stick your thumbs down into the middle of the clay and pull the sides up with your fingers. When you are finished, hopefully you have a nice pot.

The Bible speaks about God doing the same thing with His children. Throughout our lives, God will shape and mold us into His purpose and calling, but we need to be willing to be soft and allow God to shape us. If we refuse, God will discipline us in order to teach us lessons and give us character, so He can continue to mold our lives. Sadly, some people do not listen to God even when He does discipline them. God is not honored because of their stubbornness, rebelliousness, and sin. So, the next time you see a beautiful pot and think of all the time, effort, and patience the potter must have put into it, remember how God is shaping your life and making you into a person that will honor and glorify Him.

Questions:

1. How long did Joseph stay in prison before Pharaoh brought him out? (Genesis 41:1 & 14) ______________________________
2. What did the lean cows do to the fat cows? (Genesis 41:4) ________
____
____
3. Who could not interpret Pharaoh's dream? (Genesis 41:8) ________
____
____
4. Who did Joseph say would give Pharaoh the answer to his dream? (Genesis 41:16) ______________________________
____

5. What did the seven good cows and the seven good ears represent? (Genesis 41:26-29) ______________________________

____

6. What was going to happen in the land of Egypt because of the famine? (Genesis 41:30) ______________________________

____

____

7. What did Joseph tell Pharaoh he had to do to prepare for the famine? (Genesis 41:33-36) ______________________________

____

____

____

8. How did Pharaoh immediately reward Joseph for his good counsel? (Genesis 41:40-44) ______________________________

____

____

____

____

9. How old was Joseph when he stood before Pharaoh? (Genesis 41:46) ______________________________

10. What were the names of the two sons born to Joseph? (Genesis 41:51-52) ______________________________

____

Thought Questions:

1. Do you think God would still have blessed Joseph if Joseph had sinned when tempted? Why? ______________________________

____

____

____

2. What lessons do you think Joseph had learned earlier in his life to make him such a great leader before Pharaoh? ______________________________

____

____

____

____

Lesson Review:

1. In your own words, explain the difference between temptation and sin. (Lesson #13) ____
____
____
____
2. True or False: Noah and Abraham lived during the same time and could have known each other. (Lesson #4 - Time line)
3. True or False: Adam lived during the same time as Noah's father, Lamech and could have known each other. (Lesson #3 - Time line)

Supplemental Exercise: Unscramble the seven words listed below. Take the letters that are circled and rearrange them to solve the missing phrase. Hint: An Egyptian did this while he was sleeping.

☐ ☐ ◯ ☐ ☐ ☐ ◯ **R O H H P A A**

☐ ☐ ☐ ☐ ◯ ◯ **P H J S O E**

☐ ◯ ◯ ☐ **R N C O**

◯ ☐ ☐ ☐ ☐ **Y G E T P**

☐ ◯ ◯ ☐ ☐ ◯ **A I E M N F**

◯ ◯ ☐ ◯ ☐ **M R D A E**

☐ ☐ ◯ **D G O**

__ __ __ __ __ __ __   __ __ __ __ __ __ __

The Tenderness of Joseph
Lesson #15

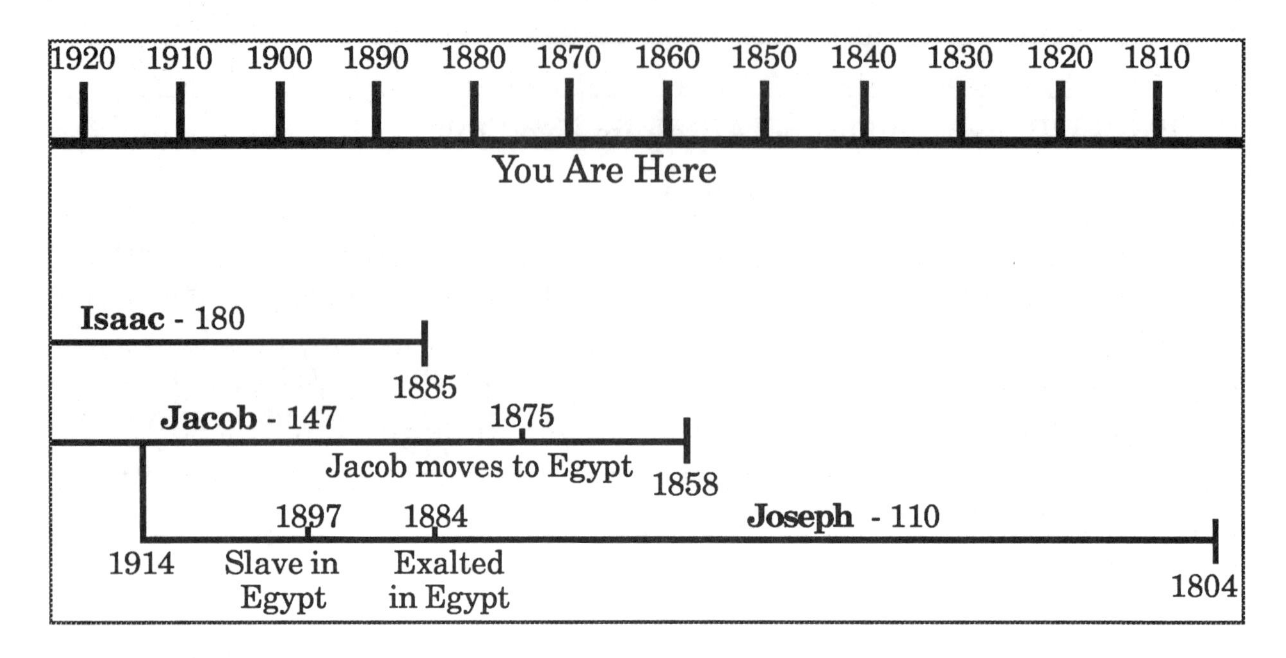

Lesson Goal: To understand that we can love other people only after we have accepted God's love and plan for our lives.

Background Text: Genesis 42-45

Memory Verse: But the fruit of the Spirit is love, joy, peace, longsuffering, gentleness, goodness, faith, meekness, temperance: against such there is no law. Galatians 5:22-23

It is hard to forgive people, especially if they have hurt us badly. In this lesson, we will see how Joseph went beyond forgiveness when he came in contact with his brothers again. He not only forgave them, but showed them compassion, tenderness, and genuine love. Why do you think Joseph was able to be so kind to his brothers? It was because he understood that although they had sinned when they mistreated him, God used that to guide and direct his life (Genesis 45:5).

There is a saying, "If life gives you lemons – make lemonade." That means if life gives you problems, turn the problems into something good that will help you. Joseph could have become bitter and hated his brothers, but he did not. Instead, he trusted the Lord to use these terrible experiences to strengthen his life and make him into the person God wanted him to be.

If Joseph had fallen into sin with Potiphar's wife, or had he become bitter toward his brothers because of their failures, that sin would have made him ineffective in serving the Lord in Egypt. However, Joseph saw that the things which happened to him were God's way of preparing him for the future. Since he had this understanding he could forgive his brothers, because even though they meant it for harm, God used it for good (Genesis 50:20). In the end, Joseph not only saved the Egyptian people from starvation, but he saved his own family as well.

Questions: Multiple choice -- circle the correct answer for each question.

1. Who stayed home while his brothers went to Egypt to buy food? (Genesis 42:4)
   *Judah
   *Jacob
   *Simeon
   *Benjamin

2. From where did the brothers come to buy food? (Genesis 42:7)
   *Mexico
   *Israel
   *Canaan
   *Jerusalem

3. What did Joseph remember when his brothers were bowing down to him? (Genesis 42:9)
   *His promise to God
   *His promise to his father
   *That he forgot to eat supper
   *His dreams

4. Who stayed in prison while the other brothers went home? (Genesis 42:24)
   *Benjamin
   *Simeon
   *Joseph
   *Judah

5. What surprise did the brothers find when they opened their sacks? (Genesis 42:27)
   *The money they had used to buy the grain along with the grain
   *Their grain had been stolen by the Egyptians
   *They had twice the amount of grain they had purchased
   *All of the above

6. Who heard Joseph when he wept? (Genesis 45:2)
   *His wife
   *All his brothers
   *The Egyptians and the house of Pharaoh
   *His father Jacob

7. Why did Joseph tell his brothers that God had sent him to Egypt? (Genesis 45:7)
   *To become a great leader
   *To save their lives
   *Because God loved Joseph
   *Because Joseph had been faithful to God

8. Who did Joseph say had sent him to Egypt? (Genesis 45:8)
   *His father
   *God
   *His brothers
   *Pharaoh

9. Where did Joseph say his brothers and father could live? (Genesis 45:10)
   *Goshen
   *Egypt
   *Canaan
   *The desert

10. What first happened to Jacob when he heard that Joseph was governor of Egypt? (Genesis 45:26)
    *He praised God
    *He sang a song
    *His heart fainted
    *He thanked his other sons for finding Joseph

Thought Questions:

1. Why do you think Joseph tested his brothers by calling them spies and keeping Simeon? ______________________________
____
____
____
____
____

2. In Genesis 42:21, the brothers were still feeling guilty about what they had done to Joseph over twenty years earlier. Why do you think they felt this way? ______________________________
____
____
____
____
____
____
____

Lesson Review:

1. How many years did the Egyptian famine last? (Lesson #14) _____
____

2. What does the term "sovereign" mean? (Lesson #12) ___________
____
____
____

3. Why did Lot choose to live near the cities of Sodom and Gomorrah? (Lesson #8) ______________________________
____
____

Unit Test #1

1. What was the first work that God gave Adam to do? (Genesis 2:15)
___
___
2. What did God take from Adam in order to make Eve? (Genesis 2:22) ___
3. What was the name of Eve's third son? (Genesis 4:25) ___
___
4. What was the name of the mountains where the ark finally landed? (Genesis 8:4) ___
5. How many times did Noah use a dove to test for dry land? (Genesis 8:8-12) ___
6. When the people built the tower of Babel, what did they use for mortar? (Genesis 11:3) ___
___
7. What did the people who built the tower of Babel do after the Lord had scattered them? (Genesis 11:8) ___
___
8. Before Job was tempted, how many children did he have? (Job 1:2)
___
___
9. Why were the herdmen of Abraham and Lot fighting? (Genesis 13:6-7) ___
___
10. How many angels came to Sodom to see Lot? (Genesis 19:1) ___
___
11. Why did Lot's wife become a pillar of salt? (Genesis 19:26) ___
___
___
12. Who did God tell Abraham to take and sacrifice? (Genesis 22:2)
___

13. What did Isaac want Esau to prepare before the blessing was given? (Genesis 27:3) ______________________________
____
14. Who dreamed that his brothers and father would worship him? (Genesis 37:9) ______________________________
15. Who was the captain of the guard and an officer in Pharaoh's army? (Genesis 37:36) ______________________________

God's delays are not denials,
He has heard your prayers;
He knows all about your trials,
Knows your every care.

God's delays are not denials,
Help is on the way;
He is watching over life's deals,
Bringing forth the day.

God's delays are not denials,
You will find Him true;
Working through life's darkest trials,
What is best for you.

Exodus Background

Author of Exodus: Moses (John 5:46-47, 7:19).

Date of Writing: 1440-1400 B.C. Exodus was written during the forty years of wilderness wanderings.

Purpose of Exodus: To show God's redemption toward His people. Redemption means to "pay a price in recovering ownership." Christ paid the price for His people and recovered them from the bondage of sin.

Outline of Exodus:

I. Israel in Egypt (1:1-12:36)
   A. God Chooses Moses (Exodus 1-4)
   B. God Sends Moses to Pharaoh (5:1-7:13)
   C. Ten Plagues (7:14-12:36)

II. Israel to Sinai (12:37-18:27)
   A. Israel Leaving Egypt (12:37-15:21)
   B. Israel Grumbles (15:22-17:7)
   C. Israel at War (17:8-17:16)
   D. Israel Establishes Order (Exodus 18)

III. Israel at Sinai (Exodus 19-40)
   A. Giving of Law and Ten Commandments (Exodus 19-24)
   B. Giving of Tabernacle (Exodus 25-31)
   C. Breaking of Law (Exodus 32-34)
   D. Building of Tabernacle (Exodus 35-40)

The Big Idea of Exodus: Exodus is an important book because it details God's redemption as He freed the Hebrew people from the bondage of the Egyptians. Following His gracious deliverance, the Lord promised to be the Israelites' God if only they would obey His law, which was given to Moses at Mount Sinai. Knowing that people are sinful and would disobey His commands, God ordered the building of the tabernacle, where sacrifices were made to atone for sins. The animal sacrifices symbolized the great sacrifice of Jesus Christ who died to forgive our sins.

It is significant to note that even before God gave the Law to Moses, His relationship with the people was established on the basis of covenants. God had made covenants with Adam, Noah, Abraham, Isaac, and Jacob. Part of the Abrahamic covenant was that his descendants would become a great nation, and the Gentiles would be included in his blessing. Several centuries later, God also established a covenant with David.

When Moses brought the law down from Mount Sinai, the Abrahamic covenant was still in effect; however, the law was added because of transgressions (Galatians 3:19). The law was necessary as a tutor to lead man eventually to Christ (Galatians 3:24). This did not end the promise to Abraham, but it expanded and fulfilled it. Even after the law was given, man was still justified by faith.

Genesis	Exodus	Numbers	Joshua	Judges	I Samuel	II Samuel	I Kings	II Kings	Babylonian Captivity	Ezra	Nehemiah
	Lev.	Deut.		Ruth		I Chron.	II Chronicles			Esther	
Job					Psalms		Proverbs				
							Eccles.				
							Song.				

Obadiah-Edom	Lament.	Haggai-Judah
Joel-Israel	Daniel	Zechariah-Judah
Jonah-Nineveh	Ezekiel	Malachi-Judah
Amos-Israel		
Hosea-Israel		
Micah-Judah		
Isaiah-Judah		
Nahum-Nineveh		
Zephaniah-Judah		
Jeremiah-Judah		
Habakkuk-Judah		

Choosing a Leader
Lesson #16

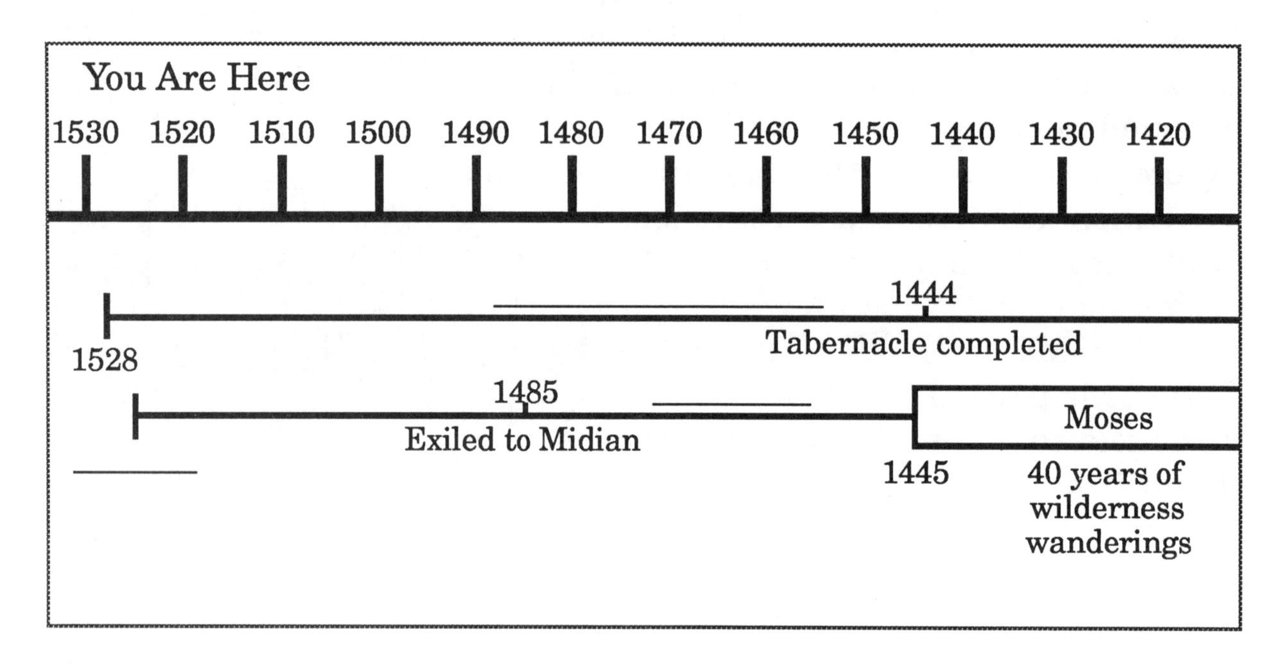

Lesson Goal: To understand that whatever we do for God, as small as it may seem, will be used to accomplish His will.

Background Text: Exodus 1:8-2:25

Memory Verse: Then Peter and the other apostles answered and said, We ought to obey God rather than men. Acts 5:29

The Israelites were in trouble. It had been 390 years since Joseph came to Egypt, and the pharaohs had forgotten all the good things he had done for their country. God had blessed the families of the Israelites so that they had grown to approximately two or three million people in population. The Egyptians were concerned about this because they feared the

Israelites would take over the nation. So, the Israelites were oppressed by the Egyptians and turned into slaves. They were forced to build large cities and received very little pay or food.

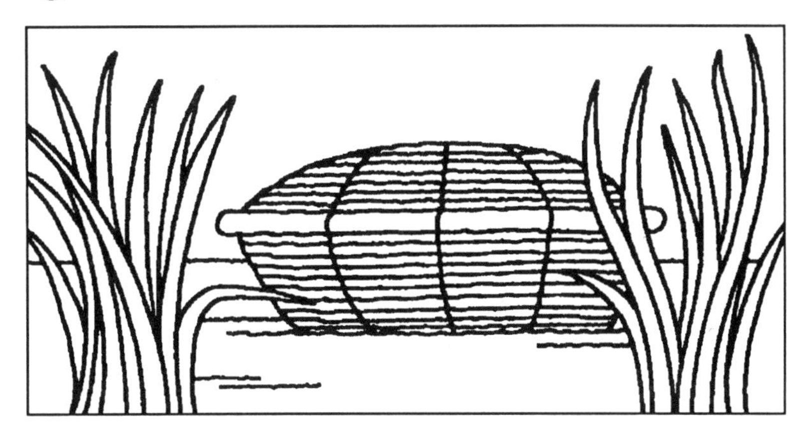

During this time, as the people became more afflicted, they began to cry out to God to save them from their bondage. That was when God raised up Moses to lead the Israelites into freedom. Before God called Moses, his parents did a very brave thing. When Moses was born, his parents disobeyed the cruel governmental laws of Egypt so they could obey the absolute law of the loving God. Pharaoh ordered all the male children to be killed, so Moses' parents disobeyed by hiding him in a basket along the river. A short time later, Pharaoh's daughter found the baby Moses in the river, so she took him to be her own child and raised him in Pharaoh's household. God honored Moses' parents and saved the life of their son because they obeyed the higher law of God.

Today, within our society, there are laws which say it is legal to kill unborn babies. Since the law says this, each year millions of mothers have their babies aborted, because people consider these children to be unwanted. What sometimes happens in society is that wicked people make laws that are different from, or contrary to, God's Law. It is during these times that God's people need to follow His Law and try to change the evil law. Just as the midwives and Moses' parents disobeyed Pharaoh's evil law, so God's people need to disobey and try to change the evil law of abortion. These small efforts are what God uses to bring about His purpose, just as God used the efforts of Moses' parents to bring a leader to deliver Israel from bondage.

Questions:

1. Whom did the Egyptians set over the Israelites to oppress them? (Exodus 1:11) ________________________________
2. What two cities did the Israelites build for Pharaoh? (Exodus 1:11)

   ____

   ____

Choosing a Leader

3. What did the King (Pharaoh) of Egypt tell the midwives to do? (Exodus 1:15-16) ____________________

____

____

4. How did God deal with the midwives? (Exodus 1:20-21) ____________________

____

____

5. Moses' parents were from which house of Israel? (Exodus 2:1) ____

____

6. How long did Moses' parents hide him? (Exodus 2:2) ____________________

____

7. Who found Moses in the river? (Exodus 2:5) ____________________

____

8. What did Moses do to the Egyptian who was fighting with the Israelite? (Exodus 2:12) ____________________

____

9. Why did Moses flee from the presence of Pharaoh? (Exodus 2:15)

____

10. What did God remember when the children of Israel cried out to Him? (Exodus 2:24) ____________________

____

Thought Questions: Ask your parents or grandparents to share an experience that they had when they were younger which God used in a greater way than they expected.

1. What was this experience? ____________________

____

____

____

2. What lessons did they learn through it? ____________________

____

____

____

____

____

____

Lesson Review:

1. What are the three major points from the outline of Exodus? (Exodus Background) ______________________________

   ____

   ____

2. What are the nine elements of the "fruit of the Spirit"? (Lesson #15) ______________________________

   ____

   ____

3. On the time line at the beginning of the chapter, complete the blank spaces with the correct information.

Supplemental Exercise: To better understand the genealogies of the Old Testament, use the chart below to design your own family genealogy. If you run out of room or need more space, you can use a separate sheet of paper.

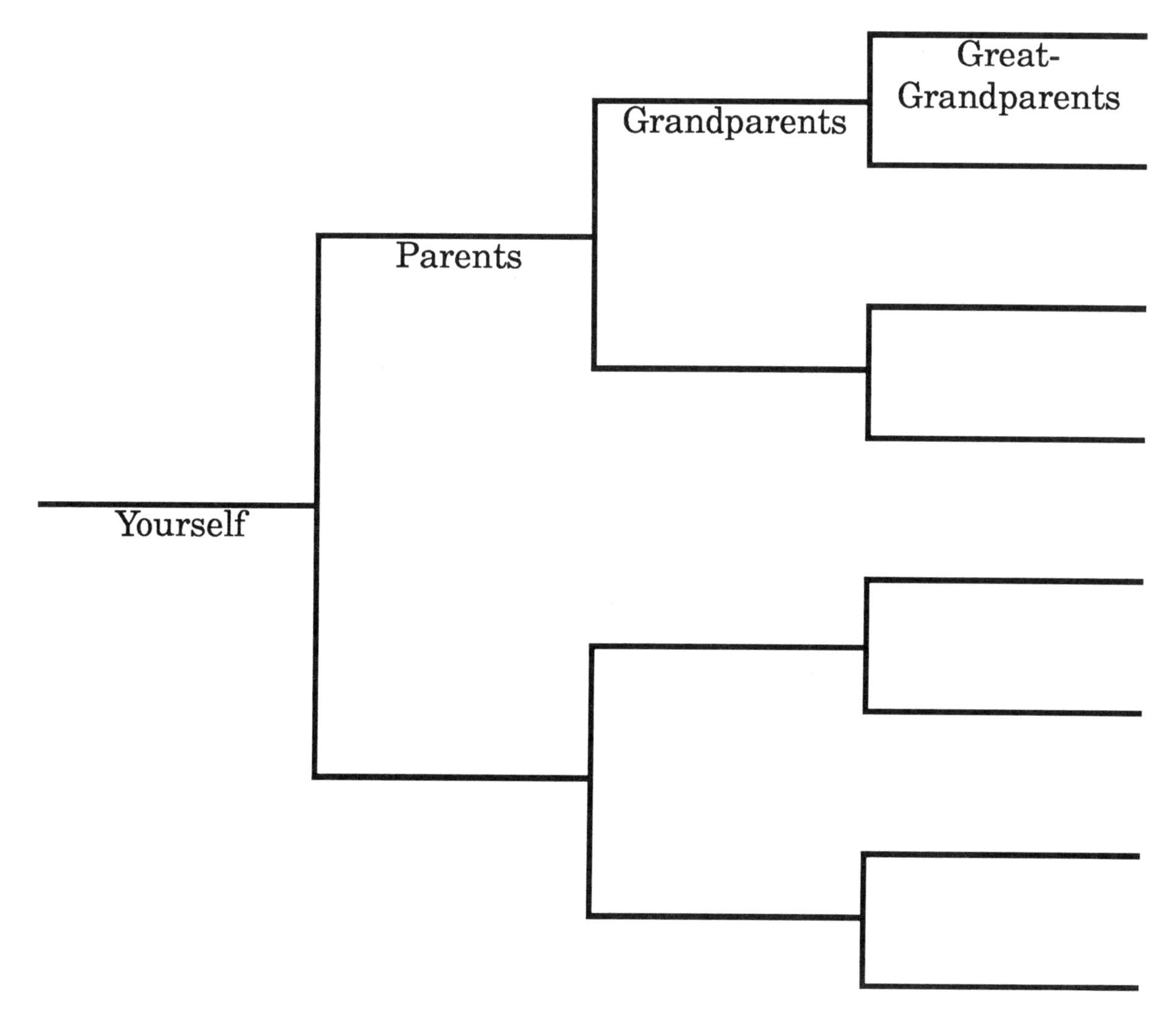

The Calling of Moses
Lesson #17

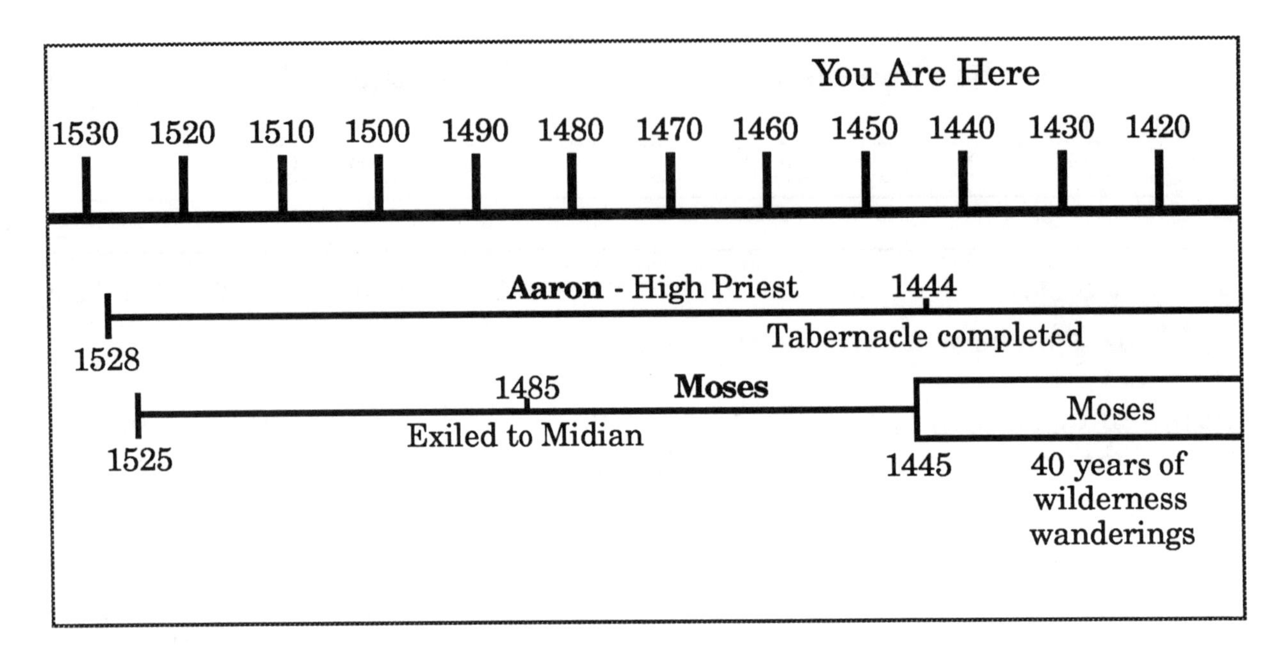

Lesson Goal: To understand that God has a specific plan and purpose for each of our lives.

Background Text: Exodus 3-4

Memory Verse: According as He hath chosen us in Him before the foundation of the world, that we should be holy and without blame before Him in love. Ephesians 1:4

Do you know what you want to be when you grow older? Perhaps you would like to be a doctor, or a construction worker, or an artist, or a baseball player, or a housewife, or a mother, or a fireman; the list could be endless. God has given us all special talents and gifts that we can use now and when we are older, no matter what type of work we do. Did you realize that God has already chosen a career for you to follow? In His will, God knows what would be best for your life.

Ephesians 1:4, which is our memory verse for this lesson, tells us that God had us specifically in mind even before He created the world.

He not only knew when and where we would be born, but he also knew everything we would do throughout our lives. Why does He love and care for us so much? Because He wants us to be blameless before Him. Just as an architect designs a house, God created and designed us. As we grow older, God will call us into the jobs and tasks that He has purposed for us. We need to do all we can to remain holy and blameless in order to fulfill God's design.

This brings us to the lesson concerning the calling of Moses. Moses was now eighty years old; he had been working as a shepherd for the past forty years. He might have been wondering if God would ever use him to help his Israelite brothers. One day while tending his sheep in the mountains, God showed Himself to Moses through the burning bush and outlined His plan to deliver Israel.

God called Moses to go to Pharaoh and lead the Israelites in Egypt out of slavery. However, Moses did not fully understand God's control and purpose in his life. Even though the Lord was directing Moses, he still raised two objections. First of all, Moses felt that the people would not accept him as their leader. No doubt Moses recalled forty years earlier when he killed the Egyptian and tried to appoint himself as judge over Israel. The people rejected him that time, so why should they accept him now? God told Moses to use his rod to do miracles as a sign to the people. This time, God had called Moses and would be directing his actions. This is an important point, because when we are following God's calling, we need to realize that God is directing our paths and not ourselves. We must not object to the Lord's leading, nor allow our thinking to get in the way of His purpose. If we begin to direct our own lives, we will make mistakes that will create problems.

Moses' second objection displayed a lack of confidence in God's ability to use him. Moses doubted his speaking ability, so God became angry and said Aaron would be the spokesman to the people. We may not be satisfied with who we are or what we look like, but that does not give us an excuse to doubt the Lord. God created us the way we are. If He would have wanted us to be or look any different, He would have made us that way. As Christians, we need to stop feeling sorry that our lives are not as wonderful as a fairy tale. We need to place our confidence in God – that He will use us in every area to which He has called us. God is not interested in our ability as much as He wants our availability.

Questions:

1. Whose flock of sheep did Moses keep? (Exodus 3:1) ______________
2. How did the angel of the Lord appear to Moses? (Exodus 3:2) _____
   ____
   ____
3. What did God say He had seen and heard? (Exodus 3:7) __________
   ____
   ____
4. What did God say that His name was? (Exodus 3:14) _____________
   ____
   ____
5. What would be "flowing" in the land of Canaan? (Exodus 3:17) ____
   ____
6. What shall every woman ask of her neighbor when she leaves Egypt? (Exodus 3:22) ________________________________
   ____
   ____
   ____
7. What was in Moses' hand? (Exodus 4:2) __________________
8. Whom did God appoint as spokesman for the Israelites? (Exodus 4:14) ____
   ____
9. What did Moses tell Aaron? (Exodus 4:28) _________________
   ____
   ____
10. What did the Israelites do when they heard that the Lord had visited them? (Exodus 4:31) ___________________________
    ____
    ____

Thought Questions:

1. What do you want to do when you get older? ____________________
2. How can you use this to glorify God? ____________________

Lesson Review:

1. What is purpose of the book of Exodus? (Exodus Background) ____
2. What relation was Rebekah to Abraham? (Genealogy Study) _____
3. Who were the twelve sons of Jacob, and who were their mothers? (Genealogy Study) ____________________

Supplemental Exercise: Go back to Genesis 3:9-12 and see if you remember how Adam tried to excuse himself for his sin. Then complete this puzzle.

The Lord 1-D called unto 6-D and said, "Where 7-A thou?" Adam said, "I heard thy 3-A in the 5-D, and I was 9-A, because I was naked; and I hid myself." God said, "Have you eaten the fruit of the 8-D that I 4-D you not to eat?" And the 2-A said, "The woman gave 2-D fruit from the tree, and I did eat."

The Ten Plagues
Lesson #18

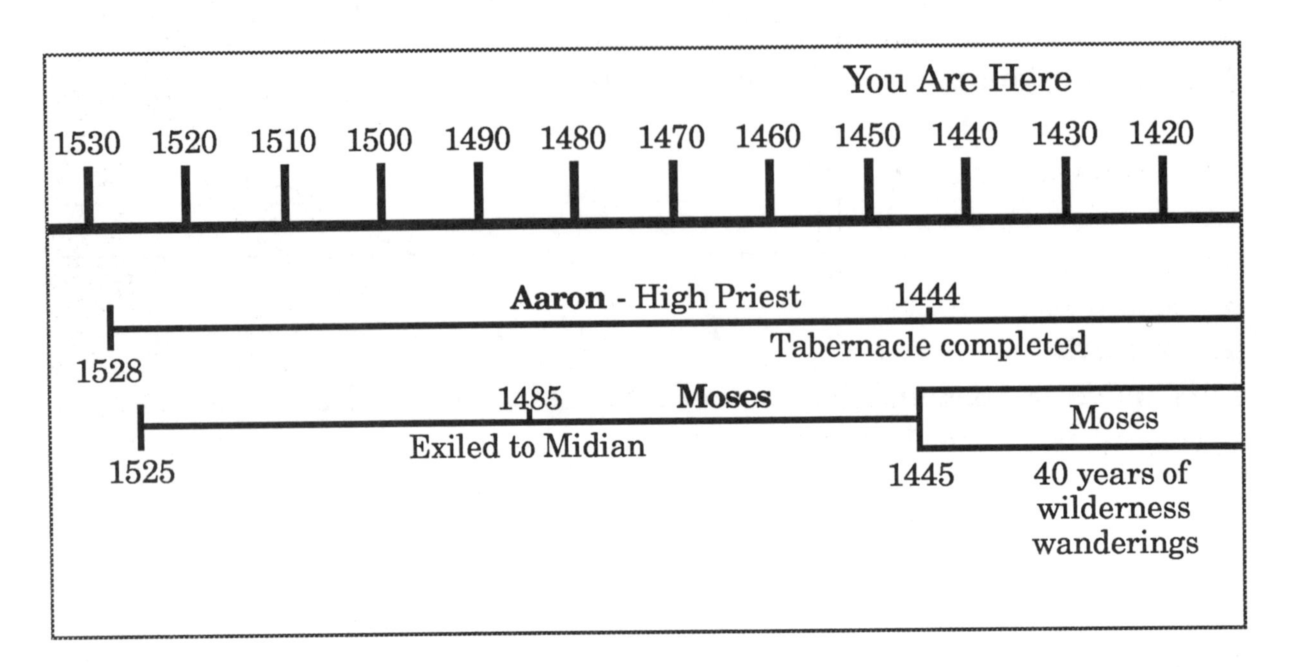

Lesson Goal: To understand the sin of hardening our hearts against God.

Background Text: Exodus 7:14-12:36

Memory Verse: For he that soweth to his flesh shall of the flesh reap corruption; but he that soweth to the Spirit shall of the Spirit reap life everlasting. Galatians 6:8

Pharaoh's heart was hardened! Do you remember a few lessons ago when we talked about our hearts remaining soft like clay so God could mold our lives? Now we have an example of a person who was so opposed to God that his heart was hard. As we study this section of Exodus on the "Ten Plagues," we will see how as the plagues became worse, Pharaoh never repented or acknowledged God as the ruler of the universe.

The warning given to us in Scripture is

very clear; hardening our hearts will lead to sin and destruction (Hebrews 3:13 and Proverbs 28:14). God uses the Bible and our conscience to speak to our hearts in the areas of conduct and righteousness. If we close our "spiritual ears" to the prompting of our

conscience, we are hardening our hearts against God. Our conscience is very quiet. Sometimes it is no louder than a whisper, so we need to pay close attention to what it says. I hope we all know what our conscience sounds like. If we do not, perhaps we are not paying close enough attention to it. Sometimes we even forget that our conscience is there, until we are planning to do something that we should not do. Then we begin to feel a slight nudging, a faint tugging of our heart, saying, "Owner, do not do this thing." As we gradually ignore the leading of our conscience, we harden our hearts and slide deeper into sin. This is what happened to Pharaoh.

Instead of hardening our hearts and ignoring our conscience, we must break down the barriers that exist between our conscience and our heart. We need to make certain that we do not have any sin in our lives that would hurt our relationship with God. Although our conscience is not the final authority like God's Word, it can be used by the Holy Spirit to lead and direct us.

Because of the hardening of Pharaoh's heart, the plagues were used as a means of discrediting the gods of Egypt. They demonstrated that the true Jehovah God of the Israelites was stronger then all the Egyptians' gods. The magicians who claimed to represent the gods of Egypt were soundly defeated. Pharaoh, who was considered divine by the people, was humbled. The great god, the Nile River, was polluted. Frogs defiled the temples of lesser gods. The greatest god in Egypt, the sun, was blotted out in darkness. Then finally, Jehovah God demonstrated his sovereignty over life and death, and won the release of the Israelites.

The Ten Plagues

Questions: Read the Bible verse above each picture, and write a brief description of the plague on the line. Shade in the triangle if the Egyptian magicians could duplicate the plague. Shade in the circle if the Bible says the Hebrews also experienced the plague.

Plague #1:
Exodus 7:17-23

△ ○

____

____

Plague #2:
Exodus 8:3-15

△ ○

____

____

Plague #3:
Exodus 8:16-19

△ ○

____

____

Plague #4:
Exodus 8:21-32

△ ○

____

____

Plague #5:
Exodus 9:3-6

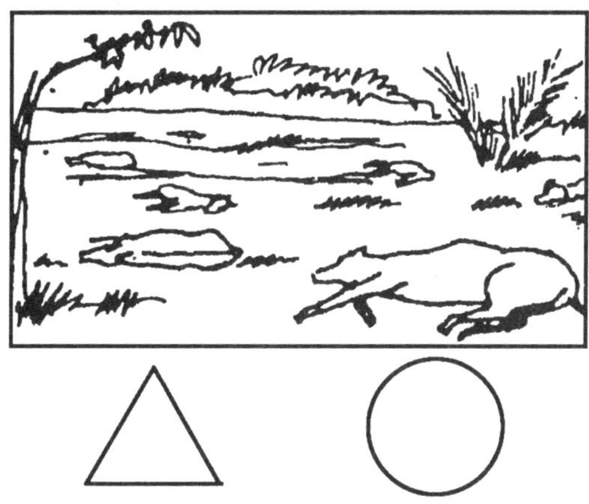

Plague #6:
Exodus 9:8-12

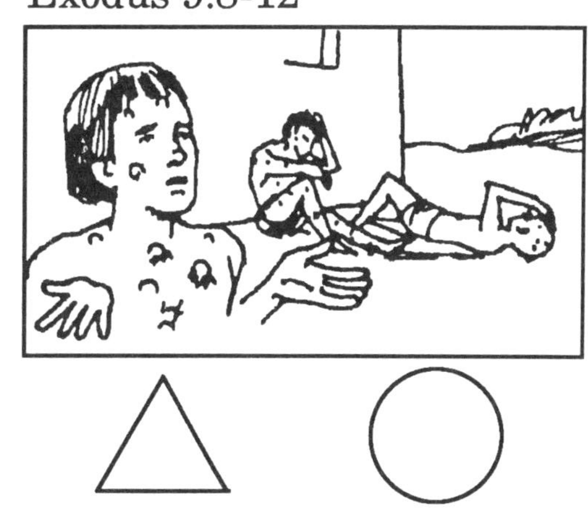

Plague #7:
Exodus 9:18-28, 34-35

Plague #8:
Exodus 10:12-20

Plague #9:
Exodus 10:21-29

Plague #10:
Exodus 11:1-12:36

The Ten Plagues

Thought Questions:

1. Why do you think Pharaoh wanted to keep the Israelites around, especially after the first couple of plagues? ____________________

____

____

____

2. How does your conscience speak to you? How can you identify it?

____

____

____

____

3. What are some things that you can do to keep your heart from becoming hard? ____________________

____

____

____

____

____

Lesson Review:

1. How old was Moses when God spoke with him through the burning bush? (Lesson #17) ____________________
2. What should Christians do if they find that their government's laws are different from God's Law? (Lesson #16) ____________________

____

____

3. What was God's purpose behind Job's suffering? (Lesson #6) ______

____

____

Crossing the Red Sea
Lesson #19

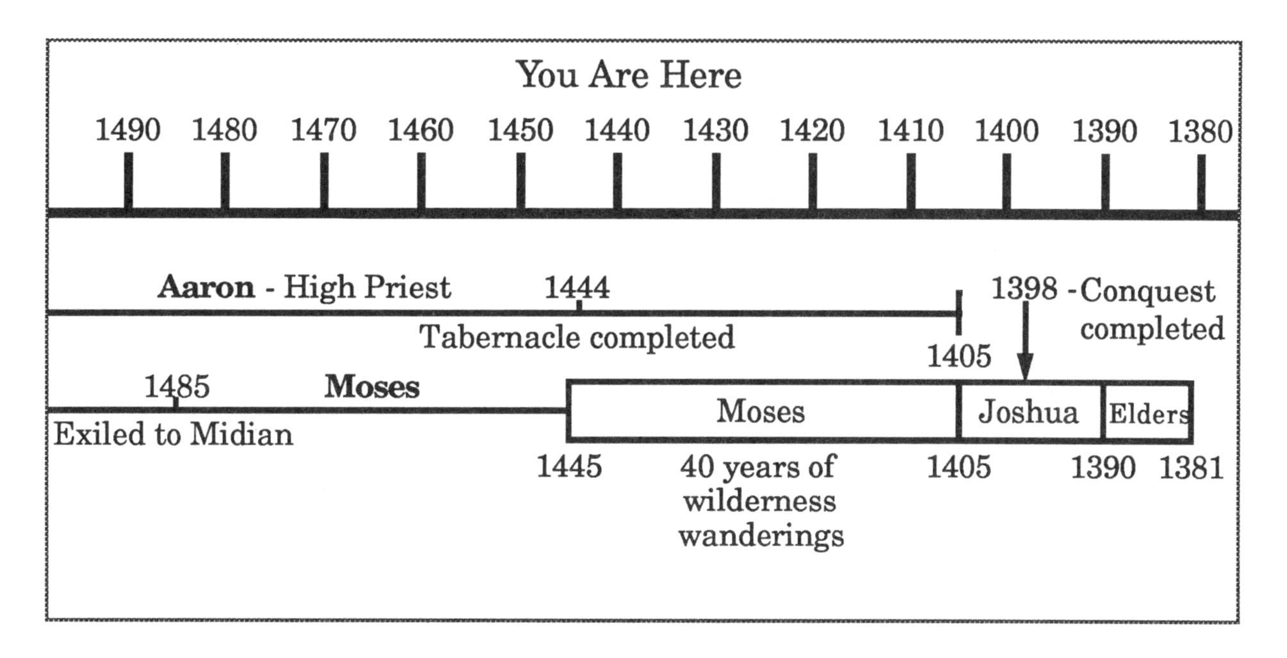

Lesson Goal: To understand that we need to trust God in the midst of fear and danger.

Background Text: Exodus 14

Memory Verse: The fear of the Lord is the beginning of wisdom. Psalms 111:10a

The Israelites were under attack. Surrounded by the desert on one side, and a large body of water (the Red Sea) on the other, with no boats and no way of escape, they had nowhere to turn. The Egyptians were traveling fast, ready to overtake the Israelites with their army of chariots. The people were terrified, knowing full well that if the Egyptians captured them, they would be tortured and killed. The Hebrews had been in subjection

to the Egyptians for over four hundred years, and they knew exactly what kind of terrible things would happen to them. "Moses," they cried, "why did you ever bring us out here? We would have been better off as slaves in Egypt than to die here in the wilderness." Moses replied, "Fear not, for you shall see the salvation that comes from the Lord. After today, you will never be bothered by the Egyptians again."

Why were the Israelites so frightened? Was it because the Egyptians were coming to get them? No, the Israelites were frightened because they were focusing their attention upon the wrong object. Instead of trusting in their salvation, which was the Lord, they were paying attention to their immediate problem, the Egyptians. They had forgotten that God was in the pillar of cloud and fire which led them through the wilderness.

Remember the story of Jesus walking on the water to the disciples in a boat during a storm (Matthew 14:22-33). The disciples first thought Jesus was a ghost, but then Peter asked to walk out to Jesus on the water to meet him. As Peter got out onto the water, he looked around at the storm and high waves, and began to sink. Peter had focused his attention on the source of his fear (the storm) rather than upon his salvation (Jesus).

What do we do when we come up against fear or danger? Do we jump into bed, tuck our heads under the covers, and cry, or do we look to Christ to help us and protect us? Fear and danger, no matter how great, have lost the battle to Christ; for God is greater than fear, sickness, and even death. If we trust Jesus, we do not even need to fear dying, because a home in heaven waits for us there.

Questions:

1. How many chosen chariots did Pharaoh take to pursue the Israelites? (Exodus 14:7) ______________________

____

2. Where did Pharaoh overtake the Israelites? (Exodus 14:9) ________

3. What did the Israelites say was better to do? (Exodus 14:12) ____

4. What was Moses to do with his rod? (Exodus 14:16) ____________

5. What did the pillar of cloud do and what was the result? (Exodus 14:19-20) ________

6. How did God cause the waters of the Red Sea to go back? (Exodus 14:21) ________

7. Who pursued the Israelites into the Red Sea? (Exodus 14:23) _____

8. How many Egyptians were alive after the sea closed in on them? (Exodus 14:28) ________

9. What did the Israelites see upon the seashore? (Exodus 14:30) ____

10. What was the Israelites' response to the Lord's great work? (Exodus 14:31) ________

Crossing the Red Sea

Thought Questions:

1. What was the difference between the Israelites' fear of the Egyptians and their fear of the Lord in 14:31? ____________________
____
____
____
____

2. In your mind, what is the difference between fear and caution? ____
____
____
____
____

3. How can fear hurt you and caution help you? ____________________
____
____
____
____

Lesson Review:

1. List the ten plagues in order of occurrence. (Lesson #18) ________
____
____
____
____
____

2. What does hardening our hearts lead to? (Lesson #18) __________
____
____
____
____

3. What two objections did Moses have when God asked him to lead the children of Israel? (Lesson #17) ____________________
____
____
____
____

The Israelites Grumble
Lesson #20

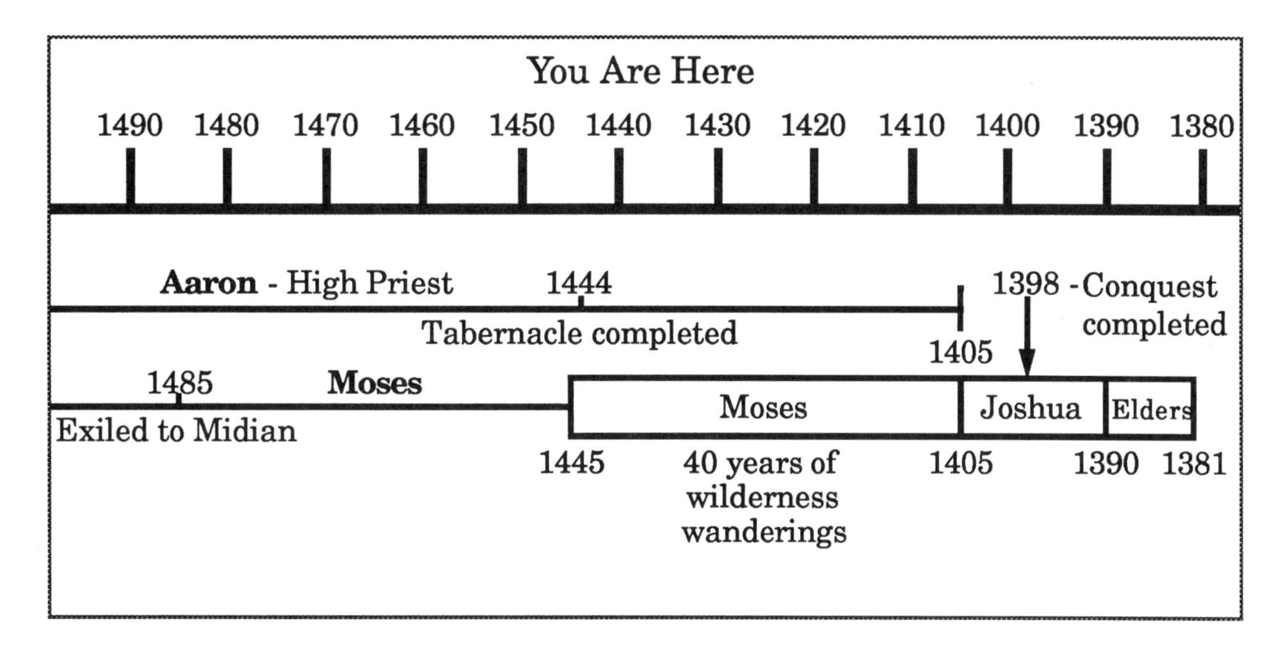

Lesson Goal: To understand the meaning of gratefulness.

Background Text: Exodus 15:22-17:7

Memory Verse: Be anxious for nothing, but in everything, by prayer and supplication with thanksgiving let your requests be made known to God. Philippians 4:6 (NASV)

Do you understand what the term "gratefulness" means? It is more than simply being thankful. It is appreciating the good things that God and other people give to you, and then openly showing that appreciation to them. During a busy day, it is very easy to forget the kind things that our parents, friends, or others do for us. How often do we really stop and say "Thank you," and then do something kind in return, like sending a card or a letter?

Part of understanding gratefulness is knowing that as Christians, we need to have the attitude of a

servant. Jesus said in Matthew 23:11 that if we want to become great in God's kingdom, we must first be the servant of everyone. The Apostle Paul called himself the bond-servant of Christ Jesus (Romans 1:1). When we have the attitude of God's servant, we are not only kind to other people, but we also give our lives to the Lord's service. Thinking of ourselves as servants is very humbling, but this is the attitude we need to have in order to be grateful.

The Israelites were not grateful. Just a few days after God delivered them from the Egyptians at the Red Sea, they were complaining that they did not have any water or food. They had already forgotten how God had saved their lives several times. It would be wise for us to learn an important lesson here. We should always be thankful to God and to others for the good things that they do for us.

Here are some important facts and figures concerning the children of Israel. Although we do not know the exact numbers, somewhere between two or three million people crossed the Red Sea. In order to take care of all the people and animals, the size of the Israelites' camp was over ten square miles. Each person was allowed one omer of manna a day (an omer is a little more than seven pints). If we could put all the manna that fell to the earth for all the people and animals in one day on a train, it would fill over 150 boxcars. Now, think of this much manna feeding the people for forty years, day after day! We definitely serve a great God who promises to supply all our needs (Philippians 4:19).

<u>Questions</u>: Please indicate your answer with either True or False.

1. ____ The people were happy and trusted God when they found the bitter waters at Marah. (Exodus 15:24-25)
2. ____ Moses cast a rock into the water. (Exodus 15:25)
3. ____ In the evening, quail came up and covered the camp. (Exodus 16:13)

4. ____ The manna melted when the sun waxed hot. (Exodus 16:21)
5. ____ The people gathered a double portion of manna on the sixth day. (Exodus 16:22)
6. ____ The people rested on the sixth day. (Exodus 16:30)
7. ____ The manna tasted like wafers made with honey. (Exodus 16:31)
8. ____ The children of Israel ate manna for fifty years. (Exodus 16:35)
9. ____ The people thirsted for God's Word, to study and memorize it. (Exodus 17:3)
10. ____ God told Moses to smite the rock to make water come out of it. (Exodus 17:6)

Thought Questions:

1. Why were the Israelites so much like children? ____________________

____

____

____

____

2. If you were Moses, what would you have done about the Israelites' ungratefulness? ____

____

____

____

____

____

Lesson Review:

1. Why were the Israelites frightened by the Egyptians? (Lesson #19)

____

____

____

2. Why did Moses flee from Pharaoh? (Lesson #16) ____________________

____

____

3. About how many miles did Abraham travel from Ur to reach Beersheba? (Map Study #1) ____________________________________

The Ten Commandments
Lesson #21

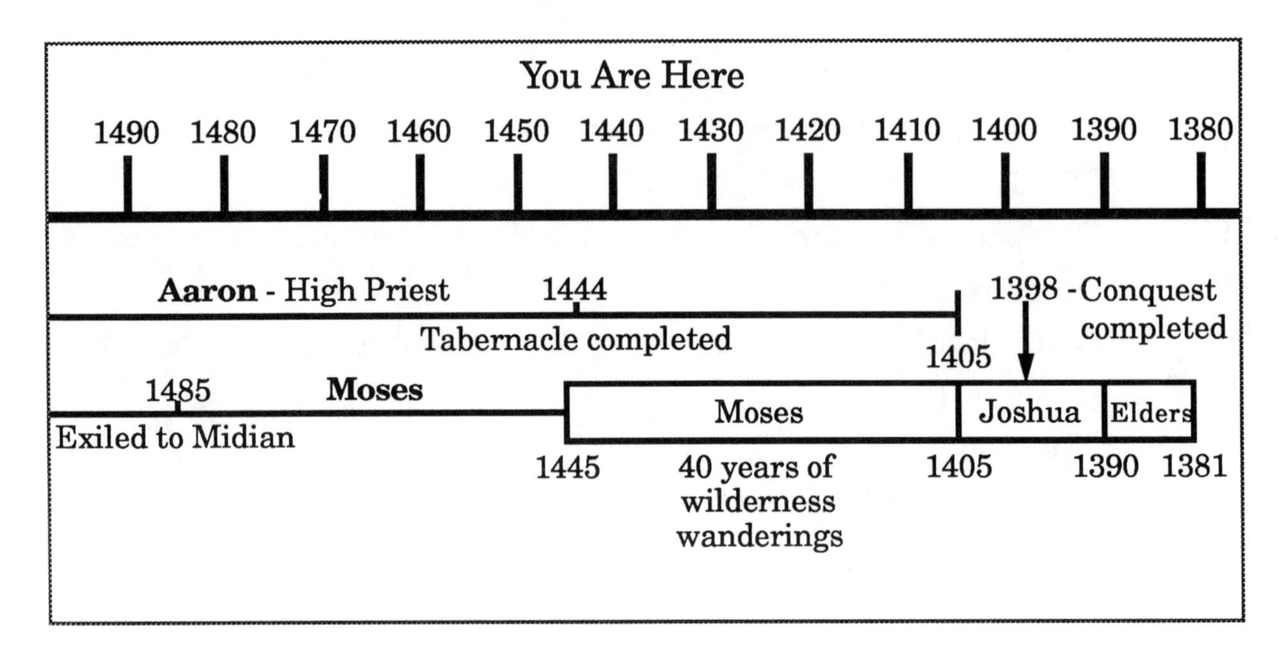

Lesson Goal: To understand the meaning and purpose for God's absolute laws.

Background Text: Exodus 20:1-23

Memory Verse: Wherefore the law was our schoolmaster to bring us unto Christ, that we might be justified by faith. Galatians 3:24

Have you ever heard of the word "anarchy"? Ask your teacher or parents to let you use a dictionary to look up the meaning. If you do not have a dictionary, the word "anarchy" means that there are no laws to govern and direct people's actions. Can you imagine what life would be like if there were no laws? People could do anything they felt like, and there would be nothing to tell them whether it was right or wrong. That would mean if a person did not like you, they could hurt you, or steal your possessions; and you would not have any laws to have them punished.

The Bible says that people need laws to show them how to live righteous lives, and to punish sin and evildoers. As Christians, we are free from the curse of sin, because Christ died on the cross for our sins. However, we still need to obey and live by God's moral laws and absolutes. If people never sinned, we would not have any need for laws. Every man is a sinner, so the law is necessary to convince the people of the need for a Savior. The law will not save a person from God's punishment of sin. That means being good is not enough to get us into heaven. We need to personally believe in Christ as our Savior in order to be saved from the punishment of sin. Therefore, the law will not save us, but it will teach us that we are law breakers in need of a Savior.

Table One

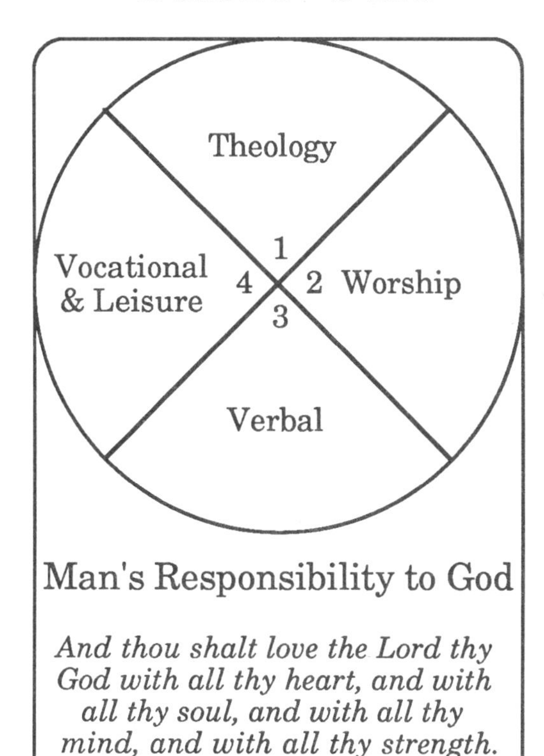

Man's Responsibility to God

And thou shalt love the Lord thy God with all thy heart, and with all thy soul, and with all thy mind, and with all thy strength.
Mark 12:30

Table Two

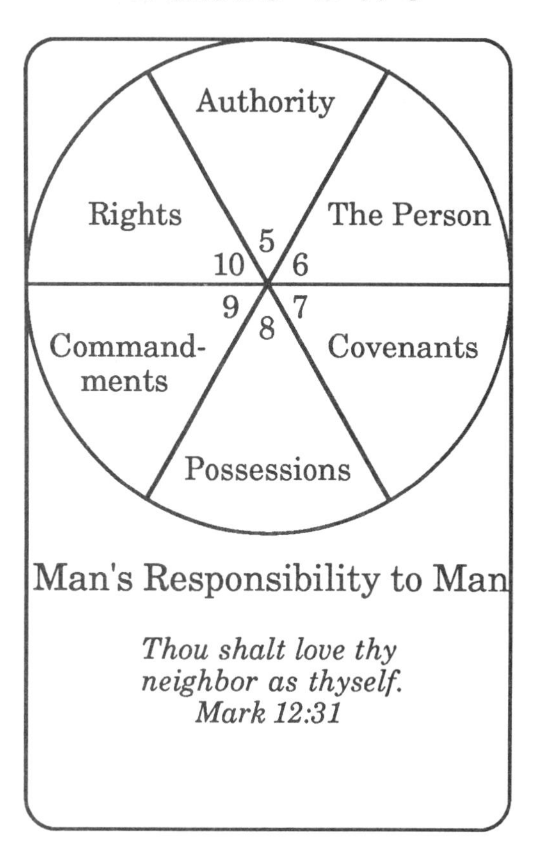

Man's Responsibility to Man

Thou shalt love thy neighbor as thyself.
Mark 12:31

The ten commandments are a summary of the laws and principles that God has given man to follow. When Christ was speaking to His disciples, He divided the ten commandments into two major areas. The first area, which is the first four commandments, is loving God with all your heart, soul, and mind. The second area, which is the last six commandments, is loving our neighbor just as we love ourselves. Love is the theme which takes priority within the Law. All the rest of the commands, laws, and principles in the Bible can be separated into these two areas, then divided into the ten commandments. Please study this chart to understand the areas covered.

The Ten Commandments

Questions: God's commandments are like signs that lead us in the right direction. Use your Bible to complete the Ten Commandments signs below.

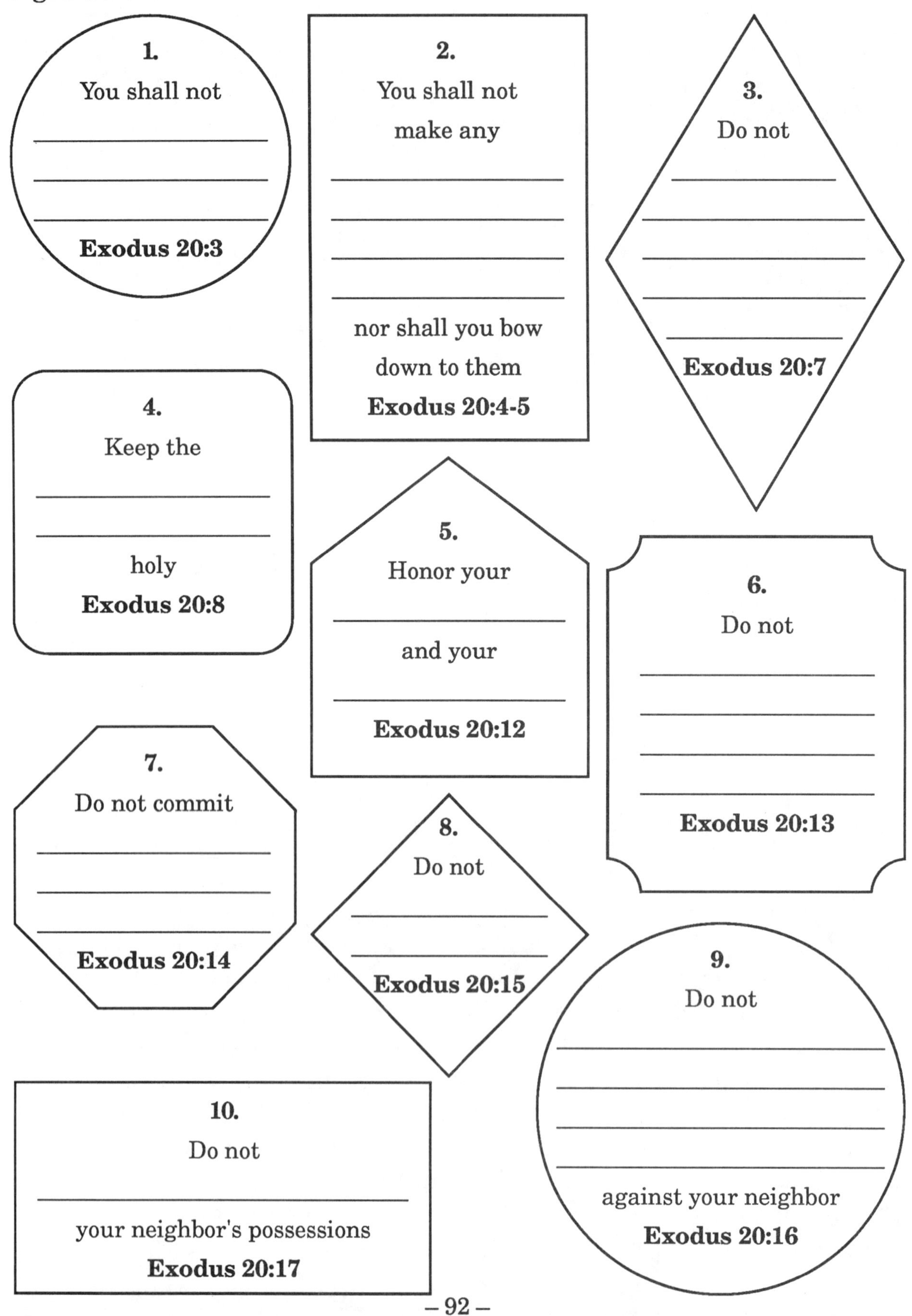

Thought Questions:

1. What do you think the world would be like if we did not have any laws or principles to guide our lives? ______________________________
____
____
____
____

2. What are the things the law can and cannot do? ______________________________
____
____
____
____

Lesson Review:

1. How much is an omer? (Lesson #20) ______________________________
____

2. What does gratefulness mean? (Lesson #20) ______________________________
____

3. What happens if we ignore our conscience? (Lesson #18) ______________________________
____
____

Supplemental Exercise: Decode the symbols to understand the message. The key is in Appendix B.

____

____

____

____

20:20

____

The Tabernacle
Lesson #22

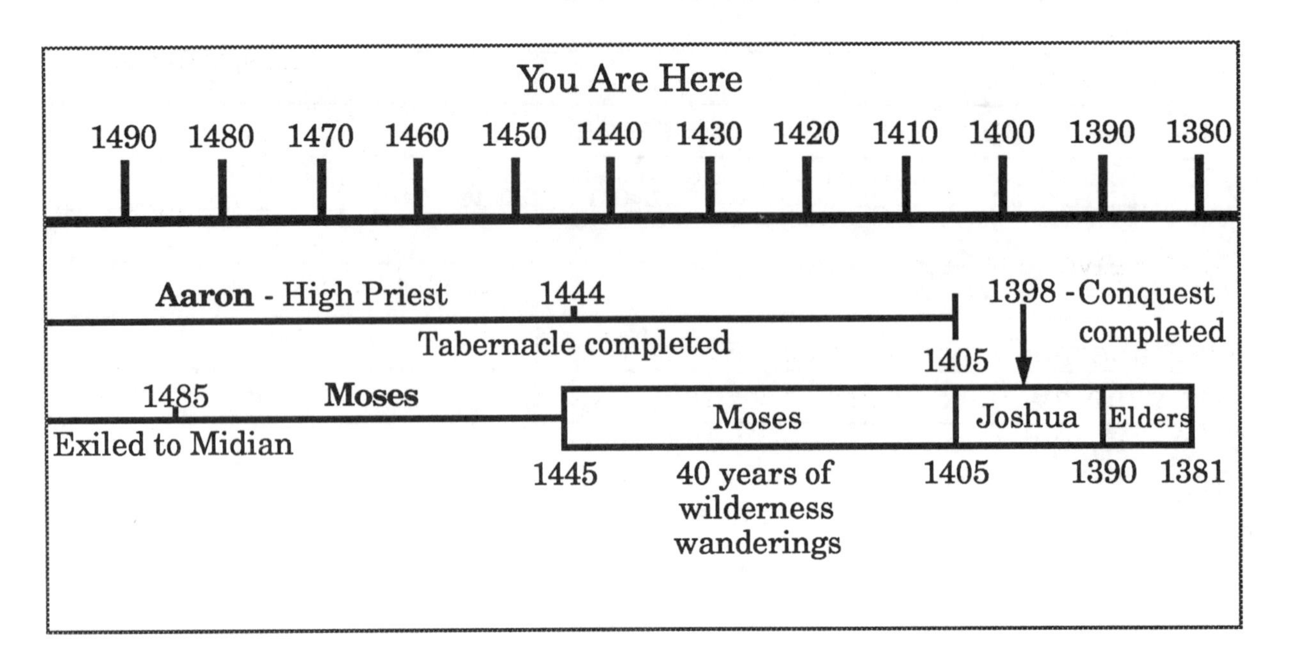

Lesson Goal: To understand that the message of the tabernacle was to point to the future Messiah.

Background Text: Exodus 25-27

Memory Verse: Lord, I have loved the habitation of thy house, and the place where thine honor dwelleth. Psalms 26:8

God gave His people the tabernacle as a means for them to have fellowship and to worship Him. It was a sanctuary, a place reserved for God to dwell among the people. The purpose of the tabernacle was to provide a means for the people to come before God and receive forgiveness for their sins. Before the tabernacle was built, the people worshiped God by building altars and offering sacrifices to Him.

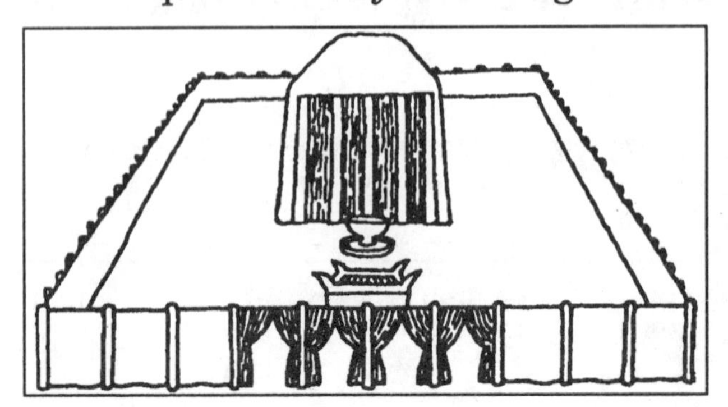

Later, according to God's specific commands, the tabernacle was replaced by a permanent temple located in Jerusalem. Although the temple was more beautiful than the tabernacle, both contained the same objects used in worship. When Christ died on the cross, His death and resurrection replaced the need for the temple. Now, Christians have their sins washed away by the blood of Christ, instead of having their sins covered by the blood of an animal (Hebrews 10:1-4). The more we know and understand about the tabernacle and the objects it contained, the better we will understand Christ Jesus and His forgiveness of our sins.

The Tabernacle

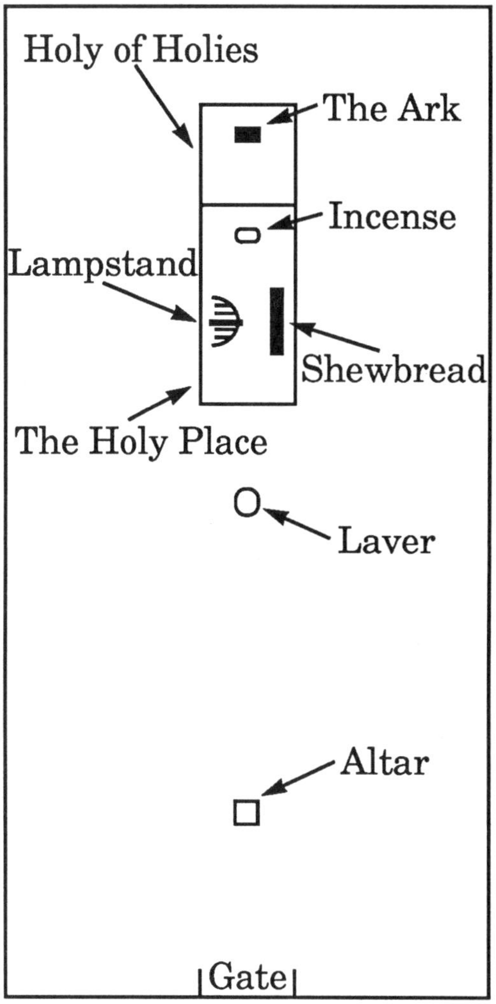

Holy of Holies
The Ark
Incense
Lampstand
Shewbread
The Holy Place
Laver
Altar
Gate

The tabernacle was a tent, seventy-five feet wide by one hundred and fifty feet long. It had one entrance facing east. To enter the tabernacle, a person had to go through this entrance or gate. The purpose of the gate was a way to enter God's presence. This gate was symbolic of Christ. John 10:9 says, "I am the door; by Me if any man enter in, he shall be saved."

The altar was seven and one-half feet long, seven and one-half feet wide, and stood four and one-half feet high. The purpose of the altar was to make sacrifices to God. The priest would kill the animal, allow the blood to run over the altar, and then burn it. Someone entering the tabernacle would not only see the altar before them, but also smell the meat burning. The altar and the shedding of blood was symbolic of Christ's death which forgave sin for all who accepted it. After the death of Christ, there was no longer any need to kill animals to make sacrifices. Believers now can worship God in their hearts and lives through the Holy Spirit within them because of the ultimate sacrifice – the death and resurrection of the Lord Jesus Christ.

The laver was a small basin for the priest to wash his hands and feet before entering the Holy Place. This is a picture of the Christian being cleansed from sin. Just as the priests had dirt removed from their bodies by washing, so Christians have sin cleansed from their lives by believing in Christ Jesus (Hebrews 10:22).

As the priest entered the Holy Place, on his right hand side was the shewbread. The purpose of the shewbread was to provide food for the priests as they went about their work in the tabernacle. The table for the bread was only two feet high, showing that the priests had to kneel to eat. The shewbread and table are symbolic of Christ, and the believer coming humbly before Him by kneeling. John 6:35 says about Christ, "I am the bread of life: he that cometh to Me shall never hunger."

In the middle of the Holy Place was the Altar of Incense. This is symbolic of the prayers that rose up to God (Revelation 8:3-4). Looking at the Altar of Incense, a person would see light smoke rising up into the tent, and smell the sweet incense in the air.

On the right hand side was the lampstand. The priests had specific instructions never to let the lampstand burn out and become dark. One purpose of the lampstand was to allow the priests to see what they were doing in the Holy Place. It is also symbolic of Christ, because John 8:12 says, "I am the light of the world: he that followeth Me shall not walk in darkness, but shall have the light of life."

Separating the Holy Place from the Holy of Holies was a veil. Once a year the High Priest would enter the Holy of Holies to atone for the sins of the people. The veil divided the place of worship and service from the presence of God. Because the people did not have the Holy Spirit indwelling them the same as Christians have today, the presence of God remained primarily in the Holy of Holies. When Christ died on the cross (Matthew 27:51-52), the veil in the temple at Jerusalem was torn in half. This was God's way of telling the people that His presence no longer existed in the Holy of Holies, but now in the hearts of believers. We now come to God, not through the veil, but through the cross of Christ (Hebrews 10:20).

Within the Holy of Holies existed only the Ark of the Covenant. The ark was three feet nine inches long, two feet three inches wide, and two feet three inches high. The ark contained the ten commandments, a pot of manna, and Aaron's rod that budded. These items were all examples of God's dealings with His children. The purpose of the ark was to provide a place for the High Priest to atone for the sins of the people. Once a year the High Priest would enter the Holy of Holies and sprinkle blood over the mercy seat which was above the ark. This blood was symbolic of Christ's blood that was shed on the cross. Now, instead of going through the High Priest, we come to God through Christ Jesus and the power of His death and resurrection. This means that we have to personally trust and believe in Christ Jesus as our Lord and Savior in order to have fellowship with God.

Questions:

1. Why did God desire a sanctuary? (Exodus 25:8) ________________

   ____
2. With what was the ark to be overlaid? (Exodus 25:11) ___________

   ____
3. What was to be on each end of the mercy seat? (Exodus 25:18) ____

   ____
4. With what was the table of shewbread to be overlaid? (Exodus 25:24) ____
5. How many branches came out of the lampstand? (Exodus 25:32)

   ____
6. What was to divide the holy place from the most holy? (Exodus 26:31-33) ____________________________________
7. Of what were the vessels of the altar to be made? (Exodus 27:3)

   ____
8. What were to be on the south side of the court? (Exodus 27:9) _____

   ____
9. What were to be made of brass? (Exodus 27:19) ________________

   ____

   ____
10. What were the children of Israel to bring for the lampstand to cause it to burn always? (Exodus 27:20) ____________________

    ____

The Tabernacle

Thought Questions:

1. Why do you think God was so specific about how He wanted the tabernacle to be constructed? ______________________________
____
____
____

2. The Bible tells us that our bodies are the temple of the Holy Spirit (I Corinthians 6:19). What can we do to make our lives a beautiful place for God to live? ______________________________
____
____
____

Lesson Review:

1. What are the four main laws in Table One of the Ten Commandments? (Lesson #21) ______________________________
____
____

2. What does the word "anarchy" mean? (Lesson #21) ____________
____

3. About how many box cars of manna a day would it take to feed all the Israelites and their animals? (Lesson #20) ____________

Supplemental Exercise: We sometimes get lost, and it is difficult to find the right way. Help this boy get out of the troublesome maze.

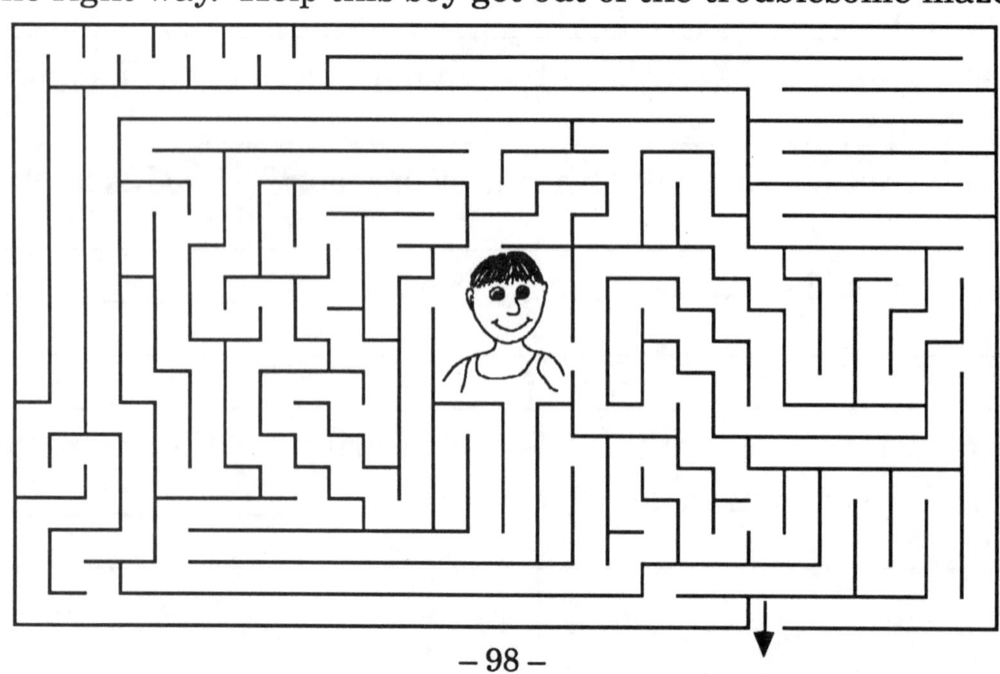

The Golden Calf
Lesson #23

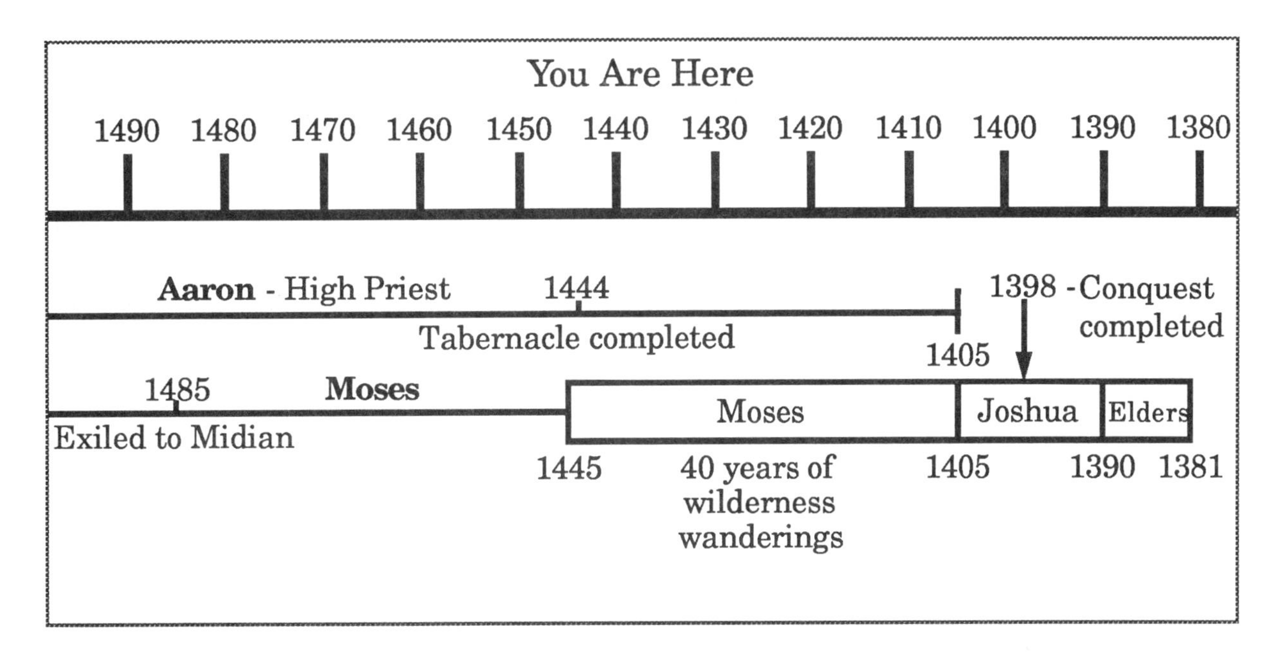

Lesson Goal: To understand that God is holy and man is sinful.

Background Text: Exodus 32

Memory Verse: For all have sinned, and come short of the glory of God. Romans 3:23

Has someone ever scolded you by saying, "I cannot leave you alone for one moment; you always seem to get into trouble"? When I was growing up, after I had done something I knew was wrong, I would shake my head and say to myself, "Why did I do that?" I knew it was wrong, and I would get punished; but I still did it anyway. Does that ever happen to you? The real question we should ask ourselves is "Why do we sin?" The Apostle Paul asked himself this same question in Romans 7:18. He said that he wanted to do good in his mind, but that his flesh (old nature) was corrupted with sin.

Whether we like it or not, we are all sinners. We were born into sin, and we will die in sin. Absolutely nothing that we can do in our own power will free us from the curse of sin. That is why we need to look to a greater power beyond ourselves to free us from wickedness, the power of Jesus Christ. Paul again says in Romans 6:13, not to give

ourselves over to sin, but over to God. By trusting and believing in Jesus Christ, He will give us the power to resist temptation and not continually sin. Although we are still sinners, we have freedom over the curse of sin through trusting in Jesus Christ. When we do not follow the Lord, we need to to humbly repent and confess that sin to God. As we do that, God will forgive us and cleanse us from all unrighteousness (I John 1:9).

Questions:

1. What did the people ask for when they saw that Moses was delayed? (Exodus 32:1) ______________________________

____

____

2. What did the people give to Aaron to make the golden calf? (Exodus 32:3) ______________________________

____

3. What did the people sit down to do? (Exodus 32:6) ______________

____

4. From what did God say the people had turned aside quickly? (Exodus 32:8) ______________________________

____

____

5. What did Moses do so that God would not destroy the children of Israel? (Exodus 32:11-14) ______________________________

____

____

____

____

6. When Joshua heard the noise, what did he think it was? (Exodus 32:17) ______________________________

____

7. What did Moses do with the tablets? (Exodus 32:19) ____________

____

____

8. What did Aaron do with the gold the people gave to him? (Exodus 32:24) ____

____

9. What did Moses say to the people while he stood in the gate of the camp? (Exodus 32:26) ____

____

10. What did God do to the people because they had made the calf? (Exodus 32:35) ____

____

Thought Questions:

1. Did Moses really change God's mind when He said He was going to destroy Israel, or was God only testing Moses? Explain your answer. ____

____

____

____

2. Is there any sin that you especially struggle with that you could use some help to overcome? How could God help you to triumph over that sin? ____

____

____

____

____

Lesson Review:

1. What was the purpose of the tabernacle? (Lesson #22) ____________

____

____

2. How did the plagues discredit the gods and rulers of Egypt? (Lesson #18) ____

____

____

3. How old was Jacob when he deceived Isaac? (Lesson #11) __________

Leviticus Background

Author of Leviticus: Moses. Over fifty times within this book it says, "The Lord spoke these words to Moses."

Date of Writing: 1440-1400 B.C. Leviticus was written during the forty years of wilderness wanderings.

Purpose of Leviticus: To illustrate God's plan of atonement; the way sinful man can come before a righteous God.

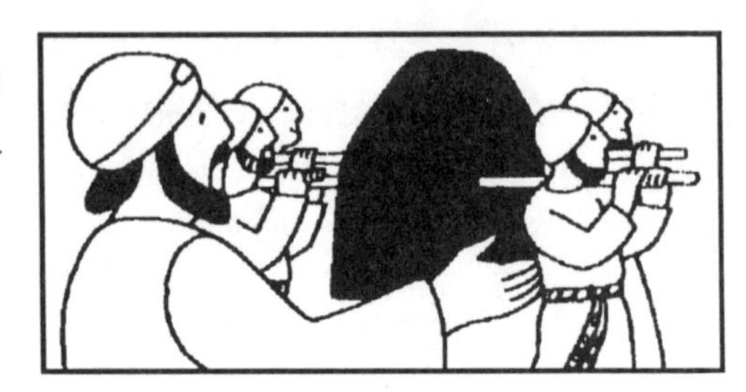

Outline of Leviticus:

I. God's Law for Offerings (Leviticus 1-7)
   A. The Five Offerings (1:1-6:7)
      1. Burnt Offering (1:3-17)
      2. Meat Offering (Leviticus 2)
      3. Peace Offering (Leviticus 3)
      4. Sin Offering (Leviticus 4)
      5. Trespass Offering (5:1-6:7)
   B. The Laws of the Offerings (6:8-7:38)

II. God's Law for Priests (Leviticus 8-10)
   A. Appointment of Priests (Leviticus 8)
   B. Acceptance of Priests (Leviticus 9)
   C. Failure of Priests (Leviticus 10)

III. God's Law for Holiness (Leviticus 11-22)
   A. Purification of Food (Leviticus 11)
   B. Purification of Bodies (Leviticus 12)
   C. Purification of Disease (Leviticus 13-14)
   D. Purification of Habits (Leviticus 15)
   E. Purification for Atonement (Leviticus 16)
   F. Purification for Animals (Leviticus 17)
   G. Purification from Heathens (Leviticus 18)
   H. Purification for Holiness (Leviticus 19-22)

IV. God's Law for His Feasts (Leviticus 23)
  A. Sabbath Day (23:1-3)
  B. Passover (23:4-5)
  C. Unleavened Bread (23:6-8)
  D. First Fruits (23:9-14)
  E. Wave Loaves (23:15-22)
  F. Trumpets (23:23-25)
  G. Day of Atonement (23:26-38)
  H. Tabernacle (23:39-44)

V. God's Law for the Promised Land (Leviticus 24-27)
  A. Consecration and Punishment (Leviticus 24)
  B. Law of the Land (Leviticus 25-27)
    1. Sabbatic Year (25:1-7)
    2. Jubilee (25:8-55)
    3. Obedience and Disobedience (Leviticus 26)
    4. Vows and Tithes (Leviticus 27)

Big Idea of Leviticus: Leviticus is one of the most difficult books in the Old Testament to study and understand. This is because it deals with technical material. Before the death and resurrection of Christ, this book was used as a handbook for the priests to guide them in their religious work.

We can now use the book of Leviticus as a guide to understanding the Old Testament law and practices. More importantly, we can use this book as a guideline for principles to follow in everyday life. Several of

the principles discussed in Leviticus are: restitution, personal responsibility and cleanliness, tithing, justice and punishment, ownership, marriage and relationships, etc.

An excellent project to further your understanding of God's Word is a Biblical principle study. Take a principle, either one listed above or another one that you would like to study, and make a chart. On the chart, list each mention of the principle and what kind of application you can make to your life. You could design the chart something like this:

Principle: Relationships

Passage	Background/Meaning	Application
19:18	Love thy neighbor as thyself	Be kind and loving to those around me, especially someone who is mean to me (name the person mean to you).
19:32	Honor the face of an old man	Respect those who are in authority over me.
19:33	Do not vex a stranger	Be kind to people I do not know in order to be a witness for God to them.

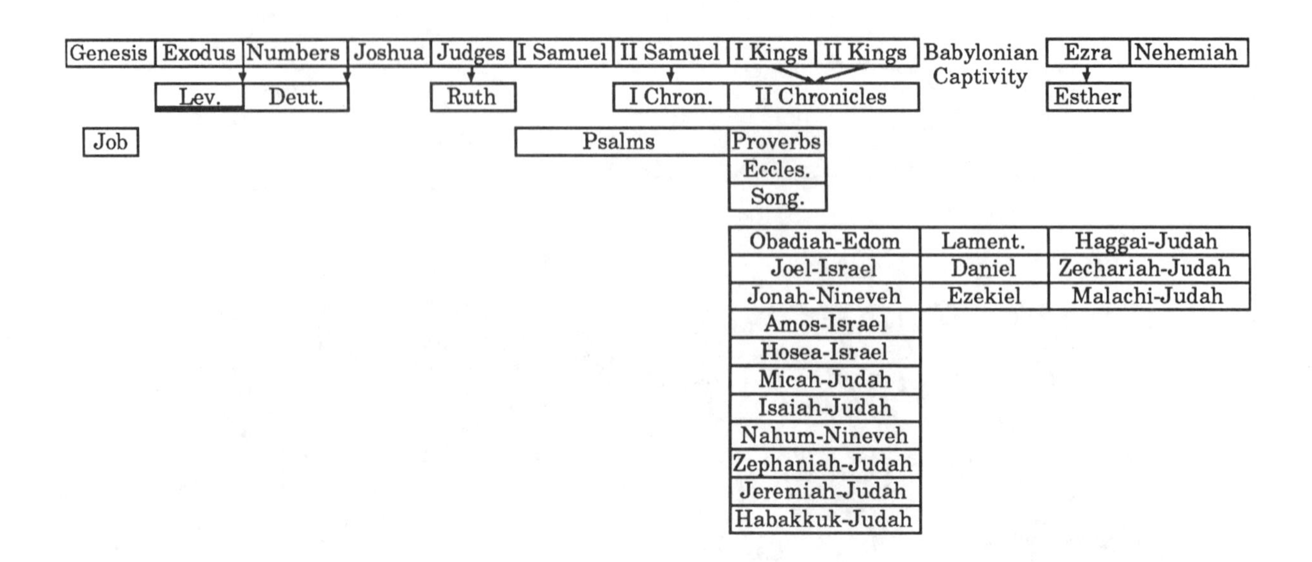

Numbers Background

Author of Numbers: Moses.

Date of Writing: 1440-1400 B.C. Numbers was written during the forty years of wilderness wanderings.

Purpose of Numbers: To show that God's children must walk by faith in order to follow Him.

Outline of Numbers:

I. Organization of the People (1:1-10:10)
   A. The First Census (Numbers 1)
   B. Division and Duties of the People (Numbers 2-4)
   C. Cleansing the Camp (Numbers 5)
   D. Spiritual Life of the People (6:1-9:14)
   E. Guiding the People (9:15-10:10)

II. From Sinai to Kadesh-Barnea (10:11-12:16)
   A. Order of Movement (10:11-10:36)
   B. Murmurings and Judgments (11-12)

III. At Kadesh-Barnea (13-14)
   A. Twelve Spies Enter Canaan and Report (Numbers 13)
   B. Israel's Response – God's Answer (Numbers 14)

IV. Wilderness Wanderings (Numbers 15-25)
   A. Laws (Numbers 15)
   B. Korah's Rebellion (Numbers 16)
   C. Priests' Duties (Numbers 17-18)
   D. Red Heifer Ordinance (Numbers 19)
   E. Deaths of Miriam and Aaron (Numbers 20)
   F. Israel's Defeats and Victories (Numbers 21)
   G. Balaam and Balak (Numbers 22-25

V. New Generation (Numbers 26-30)
   A. The Second Census (Numbers 26)
   B. Inheritance Problems (27:1-11)

- C. Joshua to Be New Leader (27:12-23)
- D. Laws of Offerings and Vows (Numbers 28-30)

VI. Preparations of Canaan (Numbers 31-36)
- A. Judgment of Midian (Numbers 31)
- B. Land Division (Numbers 32)
- C. Review of Wanderings (33:1-49)
- D. Directions for Conquest (33:50-35:34)
- E. Inheritance Regulations (Numbers 36)

Big Idea of Numbers: The book of Numbers takes its name from the two censuses found at the beginning and the end of the book. In the first thirteen chapters, God is preparing Israel to enter and take control of the land of Canaan. However, when the twelve spies that were sent into the land return and give a negative report, the people doubt God and His power to protect them. God then judges them by condemning them to stay and wander in the wilderness for a total of forty years, one year for every day that the spies were in the land of Canaan. After the forty years, the people gather at the plains of Moab, and Moses instructs them in the Law. Since the Israelites who came out of Egypt had died, their children may not have received the Law at Mount Sinai as their parents did. Moses wanted to be certain that the people were reminded of God's Law and His faithfulness to them.

One of the most important spiritual lessons that the book of Numbers teaches is that the wilderness wanderings represent a period of time in a believer's life when he stops growing spiritually, and stops walking by faith in God. The Israelites had been freed from the bondage of Egypt and were given the Law to help them to grow spiritually. They failed because their faith became weak and they stopped trusting in God. In the same sense, Christians have been freed from the bondage of sin through the death of Christ. Believers sometimes fail because they become stuck in the wilderness of sin by neglecting God and not trusting in Him. By studying the book of Numbers, the Christian can learn how not to wander in sin, but walk in righteousness (Ephesians 4:1-3).

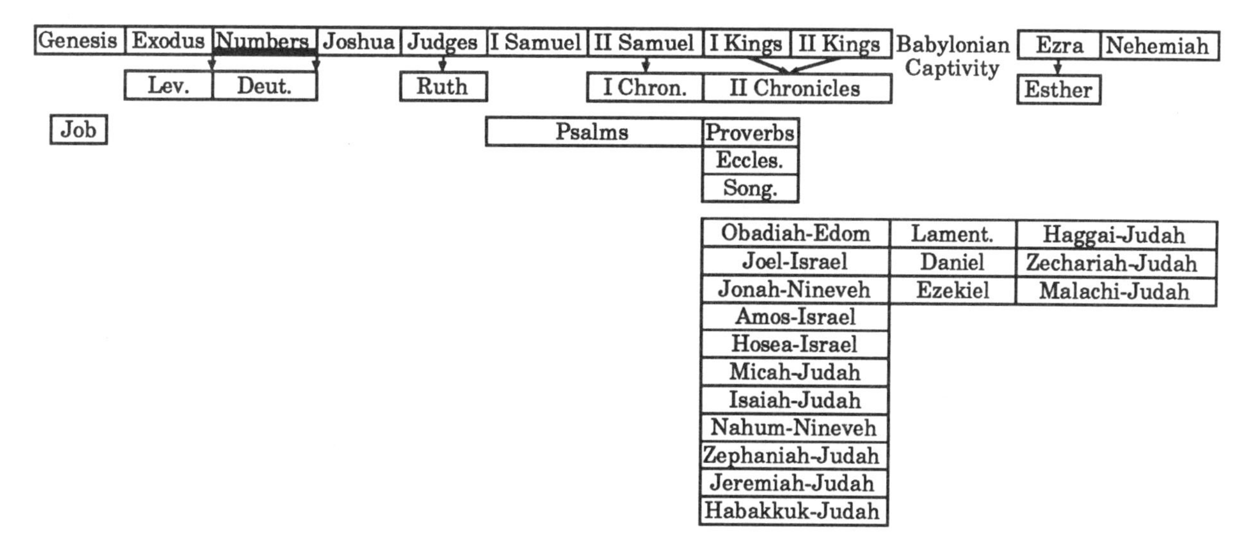

Supplemental Exercise: Read Numbers 20:1-12 and complete the crossword.

The children of Israel came to the (1–D) of Zin, and the people stayed in (3–D). Miriam, the sister of Moses, (9–D) and was buried there. Because there was not any water, the people complained, saying, "We wish God had let us die when our brethren (16–D) before the Lord!" They said that Moses should not have made them come up out of (13–A) to this (14–D) place. It is no (11–A) of (8–A), or of (7–D), or of vines, or of pomegranates; neither is there any water to drink. And Moses and Aaron went from the (11–D) of the assembly unto the (1–A) of the tabernacle, and they (7–A) upon their faces: and the glory of the Lord appeared unto them. Then the (15–A) spake unto Moses, (4–D), "Take the rod, and gather the assembly together, and speak unto the (2–A) before their (14–A); and it shall (6–A) forth water, and thou (4–A) bring forth to them water out of the rock." And Moses lifted up his (10–A), and with his rod he (12–A) the rock (5–D): and the water came out abundantly, and the congregation drank, and their beasts also. But Moses did not sanctify the Lord in the eyes of the people because he struck the rock instead of speaking to it as the Lord told him to. Therefore, God was not going to allow Moses and Aaron to bring the congregation into the (17–A) which God had given to them.

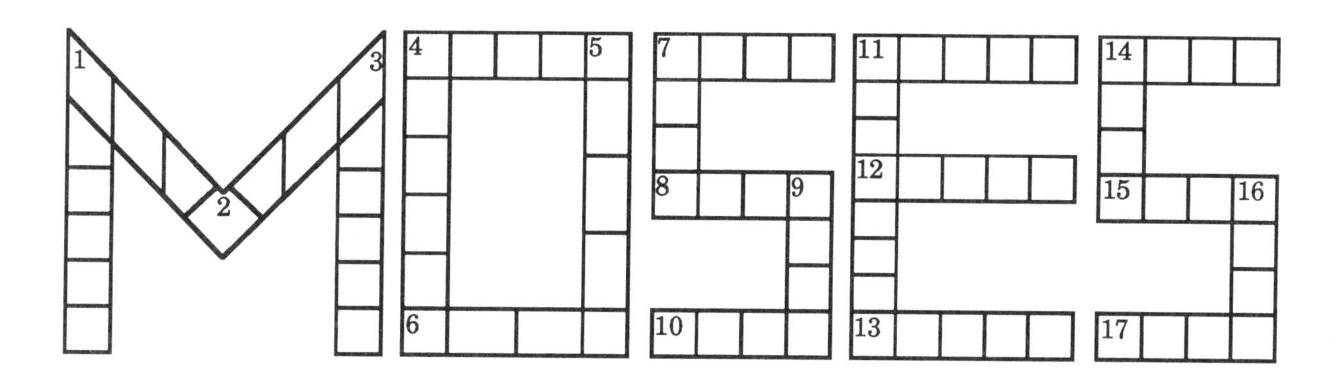

Spies in the Land
Lesson #24

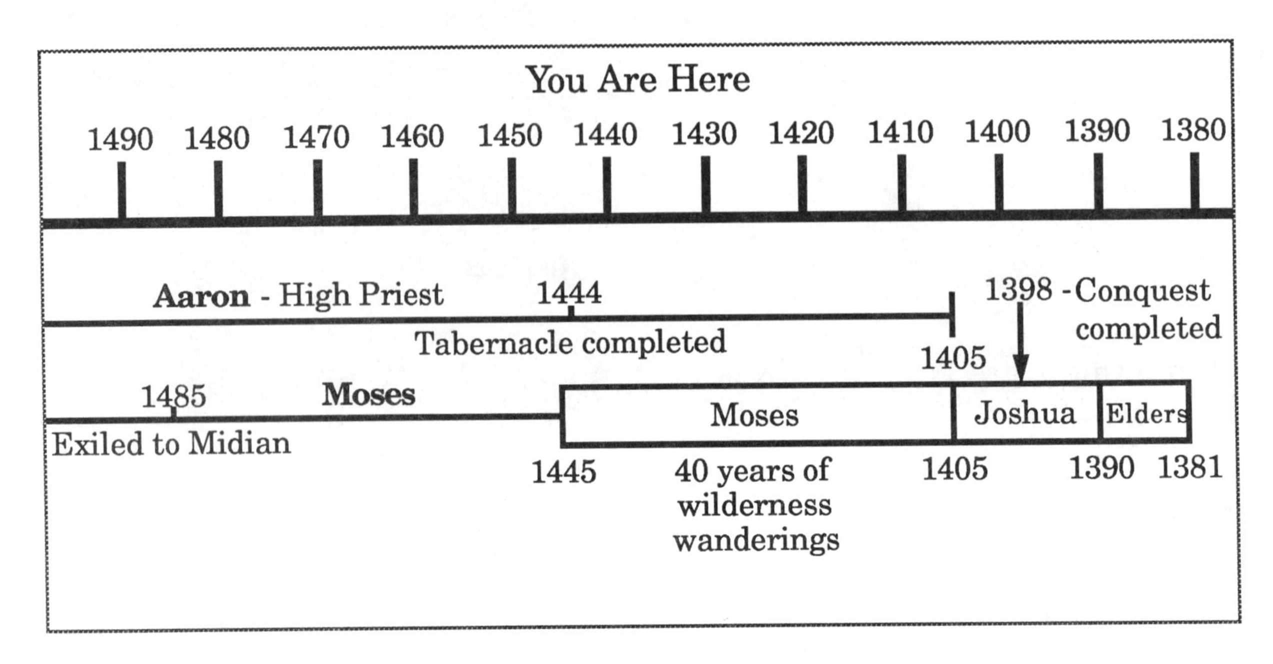

Lesson Goal: To understand that Christians need to have courage in order to serve God.

Background Text: Numbers 13

Memory Verse: Finally, my brethren, be strong in the Lord, and in the power of His might. Ephesians 6:10

It had been about one and a half years since the children of Israel had left Egypt, and it was now time for them to enter the promised land. This was the land of Canaan that God had promised to Abraham and his descendants. It was a beautiful place, flowing with milk and honey. The people must have been very excited. They had just traveled from Mount Sinai to Kadesh-Barnea through a hot, dry desert, looking for a place to make their new home. No doubt, many were thinking about planting a farm and raising some animals. Others, perhaps, were hoping to begin new trades and jobs in this land of opportunity.

To prepare the people to move into the land, God had Moses send twelve spies to search for and to discover valuable information about Canaan and the people who lived there. When the spies returned,

they did not have good news. Joshua and Caleb said that God would help them conquer the land, but ten of the twelve spies said that the Canaanites were too strong and the cities too difficult to defeat. When the children of Israel heard this, they stopped trusting God and became cowards. So God punished them by making them stay forty years in the wilderness. The spies were in Canaan forty days, so the Israelites were punished for forty years. God also said that all the people who were older than twenty years would eventually die in the wilderness, so only their descendants would enter the promised land. The only two people that God said could enter Canaan were Joshua and Caleb. This was because these men trusted God and believed in Him, even when the rest of the people did not.

Do we ever lose our courage by not trusting or believing God? God has a specific plan and purpose for each of our lives. In order to fulfill that purpose, we must have courage in Him. Ephesians chapter six commands us to wear the full armor of God so we can fight against sin and temptation. These are the things that make us become cowards. We should look carefully at our lives and ask ourselves if we have courage, so that when God's Word asks us to perform a task, we will be brave enough to do it.

Questions:

1. From where was Moses to get the twelve men to search the land of Canaan? (Numbers 13:2) ____________________________________

____

Spies in the Land

2. What did Moses tell the men to do? (Numbers 13:17) ____________

____

3. What were the men to spy out in the land? (List three or four items.) (Numbers 13:18-20) ____________

____

____

____

4. When was the city of Hebron built? (Numbers 13:22) ____________

____

5. What did the spies bring back with them from the land? (Numbers 13:23) ____________

____

____

____

6. With what did the land "flow"? (Numbers 13:27) ____________

____

7. What did Caleb say about the land? (Numbers 13:30) ____________

____

____

____

8. What did the ten spies say after Caleb? (Numbers 13:31) ____________

____

____

____

9. What type of report did the spies bring? (Numbers 13:32) ____________

____

10. Who did the spies say were giants? (Numbers 13:33) ____________

____

Thought Questions:

1. In your personal life, are there any areas where you are spiritually weak and do not have the courage to fight? Explain your answer.

____

____

____

____

2. From Ephesians six, what piece of armor could be added to or developed in your life to help you have more courage? Explain your answer. ____

____

____

____

Lesson Review:

1. About how many Israelite people came out of Egypt with Moses? (Lesson #20) ____

____

2. When was the book of Exodus written? (Exodus Background) ____

____

3. How does the Bible compare our lives to a lump of clay? (Lesson #14) ____

____

____

Supplemental Exercise: Draw a picture of the tabernacle and identify its parts. See Lesson #22 for details.

Map Study #2

Questions: Use the map at the bottom of this page to answer these questions.

1. Put an "A" next to the location where the Israelites lived in Egypt. (Genesis 47:4)

2. Put a "B" next to the location where the water was bitter. (Exodus 15:23)

3. Put a "C" next to the place which contained twelve wells and seventy palm trees. (Exodus 15:27)

4. Put a "D" next to the location where Moses went to talk with God. (Exodus 19:20)

5. Put an "E" next to the location where Moses sent twelve spies. (Numbers 13:17)

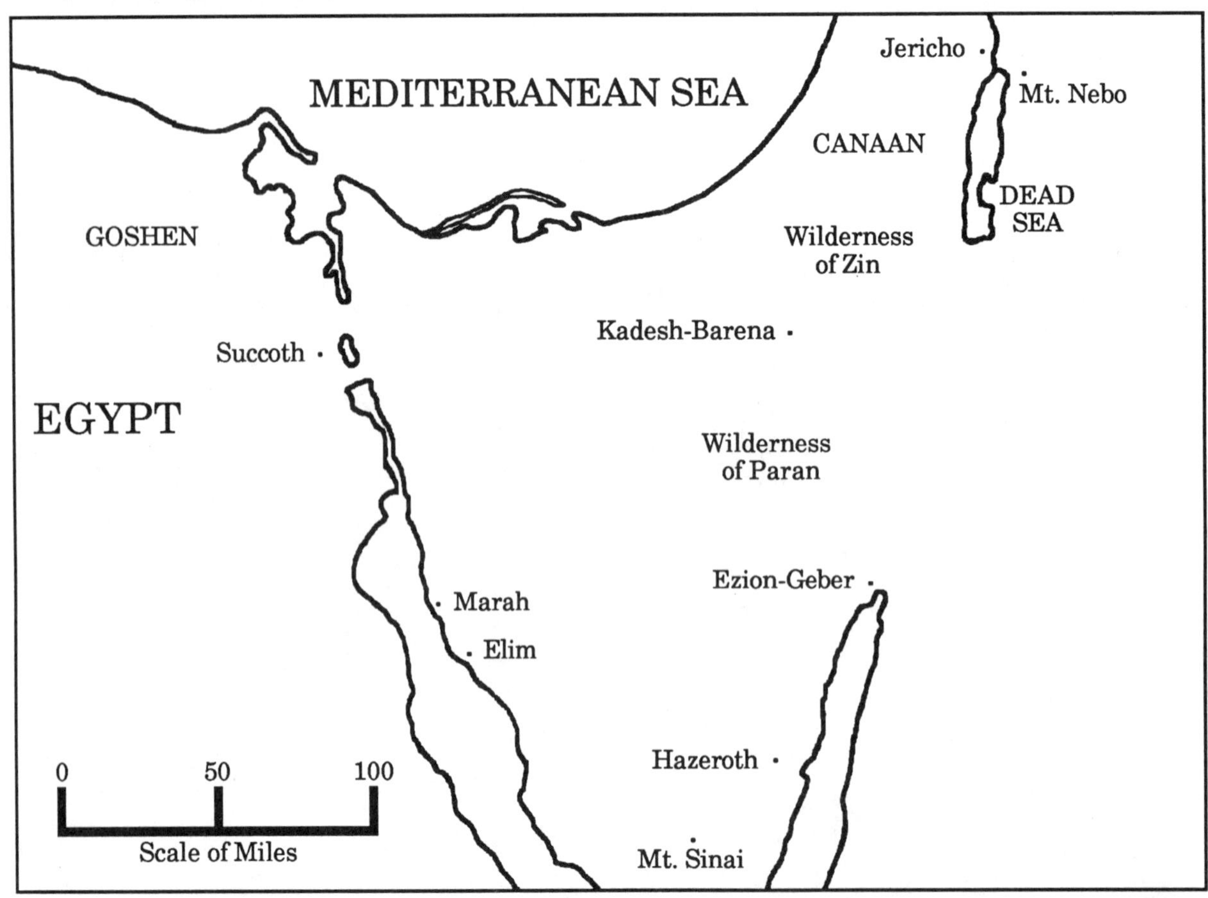

Fiery Serpents
Lesson #25

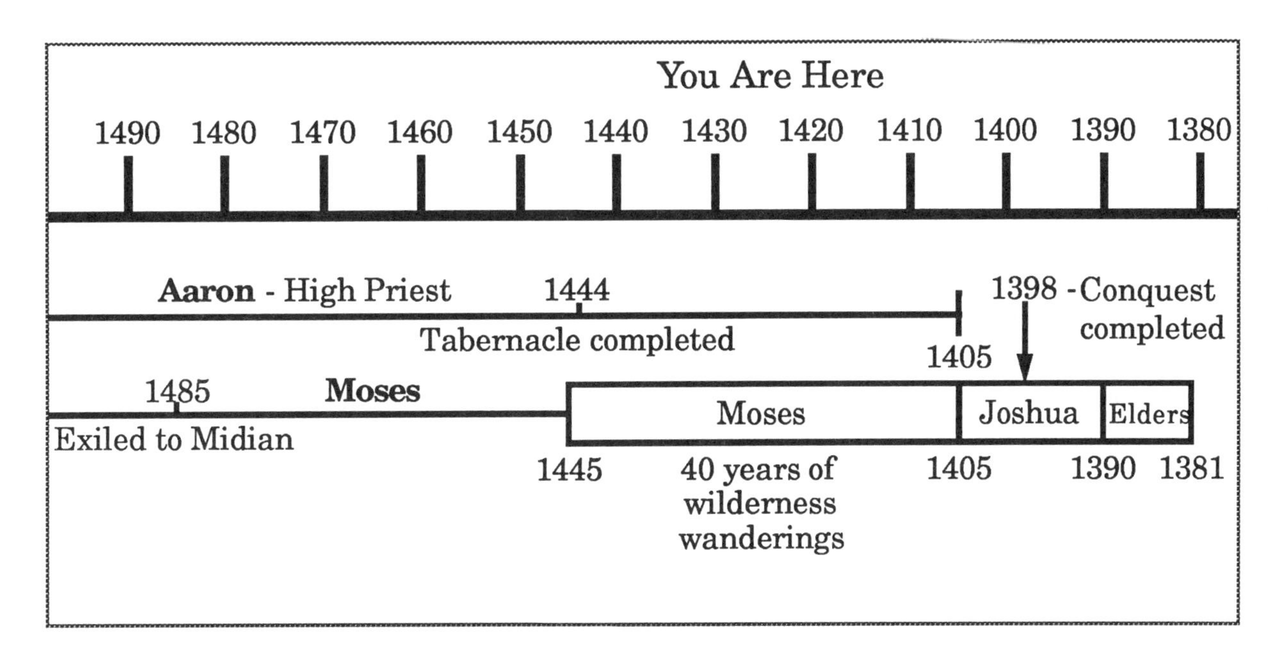

Lesson Goal: To understand that serving God means walking by faith.

Background Text: Numbers 21

Memory Verse: And as Moses lifted up the serpent in the wilderness, even so must the Son of man be lifted up. John 3:14

Look at the chair you are sitting in. Is it strong? Can it hold your weight? Now stand up, then sit back down in your seat. When you sat down, did your chair break or fall apart? Of course not! But, how did you know for certain that the chair would not break when you sat in it? When you sat down, even though you did not think about it, you put faith and trust in the chair to hold you. When you ride in a car, you have faith that the driver will be careful. When you go to the store, you have faith that the construction men built a roof that will not fall on your head. Every day you are putting your faith and trust in things and people which you hope will not fail you.

As Christians, how much more do we need to have faith that God will take care of us! Sometimes we forget about God's power and love for us, and we may lose faith in Him as the Israelites did. This not only happens when troubles or problems enter our lives, but it also

Fiery Serpents

happens when things are going well for us. Sometimes when we have been blessed by the Lord, we neglect our relationship with Him and focus our attention upon other things. We must not forget how important God is, and how much our lives depend upon Him.

In this lesson, the Israelites are once again complaining about the food and water. During the wilderness wanderings, they grumbled continually. Whenever they stopped trusting God, He had to discipline them in order to help them see how sinful and foolish they were. When Moses made the brass serpent and put it on the pole, it was symbolic of Christ's death on the cross. Just as the Israelites looked at the snake to save their physical lives, we can look to the cross of Christ to save our spiritual lives. Our walk of faith in God begins when we trust Him as Savior, and continues after we die and go to be with Him in heaven.

Questions: Match the correct answer with the proper question.

1. ____ Where did the people say Moses had brought them to die? (Numbers 21:5)
2. ____ What did the people loathe? (Numbers 21:5)
3. ____ What did God send among the people? (Numbers 21:6)
4. ____ What happened to the people after they were bitten? (Numbers 21:6)
5. ____ Who prayed for the people? (Numbers 21:7)
6. ____ Upon what did Moses set the fiery serpent? (Numbers 21:8)
7. ____ Of what did Moses make a serpent? (Numbers 21:9)
8. ____ Of whom did Moses ask permission for the Israelites to pass through the land? (Numbers 21:21-22)
9. ____ What was the city of the king of the Amorites? (Numbers 21:26)
10. ____ Who was the king of Bashan? (Numbers 21:33)

a. Moses
b. Sihon
c. Og
d. Fiery Serpents
e. Wilderness
f. Brass
g. Light bread
h. Died
i. A pole
j. Heshbon

Thought Questions:

1. How do you demonstrate your faith in the Lord Jesus? ____

2. What are some areas in your life about which you grumble and complain? ____

Lesson Review:

1. What were the three items in the Holy Place and what were their purposes? (Lesson #22) ____

2. From what mountain did Moses and the Israelites receive God's Law? (Lesson #21) ____
3. What did God say His name was when He spoke with Moses from the burning bush? (Lesson #17) ____

Balaam and Balak
Lesson #26

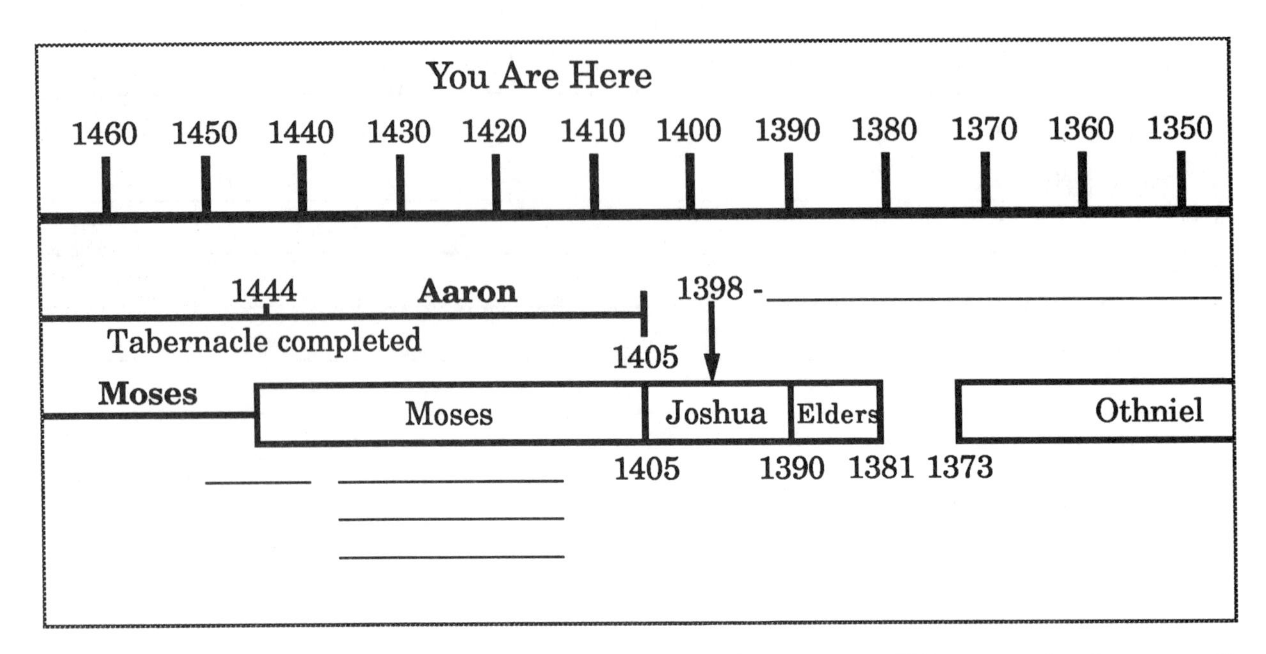

Lesson Goal: To understand that God will protect His people from evil and wickedness.

Background Text: Numbers 22:1-23:12

Memory Verse: For we wrestle not against flesh and blood, but against principalities, against powers, against the rulers of the darkness of this world, against spiritual wickedness in high places. Ephesians 6:12

Have you ever read the book *Charlotte's Web*? It is a story about a talking spider, Charlotte, who helps her good friend, Wilbur the pig. If you have never read this book, ask your parents to consider purchasing it for your library. It is an excellent story about friendship and sacrifice. In reality, we know that spiders, pigs, or any other kind of animal, cannot talk intelligently; but one time God miraculously caused a donkey to talk! In this lesson, we will study about this talking donkey and his master Balaam.

Balaam was riding on his donkey, planning to do something which was wrong, so God sent His angel to stop him. The only problem was that Balaam could not see the angel, though the donkey could. Finally, after Balaam had beaten his donkey several times in order to make him go, God opened the mouth of the donkey so it could speak to Balaam.

Balaam was a wicked man who attempted to curse the children of Israel. Further evidence of this is found in Numbers 25:1-9 and 31:16, when Balaam counseled Moab to entice Israel into Baal worship and sexual immorality. Jude 11 and II Peter 2:15 describe Balaam as an unrighteous individual who was interested only in his own financial gain.

As believers, we need to be aware that there will be unrighteous people who will try to tempt and destroy us. In response, we must remain committed to God's Word, and understand that God will protect us. Our memory verse reminds us that we do not fight against flesh and blood. We wage a spiritual war. By equipping ourselves with the full armor of God, we will have the protection and strength necessary to fight and defeat the unrighteous.

Questions:

1. Moab was sore ________________ of the people, because they were ______________. (Numbers 22:3)
2. Balak said, behold, there is a people come out of ______________, which covereth the face of the ______________. (Numbers 22:11)
3. God said unto Balaam, thou shalt not ___________ with them; thou shalt not _____________ the people: for they are ______________. (Numbers 22:12)
4. The ______________ of the ______________ stood in the way for an ________________ against him. (Numbers 22:22)

5. The ass saw the angel of the Lord standing in the __________, and his ___________ drawn in his hand. (Numbers 22:23)
6. The ass said to Balaam, what have I done to thee, that thou hast _______________ me these ______________ times. (Numbers 22:28)
7. Balaam said to the ass, because thou hast ________________ me: I would there were a ______________ in mine _____________, for now would I _____________ thee. (Numbers 22:29)
8. Balaam said to Balak, the __________ that __________ putteth in my ______________, that shall I _______________. (Numbers 22:38)
9. The Lord put a ________ in Balaam's ___________. (Numbers 23:5)
10. Balak said to Balaam, I took thee to ___________ mine enemies, and, behold, thou has _____________ them altogether. (Numbers 23:11)

Thought Questions:

1. How has the full armor of God helped to strengthen your spiritual life? (Ephesians 6:13-18) ______________________________________
____
____
____
____
2. How has God protected you in the past from individuals who may have hurt you? ____
____
____
____
____

Lesson Review:

1. What did Moses put on a pole so the children of Israel could be healed? (Lesson #25) ____
____
2. Why does Satan tempt us so to sin? (Lesson #13) _______________
____
____
____
3. On the time line at the beginning of the chapter, complete the blank spaces with the correct information.

The Judgment of the Wicked
Lesson #27

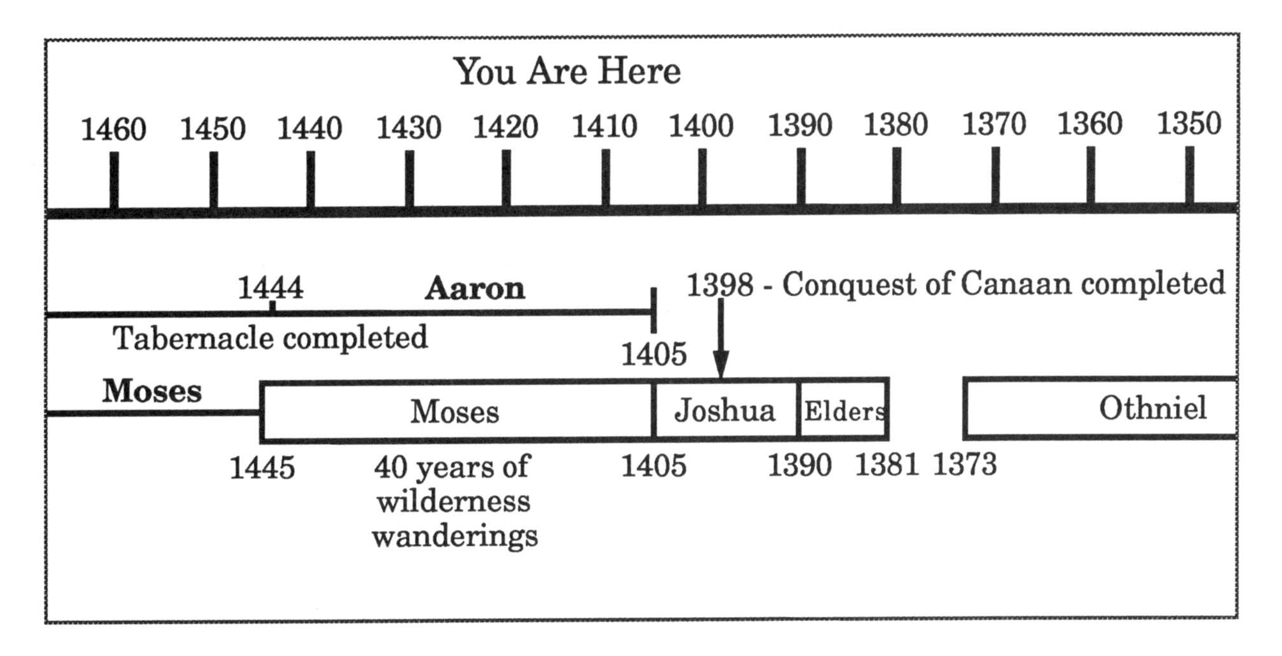

Lesson Goal: To understand that God righteously punishes sin and wickedness.

Background Text: Numbers 31:1-24

Memory Verse: Only let your conversation be as it becometh the gospel of Christ. Philippians 1:27

To the unbeliever, it may appear that God's judgment of sin and the heathen nations was too strong, even severe. Numbers 16:49 shows that 14,700 people died as a result of complaining against Moses and Aaron. Numbers 21:35 says that all the people of king Og's domain, including the women and children, were slain by the Israelites. In the passage for this lesson, Numbers 31:17-18 describes how the children of Israel were to kill all the Midianite people except the young girls. Why did God take such extreme measures against sin? God is loving and kind to those who follow Him; but He is also just, and hates all form of sin and corruption.

One way that God judged immorality and wickedness was through the children of Israel. History tells us that some of the people in and around Canaan would offer infant sacrifices in the worship of their

pagan gods. Some of the nations had a practice called "foundation sacrifices." When a home was being built, a child from the family would be sacrificed and killed, with its lifeless body placed into the foundation of the new home. This was intended to bring "good luck" to the rest of the family (they were probably lucky because they were not the ones who were sacrificed). Because of these practices, which broke God's moral Law, they deserved to be punished. God used the Israelites as His instrument to inflict His righteous judgment (Deuteronomy 9:5).

Within our society, because the morals and values of the people have declined, the medical community is discovering strange and new plagues and diseases. As much as the "experts" try to deny it, the fact cannot be hidden: people are becoming sick and dying from AIDS and other diseases because they are not obeying God's moral commandments. The solution to the AIDS problem is not better education or control, but obedience to God's Word. This country, along with the rest of the world, is being punished by God because we have failed to obey Him. People are receiving the consequences of their sin. Only when the churches begin to preach God's moral Laws, and the people begin to obey them, will God stop His punishment of this sin. God has given us laws and direction because He loves us and understands that sinful people will destroy themselves without a righteous standard to follow.

In our own lives, we may never have killed someone or robbed a bank, but we have sinned in other ways that are displeasing to God. It is necessary for us to realize that God hates sin. We need to do all we can to first defeat sin in our own lives, then to fight against sin in society. When Matthew 5:16 tells us to be the light of the world, it means we are to be shining examples of God's righteousness. Then the unsaved of the world can look upon us and find an example to follow and pattern their lives after. Our prayer should be for pure and holy lives, so that we might be good examples of righteousness and bring glory to God.

Questions:

1. Against whom were the Israelites to wage war? (Numbers 31:3) ______
2. How many people from each tribe were to be sent into war? (Numbers 31:4) ______
3. What did Phinehas bring with him into war? (Numbers 31:6) ______
4. Whom did the Israelites take captive? (Numbers 31:9) ______
5. Why was Moses angry with the captain of the host? (Numbers 31:14-15) ______
6. What was among the congregation of the Lord? (Numbers 31:16) ______
7. Whom did Moses say the Israelites were to keep alive? (Numbers 31:18) ______
8. Who was to stay outside the camp? (Numbers 31:19) ______
9. How long were the people to stay outside the camp? (Numbers 31:19) ______
10. What were the people to wash on the seventh day? (Numbers 31:24) ______

The Judgment of the Wicked

Thought Questions:

1. What areas in your life do you think God would want someone else to follow? Explain your answer. ______________________________

2. Why do you think God is glorified when other people see your good works? ______________________________

Lesson Review:

1. Why did God send the serpents to bite the Israelites? (Lesson #25)

2. How many spies did Moses send into Canaan to search the land? (Lesson #24) ______________________________

3. In the Holy Place, what did the lampstand symbolize? (Lesson #22)

4. Complete the empty boxes with the names of the books from the Chronology of the Old Testament. (Numbers Background)

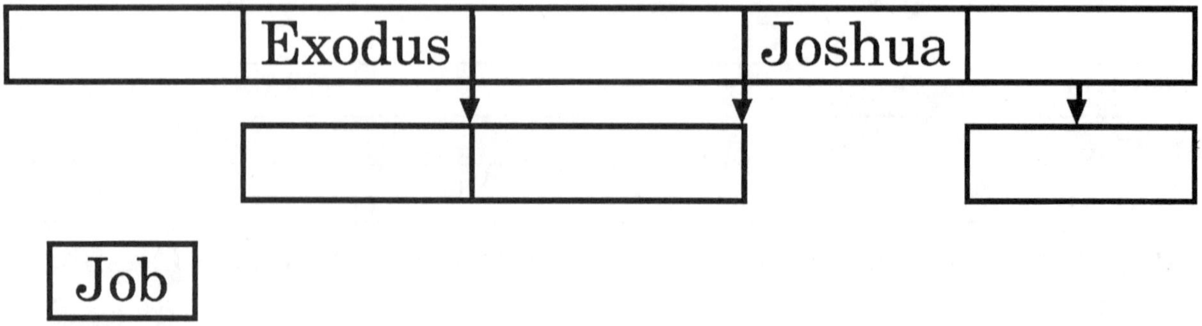

	Exodus		Joshua	

Job

Deuteronomy Background

Author of Deuteronomy: Moses. Joshua probably wrote chapter thirty-four, which gives an account of the death of Moses.

Date of Writing: 1400 B.C. Deuteronomy was written during the last few months of the wilderness wanderings.

Purpose of Deuteronomy: To establish the Law and God's covenant in the minds of a new generation of Israelites.

Outline of Deuteronomy:

I. Reviewing Israel's History (Deuteronomy 1-4)
   A. History Briefly Reviewed (Deuteronomy 1-3)
   B. Application to Obedience (Deuteronomy 4)

II. Reviewing Israel's Law (Deuteronomy 5-26)
   A. Commands Concerning God (Deuteronomy 5-11)
   B. Commands Concerning Canaan (Deuteronomy 12-26)

III. Reviewing Israel's Covenants (Deuteronomy 27-30)
   A. Law to be Recorded at Mount Ebal (27:1-8)
   B. Curses and Blessings (27:9-28:14)
   C. Results of Disobedience (28:15-68)
   D. Covenant in Moab and God's Promises (Deuteronomy 29-30)

IV. Reviewing Moses' Life (Deuteronomy 31-34)
   A. Commission to Joshua (31:1-29)
   B. Moses' Song and Blessing (31:30-33:29)
   C. Moses' Death (Deuteronomy 34)

The Big Idea of Deuteronomy: The children of Israel had wandered in the wilderness for nearly forty years. Now the time came for them to enter the promised land of Canaan. To prepare the people spiritually for their new lives, Moses reviewed the many important laws, principles, and events God had taught them since leaving Egypt. The old generation of Israelites had all died because of their disobedience to God. This new group of Israelites had not personally experienced the deliverance at the Red Sea or the giving of the Law at Mount Sinai. They needed to be reminded of God's power and purpose, and to reaffirm their commitment to the Lord through His covenant.

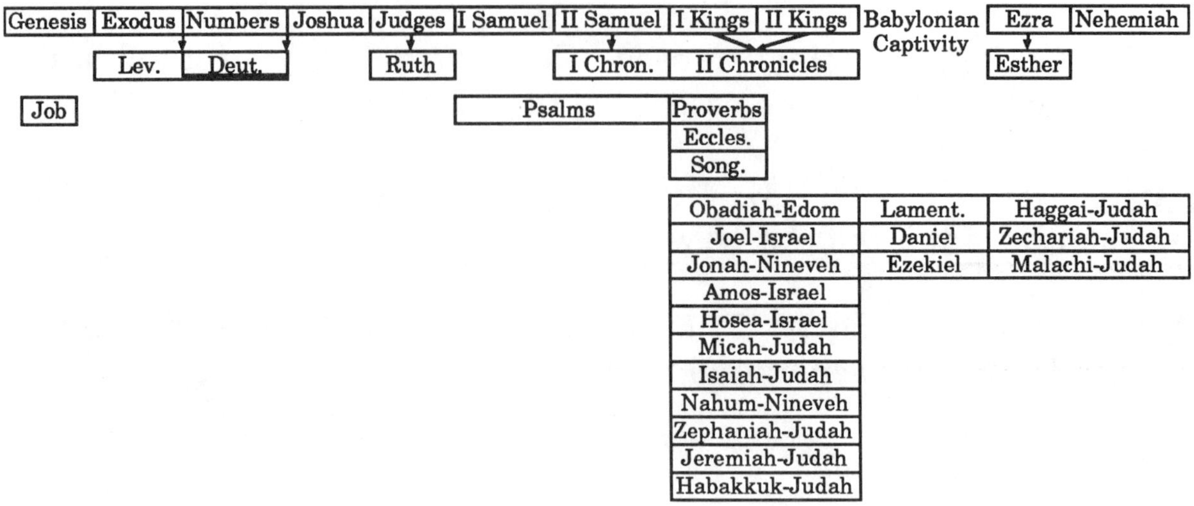

Genesis | Exodus | Numbers | Joshua | Judges | I Samuel | II Samuel | I Kings | II Kings | Babylonian Captivity | Ezra | Nehemiah

Lev. | Deut. | Ruth | I Chron. | II Chronicles | Esther

Job

Psalms | Proverbs | Eccles. | Song.

Obadiah-Edom	Lament.	Haggai-Judah
Joel-Israel	Daniel	Zechariah-Judah
Jonah-Nineveh	Ezekiel	Malachi-Judah
Amos-Israel		
Hosea-Israel		
Micah-Judah		
Isaiah-Judah		
Nahum-Nineveh		
Zephaniah-Judah		
Jeremiah-Judah		
Habakkuk-Judah		

<u>Supplemental Exercise</u>: Unscramble the seven words listed below. Take the letters that are circled and rearrange them to solve the missing phrase. Hint: Moses told Israel and Joshua to do this. The answers can be found in Deuteronomy thirty-one.

O K B O

O R N T G S

R F A E

U O L C D

T N N C V O E A

S S M E O

Y E T P G

___ ___   ___ ___   ___ ___ ___ ___   ___ ___ ___ ___ ___ ___ ___

The Changing of the Guard
Lesson #28

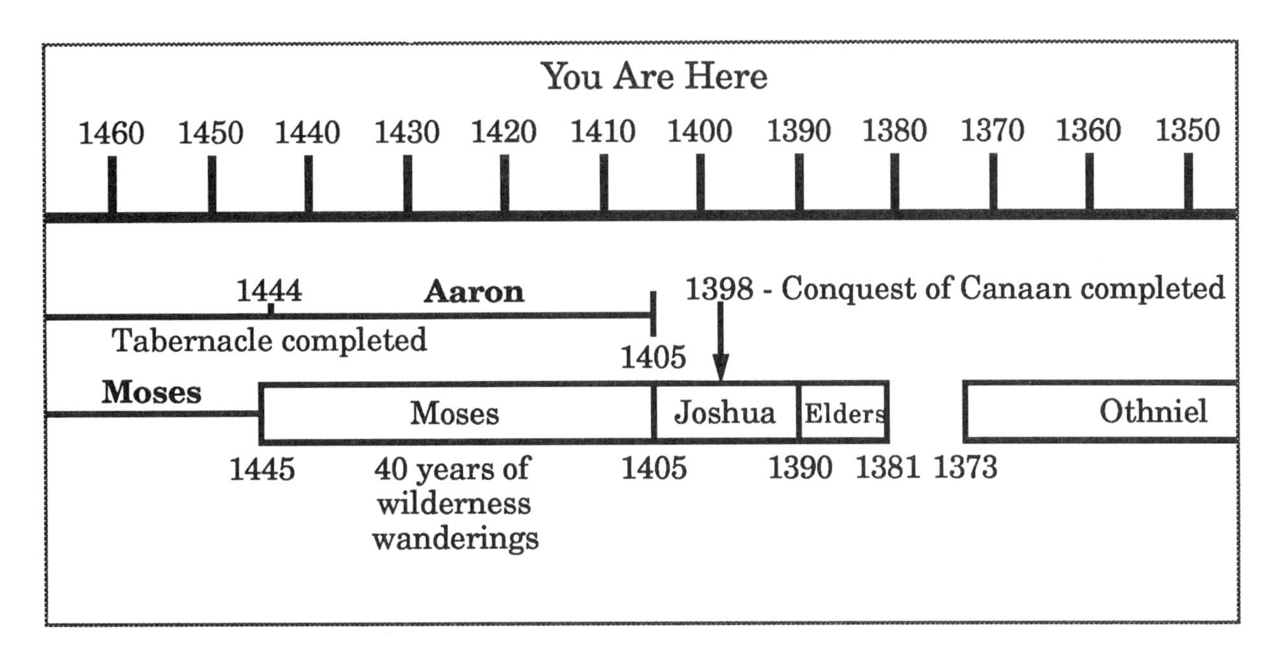

Lesson Goal: To understand that God leads and guides the steps we take by providing other people to help us grow spiritually.

Background Text: Deuteronomy 31 & 34

Memory Verse: But it is good for me to draw near to God: I have put my trust in the Lord God, that I may declare all thy works. Psalm 73:28

Have you ever visited the Tomb of the Unknown Soldier near Washington, D.C., or Buckingham Palace in London? In both places there is a ritual practiced by the soldiers called the "Changing of the Guard." In this act, the men who are patrolling an area are replaced by new guards who take over the watch. If you ever have the opportunity to visit either of these places, it is interesting to study the precise movements of the guards as they march back and forth. They are very disciplined and highly committed to their task.

In this lesson, we find that nearly forty years had passed since the children of Israel had left Egypt, and it was now time for them to enter Canaan. They had finished their wilderness wandering, and were now prepared to receive God's blessing. However, before this

The Changing of the Guard

could happen, there needed to be a "Changing of the Guard," between Moses and Joshua. It was time for Moses to die. Joshua would then take charge of the people to lead them into the promised land. This was both a sad and happy time for the people. They were sad because they were losing a great leader, but happy because they were entering Canaan.

As Joshua took command of the Israelites, God continually reminded him to be strong and courageous. Deuteronomy 31:6 says, "Be strong and of a good courage, fear not, nor be afraid of them: for the Lord thy God, He it is that doth go with thee; He will not fail thee, nor forsake thee." Joshua would succeed at his new responsibility if he continued to follow and meditate upon God's Word (Joshua 1:8).

Throughout our lives, we will be faced with new friends and changes of direction. It could be that someone close to us may die, or we may move to a new home or neighborhood. We might have to leave our friends or attend a new church. Whatever changes occur, we must not forget that God is leading us just as He led Joshua and the children of Israel. As God leads us, He often brings people into our lives to help us to grow spiritually and follow Him. Just as God directed Moses to help and lead the Hebrew people, so God also directs other people to give us help. This assistance might come from friends, our parents, a Sunday school teacher, or our pastor. God will use a variety of people to help us grow closer to Him.

Questions: Multiple choice -- circle the correct answer for each question.

1. How old was Moses when he died? (Deuteronomy 31:2)
    *100
    *120
    *150
    *600

2. Who would precede Joshua and the children of Israel into the new land? (Deuteronomy 31:3)
   *Moses
   *Joshua
   *Caleb
   *God

3. What would God do to the nations before the Israelites? (Deuteronomy 31:3)
   *Destroy them
   *Make a great people
   *Lay waste
   *Triumph over them

4. Who delivered the Law to the priests? (Deuteronomy 31:9)
   *Moses
   *Joshua
   *Caleb
   *God

5. How often was the Law to be read to the assembled people? (Deuteronomy 31:10)
   *Every week
   *Every year
   *Every seven years
   *Every fifty years

6. What did God want to be a witness for Him in opposition to the children of Israel? (Deuteronomy 31:19)
   *The Law
   *His words
   *The song of Moses
   *Joshua's words

7. What did Moses know the Israelites would do after he died? (Deuteronomy 31:29)
   *Corrupt themselves
   *Serve God
   *Follow Joshua
   *Conquer the land

8. What did God show Moses on Mount Nebo? (Deuteronomy 34:1-3)
   *The children of Israel
   *The country of Egypt
   *Mount Sinai
   *The promised land

9. Who buried Moses? (Deuteronomy 34:6)
   *Joshua
   *God
   *The children of Israel
   *Pharaoh

10. Of what was Joshua full? (Deuteronomy 34:9)
   *The spirit of the people
   *Corruption and wickedness
   *The spirit of wisdom
   *The spirit of God

Thought Questions:

1. Who has there been in your life to guide and direct you spiritually? What types of things has this person done for you? ______________
____
____
____
____
____

2. What have you done to be thankful and grateful for this person's blessing in your life? ______________________________
____
____
____

Lesson Review:

1. When was the book of Deuteronomy written? (Deuteronomy Background) ______________________________
2. What was a "foundation sacrifice"? (Lesson #27) ______________
____
____
3. What type of animal spoke to Balaam? (Lesson #26) ____________

Unit Test #2

Multiple choice -- circle the correct answer for each question.

1. Who found Moses in the river? (Exodus 2:5)
   *Pharaoh's servants
   *The daughter of Pharaoh
   *Moses' sister
   *Moses' mother

2. Whom did God appoint to speak for the Israelites? (Exodus 4:14)
   *Aaron
   *Moses
   *Joshua
   *Caleb

3. What was the tenth plague that God sent to the Egyptians? (Exodus 11:5)
   *The death of the first-born
   *The waters turned to blood
   *Frogs
   *Darkness

4. How much manna was each person to collect? (Exodus 16:16)
   *Five omers
   *One pint
   *One quart
   *One omer

5. What happened to the manna if someone tried to keep it overnight, except during the Sabbath? (Exodus 16:21)
   *It would blow away
   *It would melt
   *It would double in size
   *It would disappear

6. What is the fifth commandment of the ten commandments? (Exodus 20:12)
   *Keep the Sabbath day holy
   *Honor your father and mother
   *Thou shalt not kill
   *Thou shalt not steal

7. What was to be on each end of the mercy seat? (Exodus 25:18)
   *Priests
   *A lampstand
   *The altar of incense
   *A gold cherub

8. How many branches came out of the lampstand? (Exodus 25:32)
   *One
   *Six
   *Twelve
   *Five

9. What did the people give to Aaron to make the golden calf? (Exodus 32:3)
   *Gold coins
   *Gold necklaces
   *Money
   *Gold earrings

10. With what did the land of Canaan flow? (Numbers 13:27)
   *Milk and honey
   *Water
   *Oranges and grapes
   *Giants

11. Which two spies gave a good report about the land of Canaan and told the people that the Lord was with them? (Numbers 14:6-9)
   *Joshua and Aaron
   *Moses and Aaron
   *Moses and Caleb
   *Caleb and Joshua

12. What would happen to the people if the serpents bit them? (Numbers 21:6)
    *They would become sick
    *They would fall asleep
    *They would die
    *They would repent

13. How often was the Law to be read to the assembled people? (Deuteronomy 31:10)
    *Every week
    *Every year
    *Every seven years
    *Every fifty years

14. What did God show Moses on Mount Nebo? (Deuteronomy 34:1-3)
    *The children of Israel
    *The country of Egypt
    *Mount Sinai
    *The promised land

15. How long did Israel mourn the death of Moses? (Deuteronomy 34:8)
    *Thirty days
    *Forty days
    *Seven days
    *One year

Joshua Background

Author of Joshua: Joshua. The book uses the personal pronoun "I" when referring to Joshua, indicating that he wrote the book.

Date of Writing: Around 1400-1370 B.C. The book of Joshua spans a time of thirty years from the entrance into the land of Canaan until the death of Joshua.

Purpose of Joshua: To describe the conquest and division of the land of Canaan.

Outline of Joshua:

I. Crossing the River (Joshua 1-5)
   A. The Preparation (Joshua 1-2)
   B. The Passage (Joshua 3)
   C. The Performances (Joshua 4-5)

II. Conquering the Enemy (Joshua 6-12)
   A. The Conflicts (Joshua 6-11)
      1. Central Canaan (Joshua 6-9)
      2. Southern Canaan (Joshua 10)
      3. Northern Canaan (Joshua 11)
   B. The Victory (Joshua 12)

III. Claiming the Inheritance (Joshua 13-24)
   A. Dividing the Land (Joshua 13-21)
      1. Tribal (Joshua 13-19)
      2. Cities of Refuge (Joshua 20)
      3. Levitical (Joshua 21)
   B. Disputing with Two and One-Half Tribes (Joshua 22)
   C. Detailing Joshua's End (Joshua 23-24)

The Big Idea of Joshua: The book of Joshua is a book of victory. It details the activity of the Israelites as they moved into Canaan and possessed the land. Joshua was a great general who was eighty years old when he took over Moses' position as the leader of the Israelites. Throughout the book, we see how God's promises are fulfilled by giving the land to Israel and directing them in their fight against their enemies.

It was the Israelite's responsibility to go through Canaan and evict the heathen people who lived there. This conquest took seven years, during which time the children of Israel were faithful to the Lord. After all the major cities were defeated, another job remained – that of subduing the smaller towns and villages. This was the responsibility of the individual tribes, which they failed to fulfill. As a result, God's judgment was not completed against these wicked heathen, because they were never driven entirely out of the land. Later they would arise and attempt to destroy the children of Israel through idolatry and immorality.

Genesis | Exodus | Numbers | Joshua | Judges | I Samuel | II Samuel | I Kings | II Kings | Babylonian Captivity | Ezra | Nehemiah

Lev. | Deut. | Ruth | I Chron. | II Chronicles | Esther

Job | Psalms | Proverbs

Eccles.

Song.

Obadiah-Edom | Lament. | Haggai-Judah

Joel-Israel | Daniel | Zechariah-Judah

Jonah-Nineveh | Ezekiel | Malachi-Judah

Amos-Israel

Hosea-Israel

Micah-Judah

Isaiah-Judah

Nahum-Nineveh

Zephaniah-Judah

Jeremiah-Judah

Habakkuk-Judah

Rahab's Belief
Lesson #29

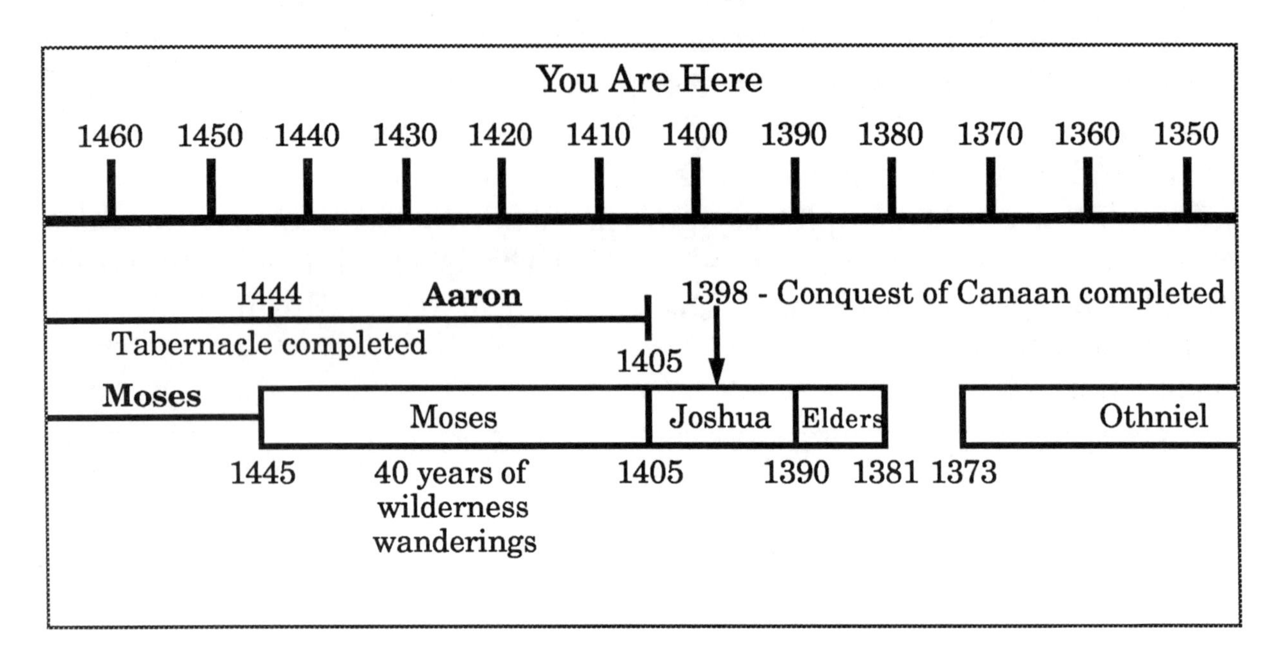

Lesson Goal: To gain a deeper understanding of our own faith and trust in God.

Background Text: Joshua 2

Memory Verse: ....The just shall live by faith. Galatians 3:11b

In our effort to study and understand the Bible, we find the same principles and lessons repeated several times. Second Peter 3:1 tells us that this is done in order to "stir up your pure minds by way of remembrance." Through His Holy Word, God continually stresses important principles that He does not want us to forget. One of these principles is **FAITH**.

Faith is important because so much of the Christian's life depends upon it. For the believer, faith can be divided into three time frames. First, there is past faith. This is the faith that is necessary to first believe in God for salvation.

Next, we have present faith. This is how we walk by trusting and believing that God will take care of all our needs and guide all our actions. Finally, there is future faith. This refers to our hope and assurance that when we die, we will be with the Lord for eternity.

Rahab had a past faith because she believed in the God of Israel. She had heard of His strength and mighty works when the Israelites left Egypt, and later when they defeated the heathen kings Sihon and Og. She had a present faith because she protected the two spies and risked her own life to save theirs. Rahab had a future faith because she trusted God to deliver and save her family when the Israelites destroyed Jericho. Because of her belief, she insured her entire family's future by making a covenant with the two spies of Israel.

Questions: Match the correct answer with the proper question.

1. ____ The two spies went to this city. (Joshua 2:1)
2. ____ The spies stayed at this person's house. (Joshua 2:1)
3. ____ The spies were hid amongst this. (Joshua 2:6)
4. ____ The men pursued the spies to this river. (Joshua 2:7)
5. ____ This had fallen upon the people of the city. (Joshua 2:9)
6. ____ The Lord dried up this water. (Joshua 2:10)
7. ____ This king was utterly destroyed. (Joshua 2:10)
8. ____ The spies escaped by using this. (Joshua 2:15)
9. ____ The spies hid here for three days. (Joshua 2:16)
10. ____ Rahab was told to put this in her window. (Joshua 2:18)

a. Terror
b. Cord
c. Jericho
d. Mountains
e. Sihon
f. Rahab
g. Scarlet thread
h. Red Sea
i. Flax
j. Jordan

Rahab's Beliefs

Thought Questions:

1. What experiences led you to your past faith? ____________________
____
____
____

2. What are you doing now to strengthen your present faith? ________
____
____
____

3. What do you hope and believe for your future faith? ____________
____
____
____

Lesson Review:

1. What are the three main points of the book of Joshua? (Joshua Background) ____
____
____

2. Joshua was filled with what? (Lesson #28) ____________________

3. What did Moses know the Israelites would do after he died? (Lesson #28) ____

Supplemental Exercise: Find and circle the words listed in the word search puzzle. Words may be forward, backward, horizontal, vertical, or diagonal.

CORD	JORDAN
COUNTRY	JOSHUA
COURAGE	KINDNESS
DESTROYED	MOTHER
EGYPT	MOUNTAIN
FATHER	PURSUED
FLAX	RAHAB
HEAVEN	ROOF
HOUSE	SCARLET
ISRAEL	SIHON
JERICHO	WINDOW

N	L	P	U	R	S	U	E	D	A	B	O	R
H	S	P	Q	E	O	H	C	I	R	E	J	D
E	L	K	M	H	K	U	V	D	E	W	O	R
A	E	I	R	T	W	T	E	S	U	O	H	O
V	A	N	X	O	A	Y	R	T	N	U	O	C
E	R	D	D	M	O	U	N	T	A	I	N	O
N	S	N	G	R	F	F	H	I	D	Y	O	U
J	I	E	T	E	C	X	D	S	R	I	H	R
W	H	S	R	A	H	A	B	B	O	O	I	A
A	E	S	C	A	R	L	E	T	J	J	S	G
D	R	E	H	T	A	F	U	T	P	Y	G	E

The Homecoming
Lesson #30

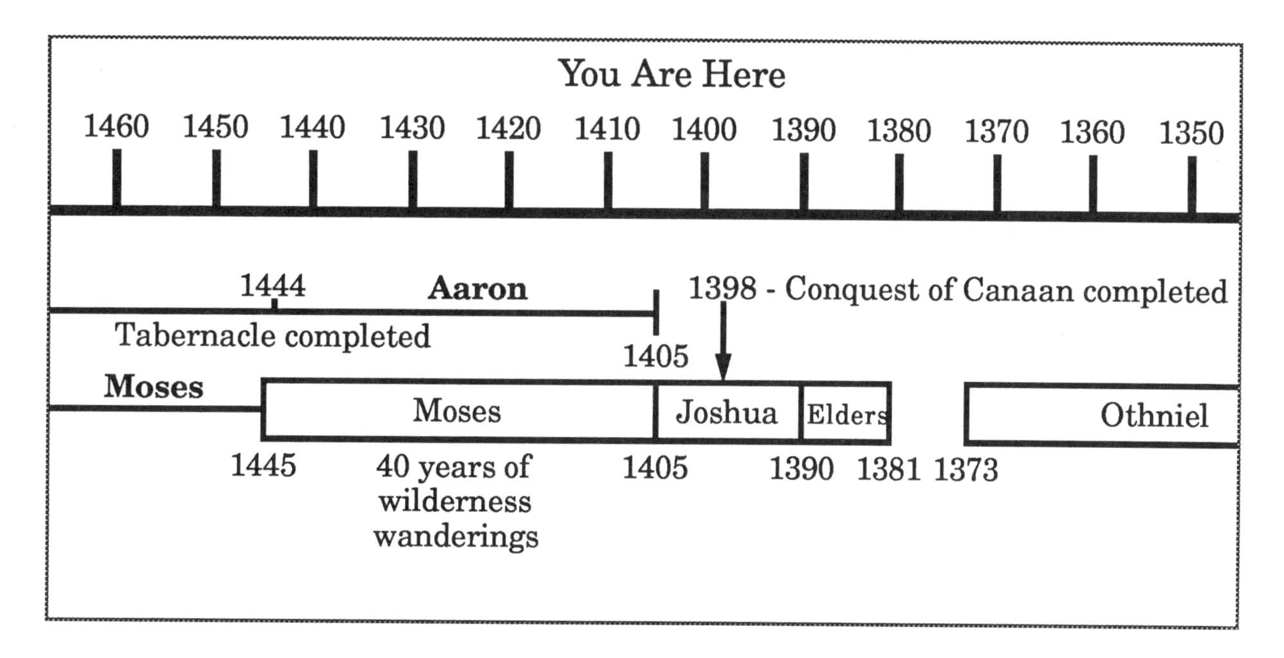

Lesson Goal: To understand that we need to establish traditions in our lives to remind us of God's kindness and goodness.

Background Text: Joshua 3-4

Memory Verse: Study to show thyself approved unto God, a workman that needeth not to be ashamed, rightly dividing the word of truth. II Timothy 2:15

The children of Israel were finally going home. Jacob and his family had left the promised land over four hundred years earlier, and now his descendants were going back to live in it. With the trials and struggles of the wilderness behind them, God's people were looking forward to a land flowing with milk and honey.

This was a time not only to look ahead to the future, but also to reflect upon the past. Joshua took that opportunity to read the

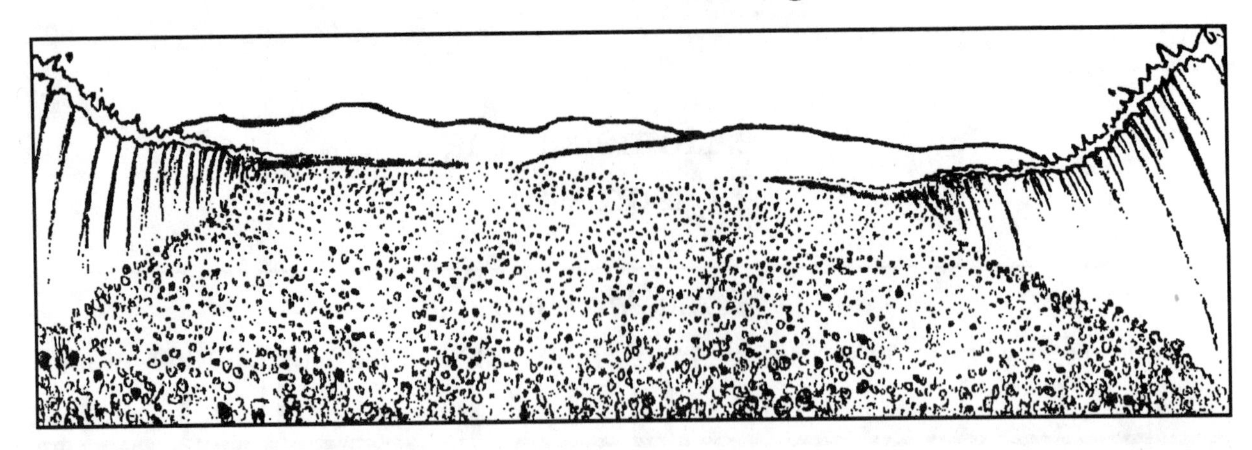

Law to the people. This was to remind them of God's covenant and what He expected of them. To confirm that His hand was upon this new generation of Israelites, God separated the waters of the Jordan just as He had done at the Red Sea. This time it was accomplished a little differently. At the Red Sea, Moses stretched out his hand, and the waters parted. Here at the Jordan, the ark of the covenant led the parting of the river. As the priests carried the holy box, their feet touched the river, and the water separated. This gave the people an opportunity to see that the source of their strength and power was from God, on the basis of His Law.

The Lord saw the importance of establishing reminders and traditions within the lives of His people so that they would not forget all He had done for them. This was why God asked to have twelve stones piled in Gilgal. In the years that followed, whenever the people and their descendants looked at the pile of stones, they would be reminded of how God miraculously brought them across the Jordan River.

In our parks and public places, we have statues and monuments that tell the stories of our heritage and history as a nation. These were placed there to remind us of the trials and great deeds of our forefathers. Many of these individuals gave their lives as they fought for freedom, but their memory and testimony live on because of their monuments.

In our personal lives, we need to build mental statues to remind us of God's kindness and goodness to us. We should never stop reading the Bible and reminding ourselves of the many times He has helped us in the past. By thinking about these things, they will help us when trials and difficulties come along. We will be reminded that as God helped us in the past, He will also help us in the future.

Questions: Multiple choice -- circle the correct answer for each question.

1. When were the people to move from their places? (Joshua 3:3)
   *In the morning
   *When they saw the priests carrying the ark
   *When Joshua told them to get up
   *In the evening

2. How far removed from the ark were the people to be? (Joshua 3:4)
   *A few feet
   *5000 cubits
   *As far as an eagle could fly in one day
   *2000 cubits

3. What would God do for Joshua the day they crossed over the Jordan? (Joshua 3:7)
   *Make him the king of Canaan
   *Help him defeat Jericho
   *Give him food and water
   *Magnify him in the sight of Israel

4. Where were the priests to stand? (Joshua 3:8)
   *By the water
   *Around the water
   *In the water
   *Near the water

5. What were the twelve men to take from the Jordan? (Joshua 4:3)
   *Twelve stones
   *Water for the people to drink
   *Fish for the people to eat
   *Nothing

6. What was the purpose of the stones piled together? (Joshua 4:6)
   *To stop the water from flowing
   *To be a sign to the people
   *To act as steps for the people to walk on
   *To frighten the enemies of God

7. Of the people who passed over the river, how many were prepared for war? (Joshua 4:13)
   *40,000
   *Two or three million
   *4,000
   *400,000

8. In what way did the people regard Joshua? (Joshua 4:14)
   *As God
   *As the enemy
   *As Moses
   *As Aaron

9. When did the people come up out of the Jordan? (Joshua 4:19)
   *The first day of the harvest season
   *After a long and cold winter
   *Before the beginning of spring
   *The tenth day of the first month

10. Where did the people camp after passing over the Jordan? (Joshua 4:19)
   *Jericho
   *The plains of Midian
   *Gilgal
   *Jerusalem

Thought Questions:

1. In your own life, how often do you read, study, and meditate in God's Word? ______________________________

____

____

____

2. What events have taken place in your life through which you can see the hand of God guiding and directing you? ______________

____

____

____

____

____

Lesson Review:

1. What three types of faith did Rahab exhibit? (Lesson #29) ________
____
____

2. What does it mean when Matthew 5:16 tells us to be the light of the world? (Lesson #27) ________________________
____
____
____

3. Of all the adult Israelites who left Egypt, which were the only two to enter the promised land? (Lesson #24) ________________
____

Supplemental Exercise: As a child I had a plaque with Proverbs 3:5-6 inscribed upon it. This I hung on the wall over my bedroom window. Every night before going to sleep, I would look at that plaque and be reminded of God's purpose and direction in my life. Since Joshua had the people pile up stones to remind them of their crossing over the Jordan River, is there something you could make which would serve as a continual reminder of God's goodness in some area of your life? When you have finished your project, put it someplace where you will see it everyday.

If you need help thinking of something to do, ask your parents or pastor for advice. They might suggest making a plaque with Scripture written on it. They may also suggest making or buying a picture that would remind you of the Lord's goodness. You should be careful to make or purchase something which you would be pleased to display in your room.

The Conquest of Jericho
Lesson #31

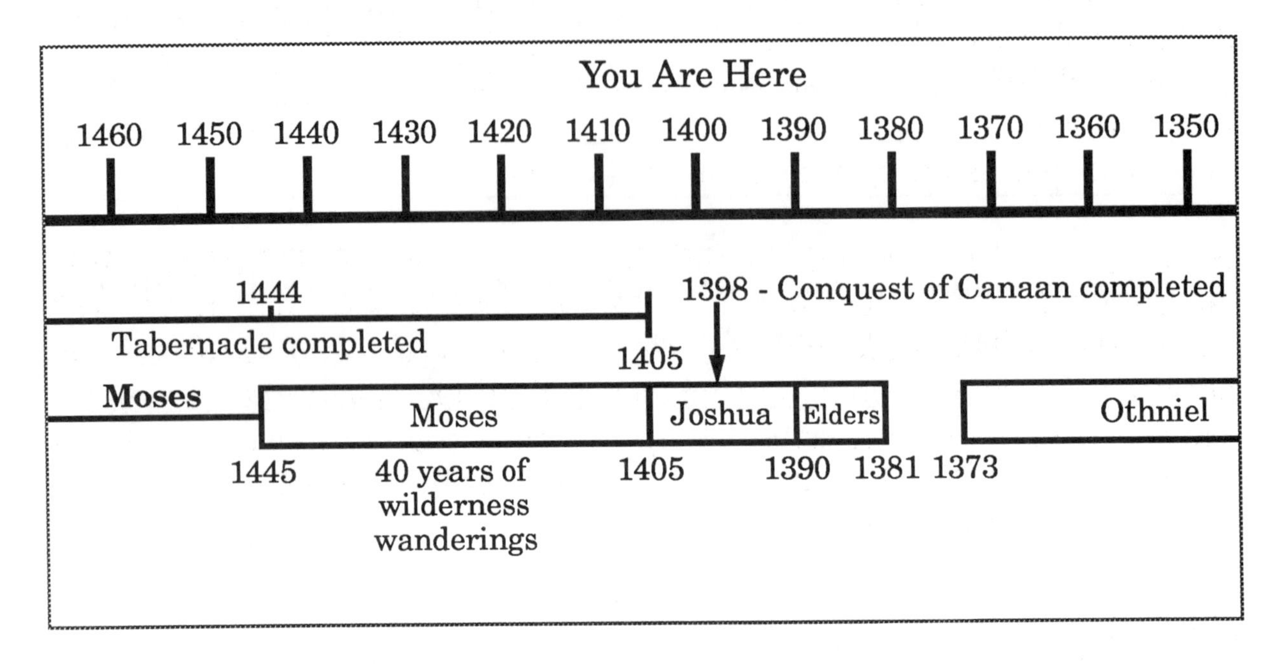

Lesson Goal: To understand the principle of determination.

Background Text: Joshua 6

Memory Verse: I have set the Lord always before me: because He is at my right hand, I shall not be moved. Psalm 16:8

Have you ever become angry while playing a game and then quit if things were not going your way? Perhaps you have jobs and tasks around the house that you should complete, but have never started. If you have homework to finish, do you get it done immediately or put it off until the last minute? We will discover from this lesson that when God gives us a job to do, He expects it to get done.

God had given the Israelites the task of marching around the city of Jericho. The people may have been puzzled by this very strange way to conquer and defeat a city. They probably were saying to themselves, "How can we defeat our enemies by only walking around them?" However, the people were determined to follow God's instructions and accomplish their task. Because of the Israelites' obedience to the Lord's directions, they were rewarded with a great victory.

Do you know what "procrastination" means? It means to postpone doing something that is supposed to be done. If the children of Israel had procrastinated when walking around Jericho, they would have never conquered the city. Procrastination is not determination; when you are determined, you give whatever energy is necessary to accomplish your task.

History and archaeology teach us that the walls of Jericho were double walls, thirty feet high. The outer wall was six feet thick, and the inner wall was twelve feet thick. There was a gap of fifteen feet between the two walls where houses and other structures were built. This is what is meant when Scripture says that Rahab's house was "upon the wall" (Joshua 2:15). Her house was one of the houses that was built between the two walls of Jericho.

Questions:

1. What had God given into the hand of Joshua? (Joshua 6:2) ________
   ____
2. How many days did the people make a single trip around the city? (Joshua 6:3) ________________________________
3. How many times were the people to go around the city on the seventh day? (Joshua 6:4) ________________________
4. What did Joshua tell the people to do after they had marched around the city for the seventh time? (Joshua 6:16) __________
   ____
5. Which family was the only one to survive the destruction of Jericho? (Joshua 6:17) ________________________
6. What would happen to the camp of Israel if someone removed an accursed thing from Jericho? (Joshua 6:18) ____________
   ____
7. What items could the Israelites take from Jericho and bring into the treasury of the Lord? (Joshua 6:19) ____________
   ____
8. What was utterly destroyed? (Joshua 6:21) ______________
   ____

9. What curse did Joshua pronounce upon Jericho? (Joshua 6:26) ____

____

____

10. What was proclaimed throughout the land? (Joshua 6:27) ______

____

Thought Questions:

1. In what area of your life do you find it easy to quit or procrastinate?

____

2. How can you determine to make that area more enjoyable and easier to accomplish? Ask your parents for advice and suggestions here. ____

____

____

Lesson Review:

1. Why was God's judgment not fully completed against the wicked heathen in the book of Joshua? (Joshua Background) __________

____

2. How long did it take the Israelites to conquer the land of Canaan? (Joshua Background) ______________________________

3. During the Old Testament times, for what was the book of Leviticus used? (Leviticus Background) ______________________

____

Supplemental Exercise: Complete the crossword from Joshua 6:12-19.

Joshua rose early in the morning, and the priests took up the 5-A of the Lord. And 4-D priests bore seven trumpets of 3-A horns before the ark of the Lord. The armed 9-D went before them. The second 2-D they went around the city once, and returned into the 6-D; so they did 11-A days. And on the seventh day it came to pass that after the seventh time they went around the city, the 10-A blew with the trumpets, Joshua said to the people, "Shout, for the 1-A hath given you the 6-A." Joshua warned the people not to take anything out of the city of Jericho, for fear they would make the camp of Israel a 8-A, and cause trouble. But all the silver and gold, and vessels of 7-D and iron, being consecrated unto the Lord, were to go in the Lord's house.

1			2		3			4
			5					
6						7		
				8				
			9					
10								
						11		

The Sin of Achan
Lesson #32

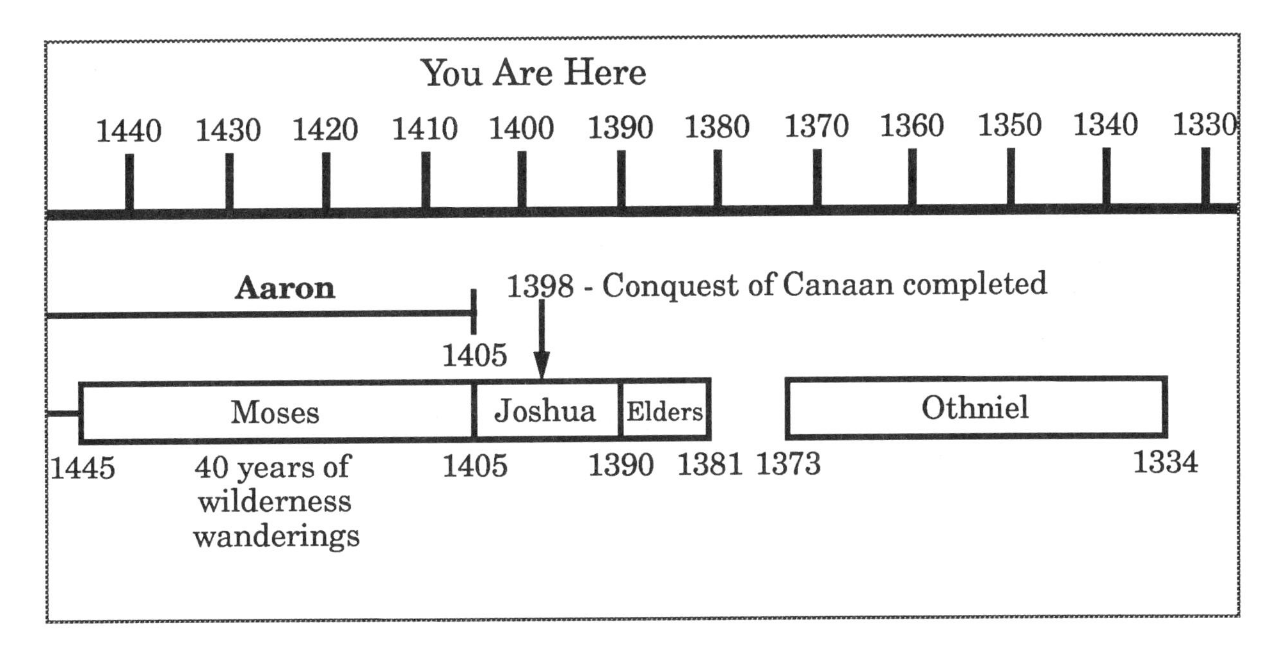

Lesson Goal: To understand the sin of covetousness and how it is different from the attitude of contentment.

Background Text: Joshua 7

Memory Verse: But godliness with contentment is great gain. I Timothy 6:6

Have you ever heard the expression "that person was green with envy"? Envy and covetousness mean almost the same thing. To covet means to desire something wrongfully, without any regard to the rights of others. It is not wrong to wish or hope for something, but when we covet, we have sinned. For example, you may want a bike or a computer for your birthday. If that wanting becomes so great that you would sin to get the thing you desire, then you are coveting. Many of the criminals in prison are there because of stealing, lying, or murder; but if you asked them what made them do these terrible things, many would tell you that they wanted something that someone else had. Their initial sin

of coveting led to more sins, which eventually sent them to prison.

What is God's answer to coveting? If we do not want to covet, what should we do? First Timothy 6:6 says that we should be content. This means that we are satisfied with whatever circumstance in life God has given to us. Now this does not mean that we stop seeking God's will, become complacent, and do nothing more to develop and strengthen our lives. Contentment is an attitude of the heart. It is an understanding that wherever God leads us, we will be satisfied in that position.

We may not be happy with the way we look, where we live, or the type of clothes we wear. We may know people who appear to have better things than we do. If we see something about ourselves that we do not like, it is not wrong to try to change it. We can brush our teeth, comb our hair, dress for a neat and clean appearance, and do the things that will help us to feel better about ourselves. Most importantly though, we can develop an attitude of contentment. We are not to feel bad because our lives are not "perfect." When we are content, we will not covet because we understand that God is directing our paths. If we can change something about ourselves, then we may go ahead and do it; but if not, then we should accept our lives the way God made them.

We can see from the life of Achan that he sinned by coveting. He stole the items from Jericho because he desired them. Then he hid those things in his tent, knowing that what he did was wrong. Because of his sin, the entire nation of Israel was punished. This should be a strong warning to us that the Lord will punish those who covet.

Questions:

1. Achan, took of the ____________ thing: and the __________ of the Lord was ____________ against the children of Israel. (Joshua 7:1)
2. The men said to Joshua, let about two or three ________________ men go up and smite ___________. (Joshua 7:3)
3. After Ai smote Israel, the ___________ of the people ____________, and became as ______________. (Joshua 7:5)
4. And Joshua rent his clothes, and fell to the ____________ upon his face before the _______ of the Lord until the eventide. (Joshua 7:6)
5. ___________ hath sinned, and they have also _________________ my ________________ which I commanded them. (Joshua 7:11)
6. O Israel: thou canst not stand before thine _____________, until ye take away the _____________ thing from among you. (Joshua 7:13)
7. He that is taken with the ______________ thing shall be burnt with __________, he and all that he hath. (Joshua 7:15)
8. Joshua said unto Achan, my son, give, I pray thee, ____________ to the Lord God of Israel, and make _________________ unto Him. (Joshua 7:19)
9. Achan said to Joshua, Indeed, I have ________________ against the Lord God of ______________. (Joshua 7:20)
10. All Israel stoned [Achan] with __________, and burned [him] with _________, after they had stoned [him] with stones. (Joshua 7:25)

Thought Questions:

1. What in your life do you feel the least happy and least contented with? ____

____

2. What practical steps can you take to improve your life and the way you feel about yourself? ____

____

____

____

The Sin of Achan

Lesson Review:

1. How many times did the children of Israel walk around Jericho on the seventh day? (Lesson #31) ________________________________

____

2. What does "determination" mean? (Lesson #31) ________________

____

____

____

3. How often was the Law of God to be read to the people assembled together? (Lesson #28) ______________________________

Supplemental Exercise: From the genealogy, complete the dotted lines with the correct information.

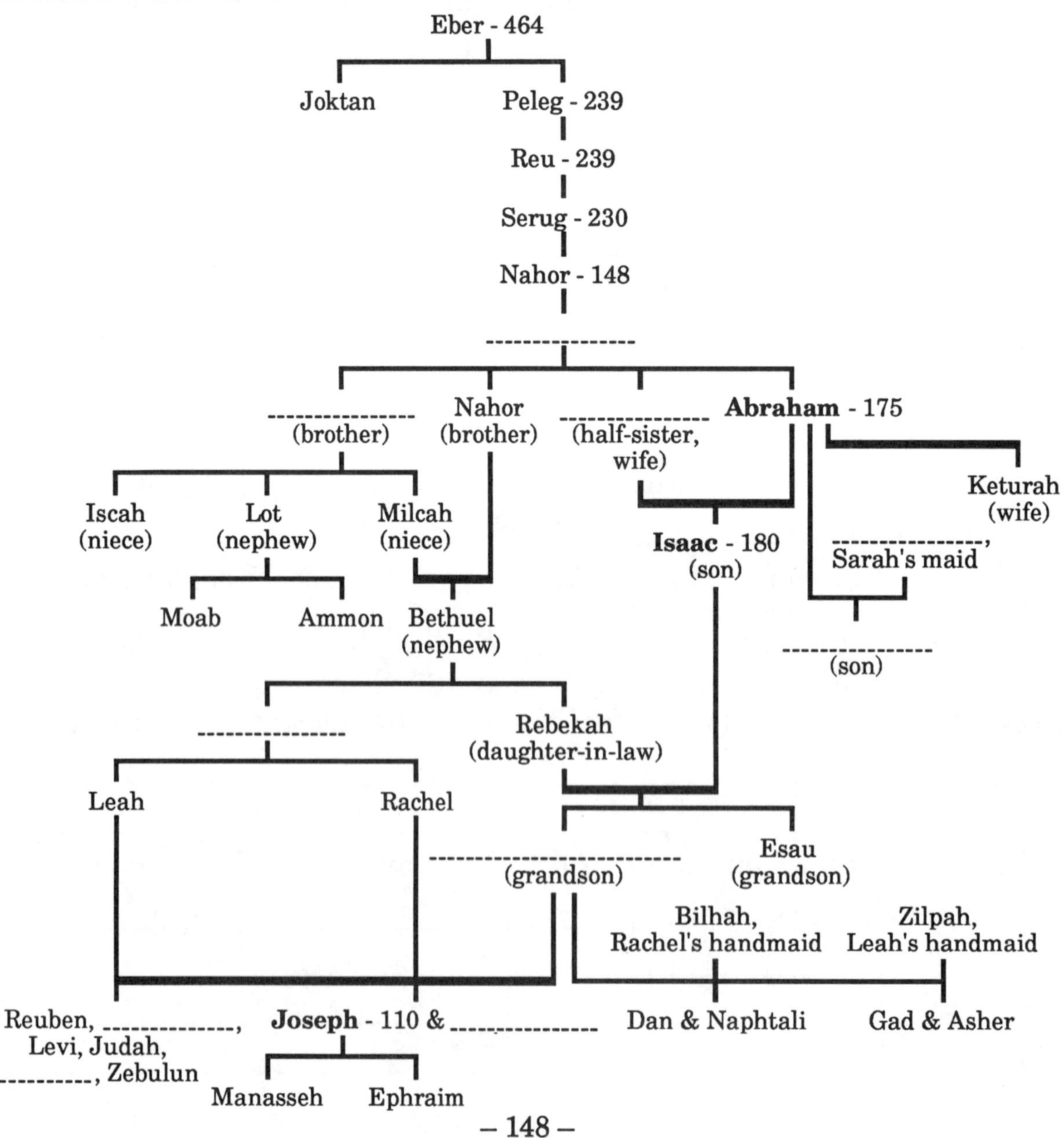

Poor Covenant with the Gibeonites
Lesson #33

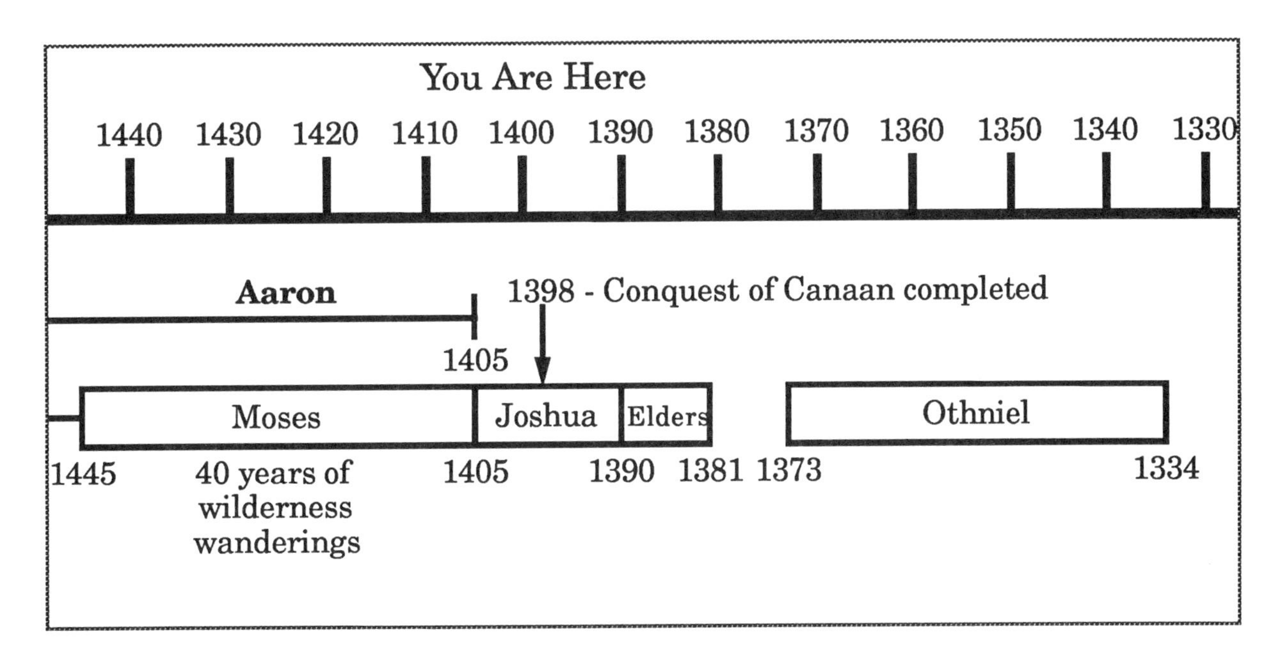

Lesson Goal: To help understand and identify wicked fools and deceivers.

Background Text: Joshua 9

Memory Verse: The fear of the Lord is the beginning of knowledge: but fools despise wisdom and instruction. Proverbs 1:7

Whenever we must make an important decision, we must first read God's Word for wisdom and guidance. Joshua and the leaders of Israel failed to do this when the Gibeonites came to them. As a result of this neglect, the children of Israel were deceived and troubled by that nation for several centuries.

As Christians, we need to be very cautious of people who may try to trick and deceive us. We can be trusting and honest with individuals, while at the same time not being foolish and gullible. "Gullible" means that we accept anything and everything someone tells us as the truth. For instance, if someone said that they were going to give us one thousand dollars if we first let them borrow one hundred dollars, we would be gullible to believe them without checking their story to see if it were true.

Poor Covenant with the Gibeonites

Ask your parents or teacher to give some illustrations of a deceiver. No doubt they have met several of these wicked people during their lives. Ask them to share with you some of their experiences and how they handled them. The Bible, especially the book of Proverbs, is very specific about foolish people, and how to avoid them. Look up the following verses and write down how God's Word helps to identify deceivers and fools and, if mentioned, how we should respond. The first two questions have been completed so you have an example to follow.

Questions:

a. Proverbs 10:18 Fools utter slander, and the person who hides hate is a liar.

b. Proverbs 12:23 Fools proclaim foolishness, but prudent men conceal the truth.

1. Proverbs 8:13 ______________________________
____
____

2. Proverbs 11:13 ______________________________
____
____

3. Proverbs 11:19 ______________________________
____
____

4. Proverbs 13:15 ______________________________
____
____

5. Proverbs 13:16 ______________________________
____
____

6. Proverbs 14:15 ______________________________

7. Proverbs 14:16 ______________________________

8. Proverbs 14:17 ______________________________

9. Proverbs 20:19 ______________________________

10. Proverbs 27:12 ______________________________

Thought Questions:

1. From your parents' illustrations and the verses in Proverbs, what steps can you take to avoid being deceived? ______________________________

2. From your parents' illustrations and the verses in Proverbs, how would you describe a person who is very wise? ______________________________

Lesson Review:

1. What is God's answer for covetousness? (Lesson #32) ______________________________

2. When was the book of Joshua written? (Joshua Background) ______________________________

3. Describe the walls of Jericho. (Lesson #31) ______________________

____

____

____

Map Review: This map represents the conquest of the land of Canaan by Joshua and the children of Israel. Study the map to identify the route the people took to gain possession of the land. Details of the conquest can be found in Joshua 8, 10, and 11.

The numbers indicate the sequence of events as the people prepared for battle.

The dotted line represents the route of the Israelites. (----)

The solid line represents the route of the Canaanites. (—)

Supernatural Victory
Lesson #34

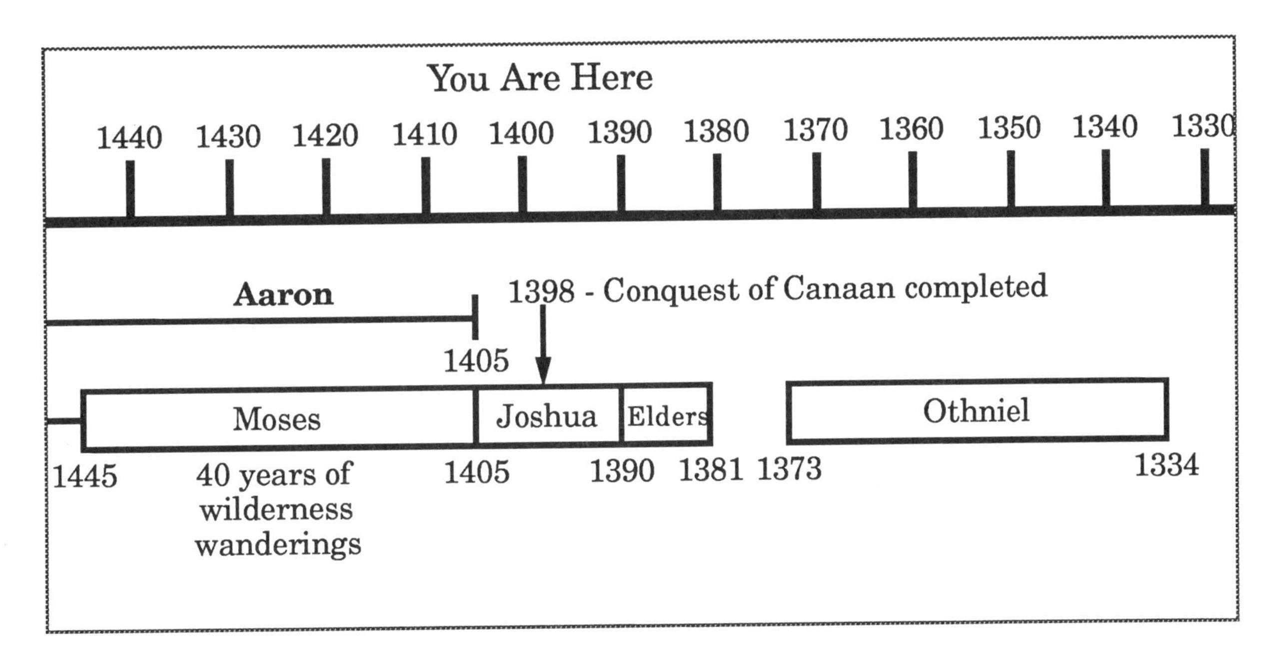

Lesson Goal: To understand that the created order is under God's control and that the Christian is to cultivate it.

Background Text: Joshua 10:1-28

Memory Verse: Fear them not: for I have delivered them into thine hand; there shall not a man of them stand before thee. Joshua 10:8

What an amazing story – to think that God has the power to stop the earth from rotating so that the sun and moon appear to stand still! It makes sense though; since God created the universe, He also controls it. However, people often do not believe in God's sovereign control over the world, so they become confused as to how they should respect and regard nature. During this day and age, most people have the tendency to view nature at two extreme levels. The first level comes from an "evolutionary perspective." If people believe that the world evolved from nothingness and chance, they generally do not respect nature. This respect is not there because they have no faith in a God Who created and controls the universe. As a result, they will manipulate nature to achieve their own desires, and if necessary, destroy it in the process.

At the other level is the "pantheistic perspective." People who hold to this belief feel that all nature has a soul and should be regarded on the same level as mankind. They believe that people could someday be reincarnated into plants and animals, or vice-versa. Therefore, they do not even want to process trees for paper or drill for oil, because it runs the risk of interrupting a part of the "natural" cycle. Their belief has led them to the condemnation found in the first chapter of Romans: "Who changed the truth of God into a lie, and worshiped and served the creature more than the Creator" (Romans 1:25). Although the protection of nature is good and important, they have taken their belief too far in an attempt to safeguard nature against mankind.

Contrary to these two perspectives, the Biblical view teaches that nature should be respected, but it also should be cultivated. God told Adam in Genesis 1:28 to subdue the earth. This meant that Adam was to gain knowledge and mastery over the environment, and bring its elements into service for mankind. God has given man nature to use and develop, but with that comes the responsibility of caring for it.

We can cultivate nature by first replenishing the items that were removed. If we cut down mature trees, we should plant new ones. We can also recycle various products to slow the consumption of the earth's natural resources. If possible, we should try to maintain the quality of the natural surroundings. For example, if a company is drilling for oil or making chemicals, they should take the necessary steps to keep pollution down and properly dispose of toxic wastes. Finally, if an area has been exhausted of one natural element, it should be turned into some other useful purpose. A good illustration of this would be garbage dumps that have been covered with dirt and turned into parks or recreational areas. The environment is not to be destroyed, nor is it to be elevated to a level that is equal to or higher than man. Instead, nature is to be nurtured and cultivated so that the next generation can also enjoy it.

Questions:

1. Over what city did Adonizedek rule? (Joshua 10:1) ______________
2. What had Adonizedek heard? (Joshua 10:1) ___________________

   ____

   ____

3. Who were the five kings (and their cities) who joined together to attack Gibeon? (Joshua 10:3) ______________________________

   ____

   ____

   ____

4. How did Joshua and the Israelites come upon the five kings and their armies? (Joshua 10:9) _______________________________

   ____

5. How did more Amorites die than were killed by the Israelites? (Joshua 10:11) ____

   ____

6. Where was it written that the sun and moon stood still? (Joshua 10:13) ____
7. Who fought for Israel? (Joshua 10:14) ________________________
8. Where did the five kings hide themselves? (Joshua 10:16) _______

   ____

9. What did Joshua ask his captains to do to the five kings? (Joshua 10:24) ____________________

____

10. How did Joshua kill the five kings? (Joshua 10:26) ____________

____

Thought Questions:

1. What should your attitude be toward the environment? __________

____

____

____

____

2. What are three specific things that you can do to cultivate nature or the environment around you? ____________________

____

____

____

Lesson Review: List these events in the chronological order as they occurred in the Bible.

______ Job suffers
______ Isaac is born
______ The Israelites are defeated by Ai
______ God creates plants
______ The twelve spies enter Canaan
______ The Israelites cross the Jordan
______ A plague of frogs
______ Manna is first provided
______ God creates animals
______ Achan is punished for his sin
______ Abraham and Lot quarrel over land
______ Joseph is sold into slavery in Egypt
______ Moses and the Israelites war against the Midianites
______ The tabernacle is built
______ Isaac dies
______ The sun and moon stand still
______ A plague of flies

Judges Background

Author of Judges: The authorship of Judges is uncertain, although tradition and history support Samuel.

Date of Writing: 1050-1000 B.C. Judges was written after the death of Samson and the crowning of Saul as king, but before David's conquest of Jerusalem (Judges 1:21).

Purpose of Judges: To detail the 300-year historical development of the children of Israel, from the conquest of Canaan to the establishment of kings ruling Israel.

Outline of Judges:

I. Introduction to Judges (1:1-3:4)
   A. Political Background (Judges 1)
   B. Spiritual Background (2:1-3:4)

II. Seven Sin Cycles (3:5-16:31)
   A. Under Othniel vs. Mesopotamia (3:5-11)
   B. Under Ehud and Shamgar vs. Moab and Philistine (3:12-31)
   C. Under Deborah and Barak vs. Canaan (Judges 4-5)
   D. Under Gideon vs. Midian (6:1-8:32)
   E. Under Abimelech vs. Shechem; Tola and Jair (8:33-10:5)
   F. Under Jephthah vs. Ammon; Ibzan, Elon and Abdon (10:6-12:15)
   G. Under Samson vs. Philistine (Judges 13-16)

III. Ungodliness Described (Judges 17-21)
   A. In the Individual (17:1-6)
   B. In the Priesthood (17:7-13)
   C. In the Nation (Judges 18-21)

The Big Idea of Judges: Just as the book of Joshua is a book about victory, the book of Judges is a book about defeat. The children of Israel failed to remove and destroy all the wicked inhabitants from the land of Canaan. They began to take on the lifestyle and actions of the heathen people and worshiped their false idols. The key verse of the book is Judges 17:6, "....but every man did that which was right in his own eyes."

Since the people set aside God's commandments and were doing what was "right in their own eyes," God disciplined and punished them. This led the people into a series of seven separate sin cycles.

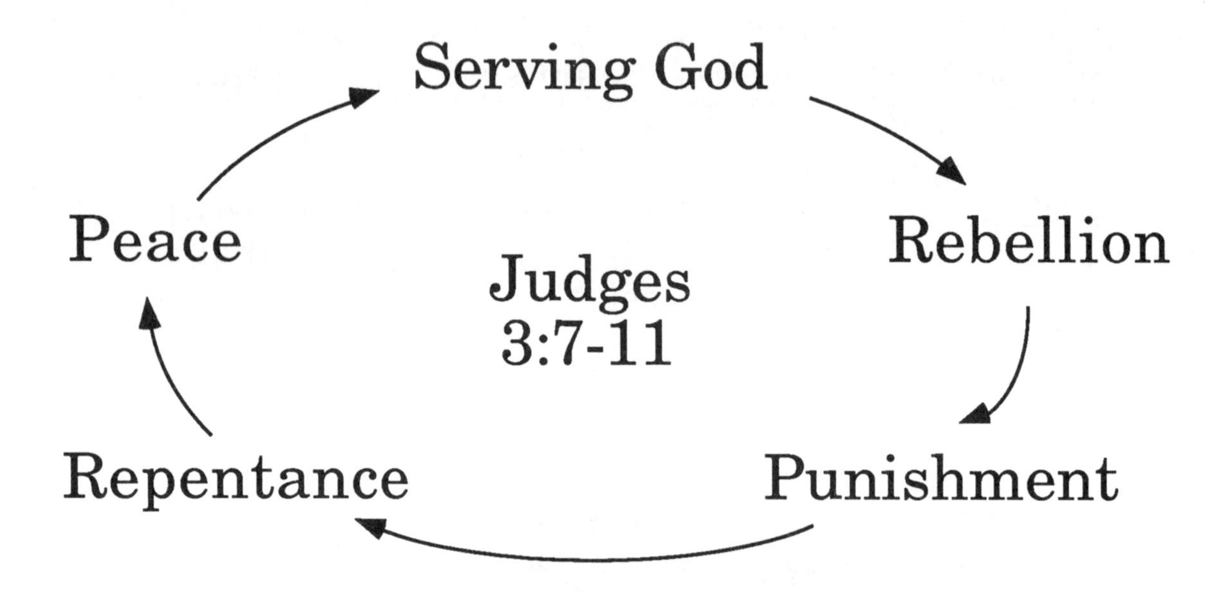

After the people rebelled and were punished, God raised up judges to lead the people into repentance and then peace. Generally, the peace was accomplished by the judge leading an army of Israelites to defeat the heathen that were oppressing them. Then after the enemies were defeated, the people would go back to serving God for a short time. Eventually, they would rebel again and needed to be punished. So the sin cycle would continue.

Genesis	Exodus	Numbers	Joshua	Judges	I Samuel	II Samuel	I Kings	II Kings	Babylonian Captivity	Ezra	Nehemiah
	Lev.	Deut.		Ruth		I Chron.	II Chronicles			Esther	
Job					Psalms		Proverbs				
							Eccles.				
							Song.				
							Obadiah-Edom		Lament.	Haggai-Judah	
							Joel-Israel		Daniel	Zechariah-Judah	
							Jonah-Nineveh		Ezekiel	Malachi-Judah	
							Amos-Israel				
							Hosea-Israel				
							Micah-Judah				
							Isaiah-Judah				
							Nahum-Nineveh				
							Zephaniah-Judah				
							Jeremiah-Judah				
							Habakkuk-Judah				

Deborah and Barak
Lesson #35

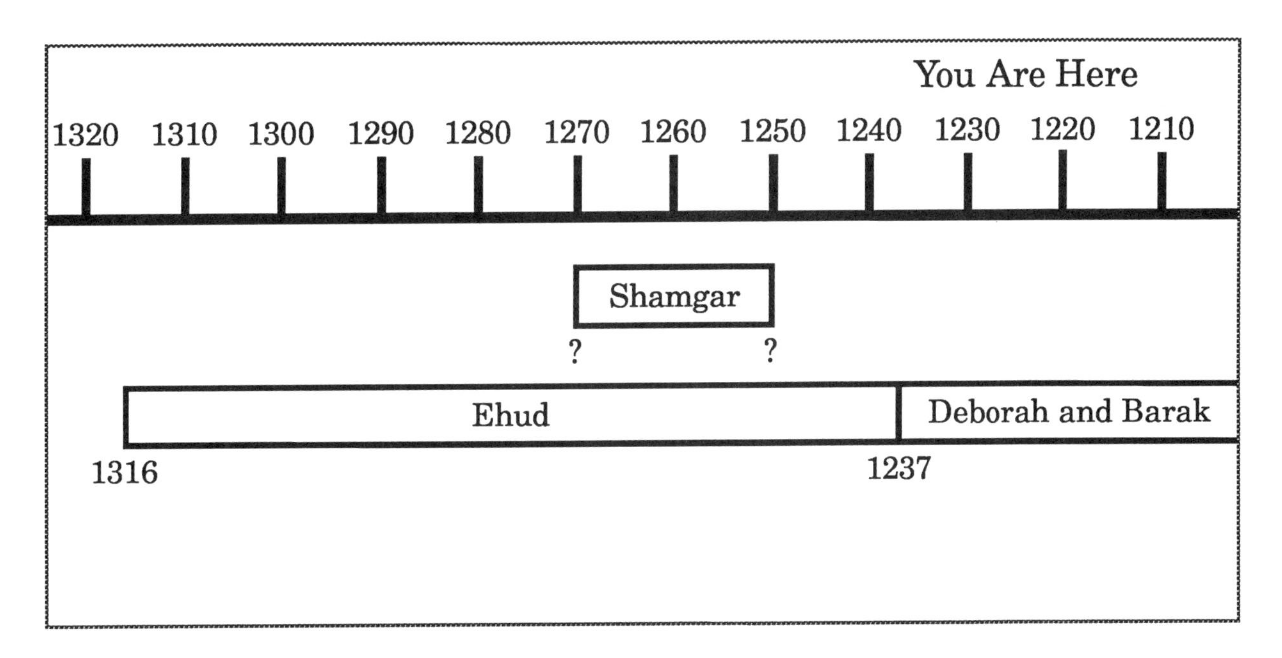

Lesson Goal: To understand the importance of women in the Bible.

Background Text: Judges 4

Memory Verse: Who can find a virtuous woman? For her price is far above rubies. Proverbs 31:10

In the third cycle of the Israelite's sin and disobedience, God delivered the people into the hands of the Canaanites. These were the same heathen that the Israelites conquered when they first possessed the promised land. However, since the Israelites did not completely destroy the Canaanites, they grew back into a strong nation which oppressed God's people. This time, instead of raising up a male judge to deliver them, the Lord raised up a female judge to save Israel.

The name Deborah means "bee," which implies that she is sweet and gives honey to her friends, but has a sharp stinger for her enemies. Deborah was aware of the way that Jabin, the leader of the Canaanites, was hurting the children of Israel. So, in her role as a judge, she called upon Barak to fight against the Canaanites. Barak, however, was fearful and asked for Deborah to go with him. Deborah agreed to this request, but said that because Barak was

Deborah and Barak

fearful, God would honor another woman (Jael) for the victory instead of him.

With God's assistance, Barak defeated the powerful and wicked Canaanites. In an attempt to escape, Sisera ran to hide in the tent of a friend, Hazor. Hazor's wife, Jael, knew that Sisera was fleeing Barak and gave him some milk to drink. This relaxed Sisera, making him sleepy. As Sisera slept, Jael killed him. Jael was a believer in God and helped the children of Israel by hammering a tent spike through Sisera's head. This explains Deborah's earlier comment to Barak concerning a woman receiving credit for the victory. Since Jael killed Sisera, she, not Barak, was honored for the destruction of the wicked leader.

There are several principles we can learn from this lesson, but we especially want to focus our attention upon the important role that women played in the Bible. We see it not only here in this lesson with Jael and Deborah, but also through many other examples in God's Word. Mary the mother of Jesus, the virtuous woman in Proverbs thirty-one, Samuel's mother Hannah, Ruth, and Queen Esther were all women who were committed to the Lord and followed His commands. God used and directed the lives of these women, and through them led His people into peace and righteousness.

Questions: Please indicate your answer with either True or False.

1. ____ The children of Israel were righteous and prospered in the sight of the Lord. (Judges 4:1)
2. ____ Sisera oppressed the Israelites for twenty years. (Judges 4:3)
3. ____ Barak said that he would not go into battle unless Deborah came with him. (Judges 4:8)
4. ____ The Lord said that He would sell Sisera into the hand of a Canaanite. (Judges 4:9)
5. ____ Sisera gathered ninety chariots to attack Barak. (Judges 4:13)

6. ____ Sisera fled from Barak on foot. (Judges 4:15)
7. ____ When Jael saw Sisera, she told him to run away and hide. (Judges 4:18)
8. ____ Jael gave Sisera some water to drink. (Judges 4:19)
9. ____ Jael hammered a nail into Sisera's heart. (Judges 4:21)
10. ____ The children of Israel prevailed against Jabin until he was destroyed. (Judges 4:24)

Thought Questions:

1. You know what Deborah's name means, but do you know the meaning of your name? If you do not, research your name and find out what it means. (Libraries generally have books that discuss names and their interpretations.) ____________________

____

____

____

2. What woman do you personally know that would fit the Biblical example of a Godly woman? What positive qualities in this woman's life would you want to have in your life? ____________________

____

____

____

____

____

Lesson Review:

1. Why was forty years chosen as the length of time for the children of Israel to wander in the wilderness? (Lesson #24) ____________________

____

____

____

2. Why do Godly people sometimes suffer? (Lesson #6) ____________________

____

____

____

3. For a total of how many days was Noah in the ark? (Lesson #4)

____

Supplemental Exercise: Go through the Bible and find an example of a Godly woman; then answer these questions. You may use one of the names found in this lesson.

1. Who is the woman? ____________________
2. Where did this woman live and where is she found in the Bible?
____
____
____
3. What does the Bible say about this woman? Give a brief description of her background. ____________________
____
____
____
____
____
____
4. Why did you choose this woman? ____________________
____
____
____
____
____
5. How did this woman glorify and serve God? ____________________
____
____
____
____
____
6. What characteristics about this woman's life do you admire the most? ____________________
____
____
____
____
____

Gideon Defeats Baal
Lesson #36

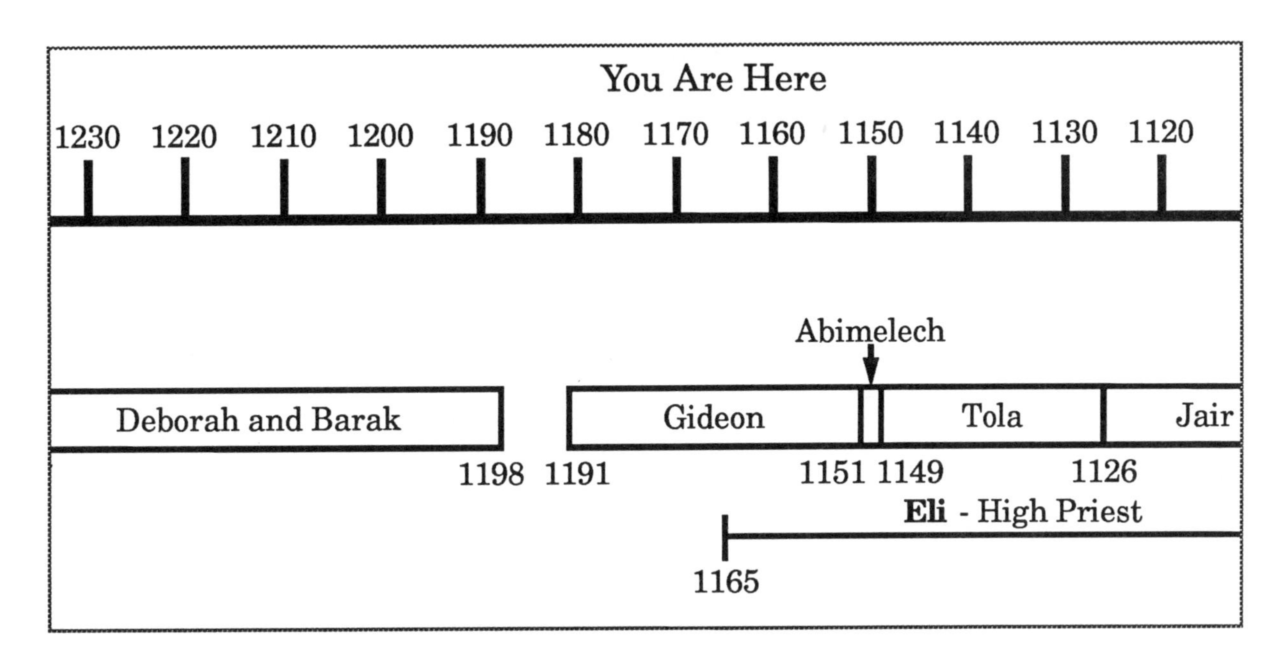

Lesson Goal: To understand that we need to tear down the idols of our heart before we can win any battles for God.

Background Text: Judges 6

Memory Verse: No man can serve two masters: for either he will hate the one, and love the other; or else he will hold to the one, and despise the other. Ye cannot serve God and mammon. Matthew 6:24

Throughout our lives, the most important battle we will fight will not be in a war; it will not be against a significant issue or social concern. The most important battle we will fight will be against the idols of our heart's desire.

What is an idol? An idol is anything or anyone that is more important to us than God. Perhaps we will not bow down to it, as Israel did to Baal; but if this person or thing replaces the Lord in our lives, it becomes an idol. An idol could be money, a sports hero, a friend, or even ourselves. Israel's idol

was Baal, who was the god of nature. Worshippers of nature hoped to receive larger grain harvests and have nice weather. Israel made the mistake of placing more emphasis upon God's creation, rather then upon God Himself.

Because of Israel's sinful actions, God gave the people over to the Midianites for seven years. The Midianites were destructive to the Israelites and robbed them of most of their food and animals. God called upon Gideon, who was the least in a very poor family from one of the morally weakest tribes in Israel, to destroy the idols of Baal and deliver the children of Israel from bondage. Gideon was called "Jerubbaal," which meant "Baal will fight," because he tore down the idol of Baal. Before Gideon could fight the Midianites, he had to get rid of anything that was coming between God and His people. The real enemy of the Israelites was their own sin. Sin was the cause of their problems. The Midianite persecution was only the result of their sin.

Israel found it was easy to focus their attention upon the Midianite army of 135,000 men and forget about Baal. In our personal lives, it is also easy to see only the result of our sin and neglect the sin's source, which could be the idols in our lives. God is calling us to be Gideons. First, we should destroy the idols in our lives, and then go to our family and our community and destroy the idols there. The most important battle we will fight will not be against the problems of the world, but against the idols in our hearts (Ezekiel 14:3-4).

Questions:

1. What did the Midianites destroy? (Judges 6:4) ________________

____

2. Where did the angel of the Lord sit? (Judges 6:11) ______________

____

3. How did Gideon describe his family and himself? (Judges 6:15)

____

4. What did Gideon prepare for the angel? (Judges 6:19) __________

____

____

____

5. What did Gideon use to throw down the altar of Baal? (Judges 6:25) ________________________________

6. How many men did Gideon take with him to tear down the altar? (Judges 6:27) ____________________________

7. Into which tribes did Gideon send messengers? (Judges 6:35) _____

____

8. What was the first test that Gideon desired from God? (Judges 6:37) ________________________________

____

____

9. What was the second test that Gideon desired from God? (Judges 6:39) ________________________________

____

____

10. Why did Gideon ask God for these two miracles? (Judges 6:36-37)

____

____

Thought Questions:

1. Study Gideon's family background. Why do you think God chose him? ________________________________

____

____

____

____

2. What can you do to tear down idols and keep them from entering your life? ______________________________

____

____

____

____

Lesson Review:

1. Who killed Sisera and how? (Lesson #35) ______________________________

____

____

2. Throughout the book of Judges, into how many sin cycles did the children of Israel fall? (Judges Background) ______________

3. What was the source of Achan's sin? (Lesson #32) ______________

____

Supplemental Exercise: Complete the crossword from Judges six.

– Across –

2. What was Joash (v. 11)
5. The Spirit of the Lord came upon this person (v. 34)
7. The men said this would happen to Gideon (v. 30)
9. "And [Gideon] ______ messengers" (v. 35)
10. Gideon's father (v. 11)
11. "In whose ______ ye dwell" (v. 10)
12. The number of servants who helped Gideon (v. 27)
13. Gideon was to throw this down (v. 25)
14. "The Lord ____ them into the hand of Midian" (v. 1)
16. The Midianites came as this (v. 5)
18. Gideon feared the men of this place (v. 27)
19. The Lord sent this person (v. 8)
20. None of this was left for Israel (v. 4)

– Down –

1. "If [Baal] be _______, let him plead for himself" (v. 31)
3. Fire did this out of the rock (v. 21)
4. "They ____ into the land to destroy it" (v. 5)
5. Gideon was to cut down the wood of this place (v. 26)
6. When Gideon threw down Baal (v. 27)
8. This sat under an oak (v. 11)
11. He delivered Israel into the hand of Midian (v. 1)
12. Gideon blew this (v. 34)
13. Gideon was not to fear the gods of these people (v. 10)
15. "It be dry upon all the ________ beside" (v. 37)
17. Gideon found grace in God's ____ (v. 17)

Map Study #3

1. Put an "A" next to the city where the walls fell down. (Joshua 6:1, 20)

2. Put a "B" next to the city from which the people came who tricked Joshua and the leaders of Israel into making a covenant with them. (Joshua 9:1-6)

3. Circle the names of the two tribes that Barak called to help in fighting Sisera. (Judges 4:10)

4. Put a "C" next to the city where Jabin was the king. (Judges 4:17)

5. Cross out the tribe from which Gideon came. (Judges 6:15)

6. Trace the route, and number the steps which Joshua and the children of Israel took to conquer the land of Canaan. (Lesson #33)

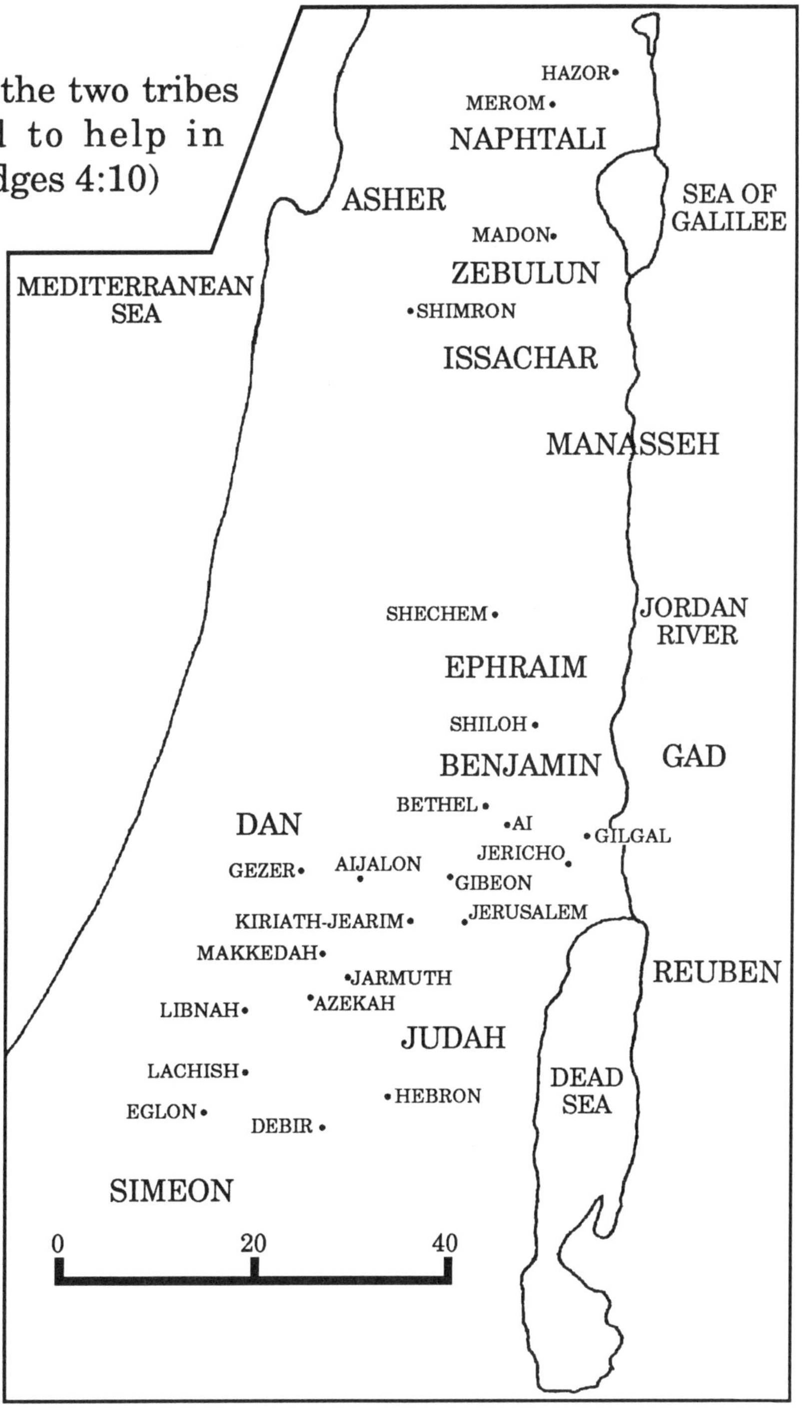

Gideon Defeats Midian
Lesson #37

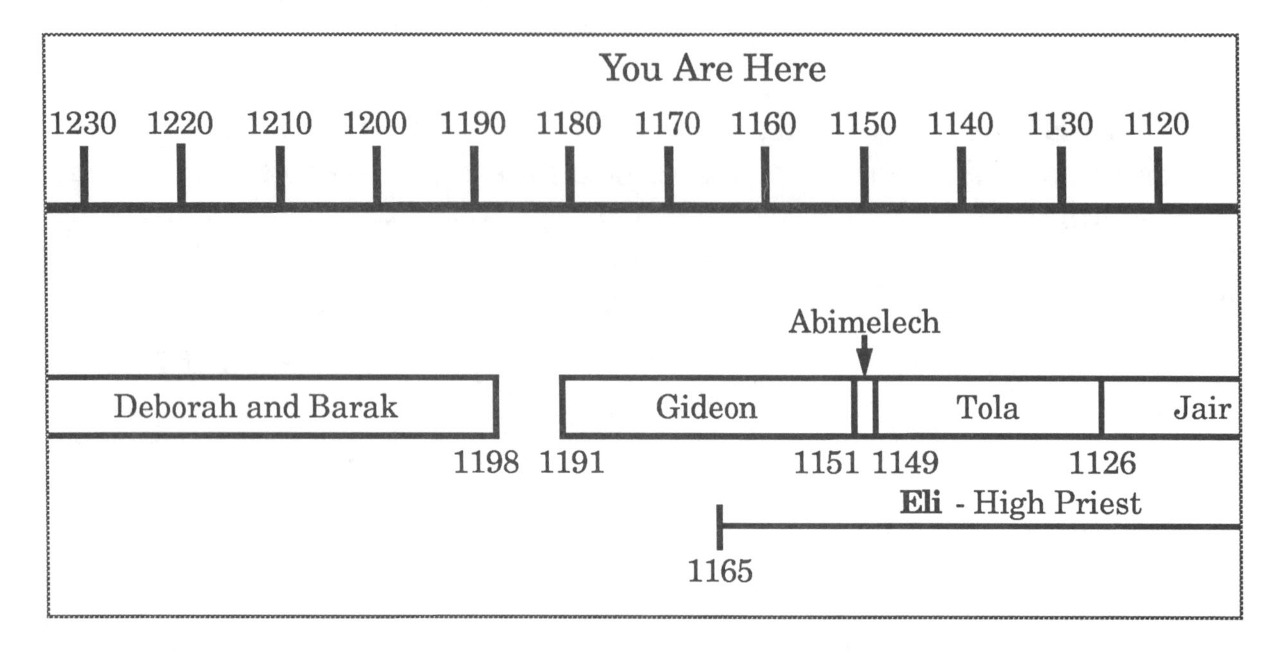

Lesson Goal: To understand that God's enemies are defeated by the Gospel.

Background Text: Judges 7

Memory Verse: But the salvation of the righteous is of the Lord: He is their strength in the time of trouble. Psalms 37:39

As we studied in our last lesson, Gideon's most important mission was to destroy the idols of Baal. Once that was completed, he had the simpler task of destroying an army of 135,000 men. It may seem strange that defeating an army of this size would be easy, but we cannot forget that God was fighting for Israel. From this Biblical example, we will discover how to use the Gospel to defeat sin and corruption after the idols in our lives have been destroyed.

During the night, Gideon took three hundred men with trumpets, torches, pitchers, and swords, and surrounded the camp of Midian. This illustration can be likened to

the Christian defeating sin with the message of Christ Jesus. God has called each of us to go into the world and, if necessary, wage spiritual warfare against those who oppose His message. This can be a very frightening task, but we must realize that since God is on our side, nothing can defeat us.

Gideon fought against immense odds but experienced victory, because the unseen Lord fought for him. In a similar fashion, the Church, equipped with the sword of God's Word (Ephesians 6:17), fights against the corruption of sin and triumphs over it. God is fighting for the Church, just as He did for Gideon.

When Gideon and his men blew their trumpets and broke their pitchers to expose the light of the torches, they were announcing to the Midianites that judgment had come. Part of the Gospel's message is to explain to the unbeliever that he is a sinner bound for hell. Unless he repents of his wickedness and commits his heart to the Lord, he eventually will be judged by God and condemned to eternal punishment.

It is the responsibility of the Christian to take the Gospel of Jesus Christ into every walk of life. When we find sin in the world, we are to fight against it and defeat it. As we have seen from this illustration of Gideon, the Lord has already given the victory into our hands. All we need to do is have faith and be obedient to what God's Word commands.

Questions:

1. Gideon and the people rose up early, and ________________ beside the well of ________________. (Judges 7:1)
2. Because they were fearful, there returned of the people __________ and two ________________. (Judges 7:3)
3. Every one that ________________ of the water with his tongue, as a dog lappeth, him shalt thou set by ______________. (Judges 7:5)
4. By the three ________________ men that lapped will I save you, and deliver the Midianites into thine ______________. (Judges 7:7)
5. If thou fear to go down, go thou with ________________ thy servant down to the ______________. (Judges 7:10)
6. The ______________ and the ________________ and all the children of the ____________ lay alone in the valley like ________________. (Judges 7:12)
7. A cake of ________________ bread tumbled into the host of Midian, and came unto a ____________, and smote it that it ____________, and overturned it, that the tent lay ______________. (Judges 7:13)
8. For into Gideon's hand hath __________ delivered ______________, and all the host. (Judges 7:14)
9. When _____________ heard the telling of the ______________, and the interpretation thereof, that he ________________. (Judges 7:15)
10. The three companies cried, "The ____________ of the ___________, and of Gideon." (Judges 7:20)

Thought Questions:

1. Why did God want Gideon to have only three hundred men with him and not several thousand? ______________________________

____

____

____

____

____

2. Who has God placed in your life to whom you can bring the message of the Gospel? ______________________________

____

Lesson Review:

1. What is the most important battle you will fight? (Lesson #36) ____

____

____

2. How many men did the Midianites have in their army? (Lesson #36) ______________________________

3. What are the two extreme perspectives that people have about the environment? (Lesson #34) ______________________________

____

____

Supplemental Exercise: Find and circle the words listed in the word search puzzle. Words may be forward, backward, horizontal, vertical, or diagonal.

AMALEKITES	GIDEON	MIDIANITES	SWORD
ASHER	GRASSHOPPERS	MOREH	TENT
BARLEY	JERUBBAAL	MOUTH	TRUMPETS
CAMELS	KNEES	NAPHTALI	VALLEY
EARS	LAMPS	PHURAH	WATER
EPHRAIM	LAPPETH	PITCHERS	WORSHIPED
FEARFUL	MANASSEH		

```
V A L L E Y P I T C H E R S Z I
K L S W O R D E P I H S R O W B
J M O N A P H T A L I E R E W S
H E S S A N A M T R P E T N E T
T J R H L A M P S P H Q P T J E
E S A U G E Y I O S U T I E F P
P P E H B E M H A N R N U E O M
P U H E L B S A O F A E A O O U
A F S R N S A E C I H R T R M R
L N A G A K D A D D F K E A M T
D B V R X I A I L U L H U B W N
A Y G C G A M A L E K I T E S C
```

The Destruction of the Wicked
Lesson #38

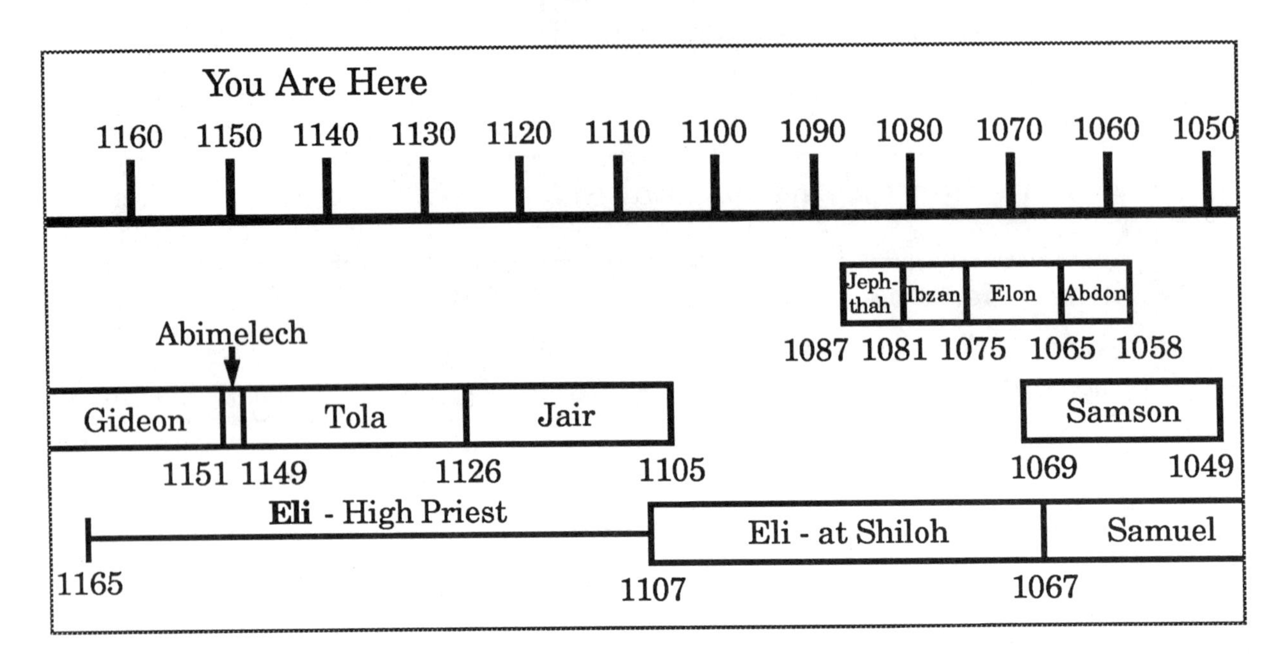

Lesson Goal: To understand that the wicked will eventually be punished for their actions.

Background Text: Judges 9

Memory Verse: For evildoers shall be cut off: but those that wait upon the Lord, they shall inherit the earth. Psalms 37:9

In the book of Psalms, Asaph asked God why wicked people prosper and are successful, while righteous people are afflicted. Psalm 73:3 says, "For I was envious at the foolish, when I saw the prosperity of the wicked." Asaph was concerned, because he wondered why he should live a good life if the evil person succeeds. God's response is found in Psalm 37:10, "For yet a little while, and the wicked shall not be: yea, thou shalt diligently consider his place, and it shall not be." The Bible is very clear that although it appears that the wicked person is succeeding, God will eventually bring him to ruin.

Abimelech was a wicked judge who appeared to be successful. However, after three years, God brought an end to Abimelech and his evil ways. The principle to focus upon is that ungodly people will eventually destroy themselves. Evil, because of its very nature, is

self-destructive. Abimelech was killed when his wicked army was fighting a civil war against another group of evil people.

It is reassuring to realize that as Christians, we do not need to worry about the possible success of the wicked. God will eventually bring them to ruin. It is enough that we continue to live in righteousness and serve God. Psalms 37:34 encourages us to "Wait on the Lord, and keep His way, and He shall exalt thee to inherit the land: when the wicked are cut off, thou shalt see it."

Questions: Multiple choice -- circle the correct answer for each question.

1. When Abimelech went to Shechem, to whom did he speak? (Judges 9:1)
   *His father
   *God
   *His mother's brethren
   *The people of the city

2. How much money did Abimelech's brethren give him to hire a worthless group of followers? (Judges 9:4)
   *Thirty pieces of silver
   *Threescore and ten pieces of silver
   *Thirty pieces of gold
   *Threescore and ten pieces of gold

3. Where did Abimelech kill the sons of Jerubbaal? (Judges 9:5)
   *Upon one stone
   *In the city
   *In the river
   *In the country

4. Because he hid himself, who was the only son of Jerubbaal that lived? (Judges 9:5)
   *Gideon
   *Barak
   *Jotham
   *Zebah

5. In Jotham's story, what eventually ruled over the trees? (Judges 9:14-15)
   *The olive tree
   *The fig tree
   *The grape vine
   *The bramble

6. Abimelech was the son of whom? (Judges 9:18)
   *Jotham
   *Jerubbaal's (Gideon's) maidservant
   *The men of Shechem
   *The house of Baalberith

7. Who did God send between Abimelech and the men of Shechem? (Judges 9:23)
   *Jotham
   *A righteous judge
   *The angel of the Lord
   *An evil spirit

8. What did Abimelech sow with salt? (Judges 9:45)
   *The city
   *The meat
   *The sacrifice
   *The food

9. What did a woman throw to break Abimelech's skull? (Judges 9:53)
   *A spear
   *A sword
   *A millstone
   *A jug of water

10. What came upon the evil men of Shechem? (Judges 9:57)
    *A plague
    *The wrath of God
    *The curse of Jotham
    *The blessing of Abraham

Thought Questions:

1. Since the wicked will be punished for their actions, what does this teach you about living a righteous life? ____

2. What is the meaning of Jotham's story in Judges 9:7-15? ____

Lesson Review:

1. How do we defeat the enemies of God? (Lesson #37) ____

2. What is an idol? (Lesson #36) ____

3. What should our response be toward God's authority? (Lesson #10) ____

Jephthah's Vow
Lesson #39

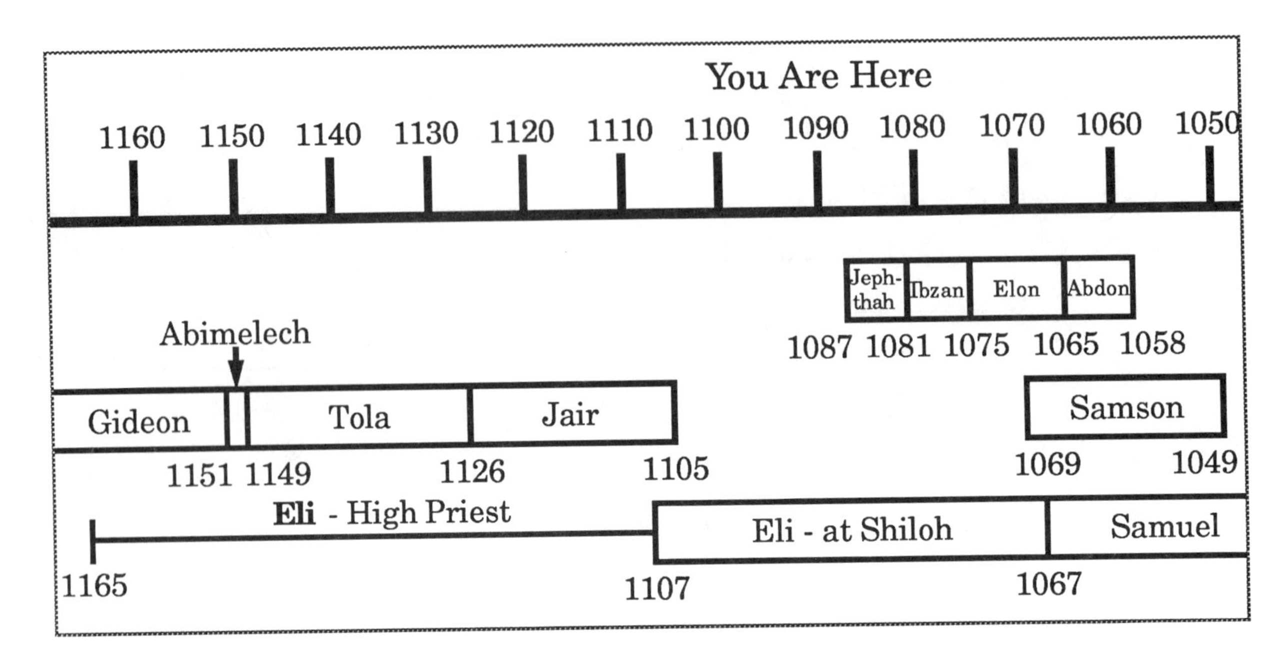

Lesson Goal: To understand that we need to control the tongue.

Background Text: Judges 11

Memory Verse: Even so the tongue is a little member, and boasteth great things. Behold, how great a matter a little fire kindleth! James 3:5

Do you know what the book of James says is one of the most difficult things in the world to tame and control? It is not a lion, bear, dog, cat, or horse. We can tame animals and teach them to do tricks. One of the most difficult things in the world to tame and control is the tongue. Have you ever noticed how a large ship is directed by a very small rudder? Whichever direction the captain turns the rudder, that is the direction the ship will go (James 3:4). The rudder can be most useful, as long as it is used to steer the ship properly. However, if the rudder is misused, the ship could hit something and sink. The tongue is like the ship's rudder, because with it we control our lives. Although the tongue is a small part of the body, it is very difficult to manage. We can use the tongue for good things that will bless both God and man. Or, we can use it to say evil things which could hurt ourselves and those around us.

In this lesson, we will learn about a judge named Jephthah. Before Jephthah went into battle, he made a promise to God in order that he might have victory. He promised that after he returned from battle, "that whatsoever cometh forth of the doors of my house to meet me ... shall surely be the Lord's, and I will offer it up for a burnt offering" (Judges 11:31). No doubt, Jephthah was expecting one of his servants to meet him when he arrived. Instead, the only child he had, his own daughter, came out to greet him.

When we study God's Word, we need to be careful how we interpret Scripture so we can understand its true meaning. Did Jephthah kill his daughter by burning her on the altar, or did his vow mean something different? As we consider this issue, we need to understand that the Bible does condemn human sacrifices (Leviticus 18:21; Deuteronomy 12:31). In addition, Judges 11:37-40 indicates that Jephthah's daughter was upset not because she was going to die, but because she would not get married. Finally, the most accurate translation of Judges 11:31 would be, "It shall surely be the Lord's, and I will offer to Him (i.e., to God) a burnt offering." The correct understanding of this passage would be that Jephthah's daughter was given as a servant of the tabernacle, where she would not get married, and live the rest of her life. She was a living sacrifice, devoted to perpetual celibacy in her service to the Lord.

From this lesson we can see that Jephthah's rash vow warns us to be very careful about the things that we say with our tongue. Unless we learn to control the things we say, we are headed for trouble. No doubt each of us has had times when we have said something and later wished that we had not said it. Many people have ruined their lives because they did not manage the things that they said. James chapter three explains that in order to tame the tongue, we need to seek Godly wisdom. This wisdom will give us the strength to control the things that we say.

Practically speaking, one of the best ways for us to control our tongues is to follow the same steps that we use when we cross the street. When we come to a street, we stop, look both ways, and listen for traffic; if the way is clear, then we cautiously move ahead. With our tongue, we should stop and not say anything, think about what we are about to say, and make certain that it should be said. Then, if what we are planning to say is good, we should cautiously proceed with our statement. This is not any guarantee that our tongues will not get us into trouble, but at least by following these steps, we can gain a better control of the things that we say.

Questions:

1. To what land did Jephthah flee? (Judges 11:3) ________________
2. Who made war against Israel? (Judges 11:4) ________________
3. Who went to fetch Jephthah? (Judges 11:5) ________________
4. What did the elders of Gilead and the people make Jephthah? (Judges 11:11) ________________________________
____
5. To what did the king of Ammon not harken? (Judges 11:28) ______
____
6. What came upon Jephthah? (Judges 11:29) ________________
7. What was Jephthah's vow? (Judges 11:31)________________
____
____
8. How many cities did Jephthah defeat? (Judges 11:33) ____________
9. Who came out of Jephthah's house to meet him? (Judges 11:34)
____
10. What request did Jephthah's daughter have before he fulfilled his vow? (Judges 11:37) ________________________
____

Thought Questions:

1. Give an illustration showing how your tongue has gotten you into trouble. ________________________________
____
____
____
2. How can you do a better job controlling the things that you say?
____
____
____

3. Is there someone to whom you should apologize because you said something that you should not have. Why? ______________________

____

____

____

Lesson Review:

1. How did Abimelech die? (Lesson #38) ______________________

____

____

2. Draw the diagram of the sin cycle. (Judges Background)

3. What are the six commandments on table two of the Ten Commandments? (Lesson #21) ______________________

____

____

____

Supplemental Exercise: Decode the symbols to understand the message. The key is in Appendix B.

____

____

____

____

12:36

____

Samson's Strength
Lesson #40

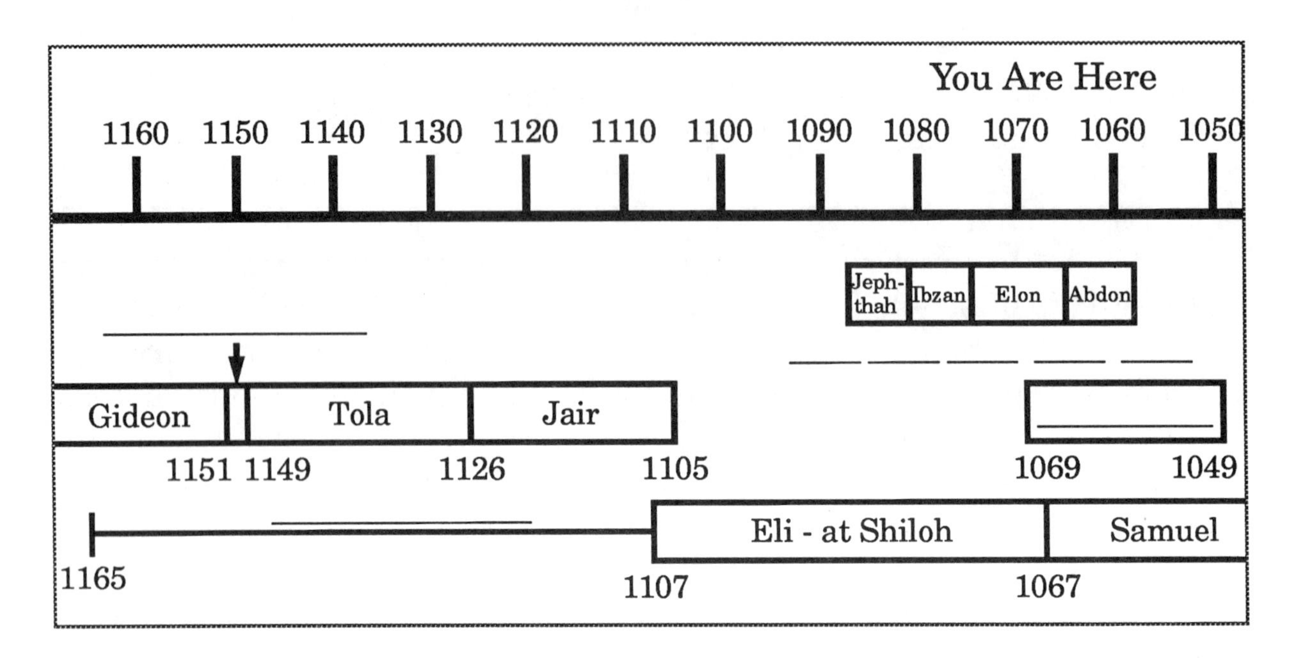

Lesson Goal: To understand that Samson's strength, like our own spiritual strength, is dependent upon our commitment to the Lord.

Background Text: Judges 14-15

Memory Verse: Have not I commanded thee? Be strong and of a good courage; be not afraid, neither be thou dismayed: for the Lord thy God is with thee whithersoever thou goest. Joshua 1:9

To fully understand the story of Samson, it is necessary to study the historical background behind this lesson. As a result of the Israelite's seventh sin cycle, the people were in subjection to the Philistines. The Philistines did not harshly mistreat God's children, but they did rule over them. Both groups agreed that if the Israelites did not trouble the Philistines, they in turn would not oppress the Israelites. Since the Philistines were distant relatives of the Egyptians, it was as though the Hebrews were in bondage again in Egypt.

The Israelites had fallen asleep spiritually, and needed something to awaken them and move them into action. As God's servant, Samson harassed the Philistines in order to arouse the children of Israel. He also sought to punish the Philistines for their domination over God's

children. Samson's role as judge was to lead the Hebrew people to repentance and deliver them from the Philistines.

Even though Samson was not completely faithful to the Lord during this time in his life, he did use the special abilities that God had given him to judge and direct the people of Israel. It is important for us to understand that as God's children, we have each received special gifts and abilities. If we are not committed to the Lord, we will not have the spiritual strength to resist temptation. If we are not faithful to His Word, we will not be able to use our spiritual gifts. The measure of our success in our service for the Lord is directly related to the level of our commitment to His Word. It should be our goal to serve the Lord with joy and gladness, and to remain faithful to everything that the Bible teaches.

Questions:

1. Where did Samson go? (Judges 14:1) ____________________
2. What did Samson's father and mother not know? (Judges 14:4)

   ____

   ____
3. What came mightily upon Samson? (Judges 14:6) ______________

   ____
4. What was in the carcass of the lion? (Judges 14:8) ____________

   ____
5. How many days did Samson give the Philistines to answer the riddle? (Judges 14:12) ______________________________
6. What did the Philistines say they would do to Samson's wife if she did not tell them the riddle? (Judges 14:15) ________________

   ____
7. How many foxes did Samson catch? (Judges 15:4) ______________
8. What did the Philistines do to Samson's wife? (Judges 15:6) _____

   ____
9. How many men of Judah went to capture Samson? (Judges 15:11)

   ____

10. What did Samson use to kill one thousand Philistines? (Judges 15:15) ______________________________

Thought Questions:

1. Define in your own words what "to fall asleep spiritually" means?
____
____
____
____

2. What are some things that you can do so you will not fall asleep spiritually? ______________________________
____
____
____
____

Lesson Review:

1. What is a practical way to control your tongue? (Lesson #39) _____
____
____

2. How many spies did Moses send into the land of Canaan? (Lesson #24) ______________________________

3. On the time line at the beginning of the chapter, complete the blank spaces with the correct information.

Samson's Weakness
Lesson #41

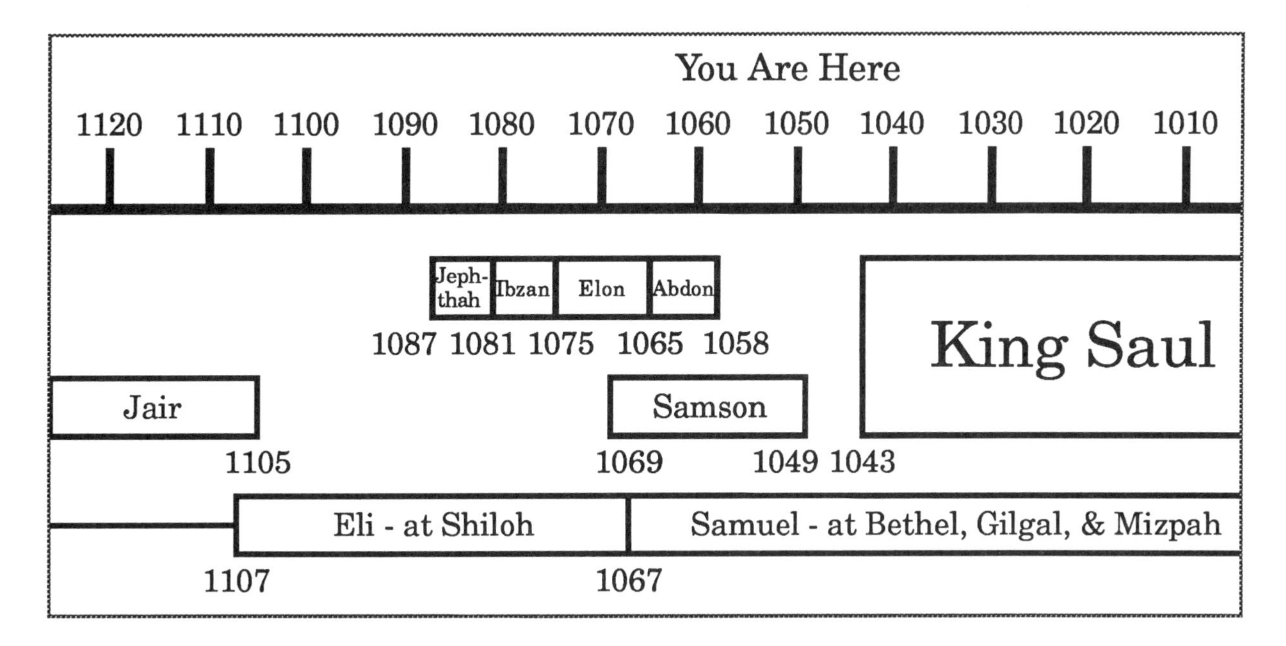

Lesson Goal: To understand that our spiritual strength is lost when we become weak in our commitment to God.

Background Text: Judges 16

Memory Verse: The Lord is my light and my salvation; whom shall I fear? The Lord is the strength of my life. Psalms 27:1

After almost twenty years of leadership for Israel, Samson succumbed to the same type of sin into which the nation of Israel had fallen. Samson accepted the Philistine culture, and so sought after the earthly pleasures which it had to offer. There is a contrast between this part of Samson's life and his earlier ministry. When Samson first became a judge, he sought out the Philistines to punish them for their sins and lead the Israelites to repentance. Now Samson went to the Philistines to partake in their pleasures.

Near the end of Samson's life, his commitment to the Lord weakened. This is seen most clearly through his relationship with Delilah. Day after day, Delilah would ask Samson to reveal the secret of his strength. By gradually wearing down his resistance, Samson gave in to Delilah and told her the private things of his heart.

Samson's Weakness

When Samson's hair was cut, the Bible tells us that the Lord departed from Samson. There was no magical secret to Samson's long hair that gave him his strength. Samson's strength came from the Lord. His hair was only an outward sign of this commitment to God. The reason Samson had long hair was because he was a Nazarite. Immediately after his hair was taken from him, his vow as a Nazarite was broken. The Lord then left Samson when he broke his vow, and the outward sign of his commitment was removed.

This principle is very clear for us to follow: if we do not stay committed to God, we will eventually fall away from Him. This is not to imply that we can lose our salvation, but that we can become weak in our faith. It is sad to consider what happened to Samson, but encouraging to realize that at the end of his life, he reestablished his faith with the Lord.

Throughout our lives, we will face many trials and temptations. We must purpose in our hearts to stay away from sin and pursue the righteousness of God. Second Timothy 2:22 says, "Flee also youthful lusts: but follow righteousness, faith, charity, peace, with them that call on the Lord out of a pure heart." When we obey this verse, we will have the spiritual strength to defeat sin, and live a life that is honoring and pleasing to God.

Questions:

1. Where did Samson see a harlot? (Judges 16:1) ________________
2. What did Samson do at midnight? (Judges 16:3) ________________

   ____
3. What was the name of the woman that Samson loved? (Judges 16:4) ________________________________
4. What did each of the lords of the Philistines give to Delilah? (Judges 16:5) ________________________________
5. The third time when Samson responded, what did he say would make him weak? (Judges 16:13) ________________________

   ____

6. What had Samson been from his mother's womb? (Judges 16:17)
____

7. How many locks of hair did Samson have on his head? (Judges 16:19) ______________________________
____

8. Who did the Philistines say had delivered Samson into their hands? (Judges 16:23) __________________________

9. What did Samson ask to lean upon? (Judges 16:26) __________

10. How many Philistines died when Samson died? (Judges 16:27-30)
____

Thought Questions:

1. In what areas of your life have you sinned and accepted the ungodliness of the world? ____________________
____
____
____

2. Samson sinned because he accepted the culture and lifestyle of the sinful Philistines. What does this tell you about your own attitude toward today's culture? ____________________
____
____
____
____
____

Lesson Review:

1. What was Samson's role as a judge? (Lesson #40) __________
____
____

2. When is it moral to disobey civil laws? (Lesson #16) __________
____
____

3. What are the three ways the Bible tells us to fight temptation? (Lesson #13) ____________________________
____
____

Ruth Background

Author of Ruth: The authorship of Ruth is uncertain, although history and tradition suggest that possibly Samuel wrote the book of Ruth after he anointed David as King of Israel.

Date of Writing: 1000 B.C. The book covers a span of ten years during the period of the judges.

Purpose of Ruth: Ruth was written in order to give us insight into a happier time during the period of the judges. It was also written to show God's providence as He brought Boaz and Ruth together. Boaz and Ruth were the great-grandparents of King David and part of the royal bloodline of Joseph, the step-father of Jesus.

Outline of Ruth:

I. Ruth's Religion (Ruth 1)
   A. Her Suffering (1:1-5)
   B. Her Choice (1:6-22)

II. Ruth's Reaping (Ruth 2)
   A. Her Work (2:1-3)
   B. Her Provision (2:4-17)
   C. Her Report (2:18-23)

III. Ruth's Rising (Ruth 3)
   A. Naomi's Advice (3:1-5)
   B. Ruth's Actions (3:6-9)
   C. Boaz's Acceptance (3:10-18)

IV. Ruth's Rewarding (Ruth 4)
   A. A Marriage (4:1-12)
   B. A Family (4:13-17)
   C. A Genealogy (4:18-22)

The Big Idea of Ruth: The book of Ruth tells the beautiful story of God's love for the Jewess, Naomi and the Moabitess, Ruth. After the death of Naomi's husband and two sons, she told her daughters-in-law to leave her and find new husbands. Orpah left, but Ruth stayed and devoted herself in service to Naomi and her God. Noble Boaz acted for God in rewarding Ruth's loyalty when he bought Naomi's lost property and married Ruth. Just as Boaz purchased a forfeited inheritance and married Ruth, so also Christ purchased salvation for sinners, by dying on the cross and then making the church His bride (Matthew 19:29; Ephesians 5:22-33; I John 4:7-11).

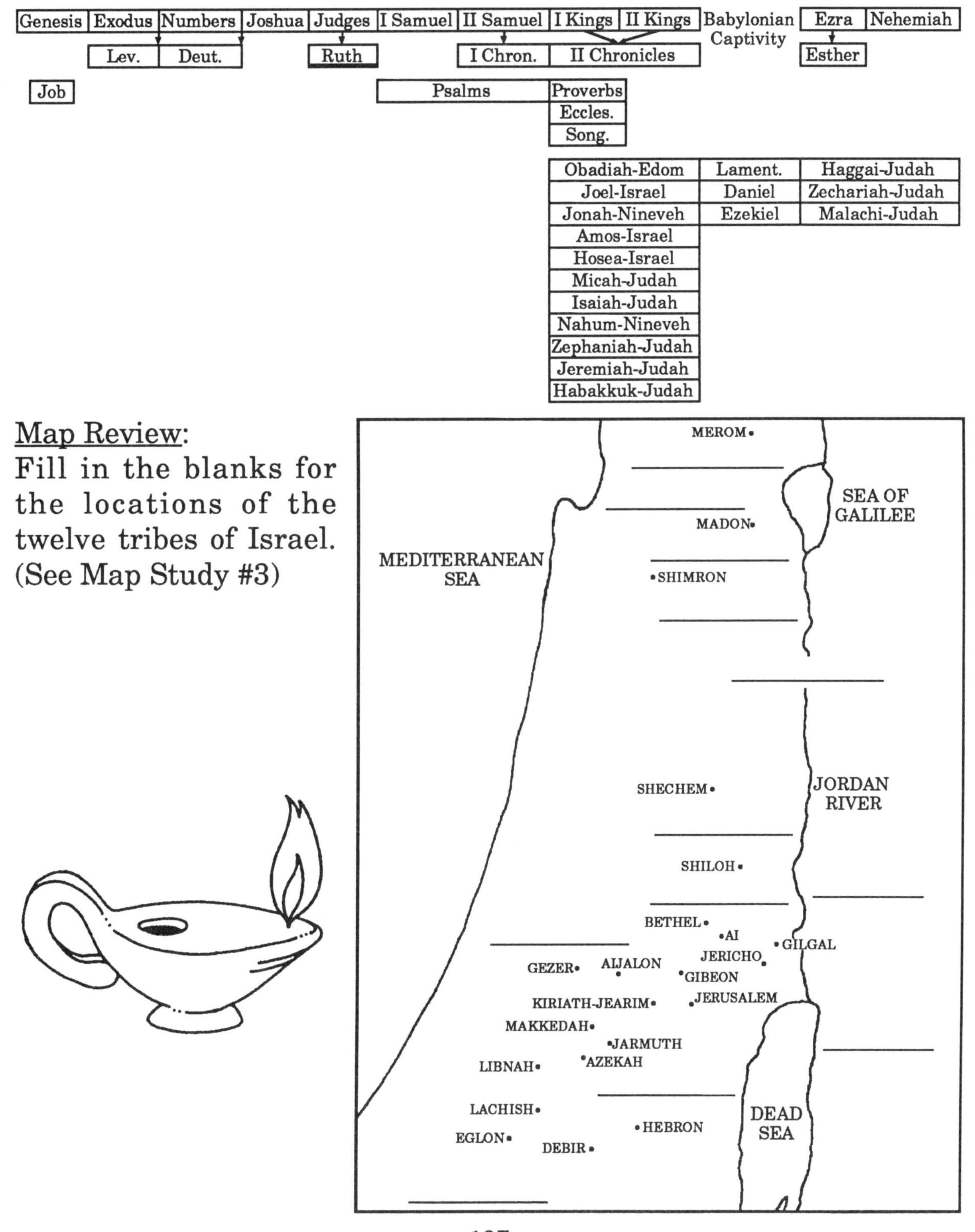

Map Review:
Fill in the blanks for the locations of the twelve tribes of Israel. (See Map Study #3)

Boaz and Ruth
Lesson #42

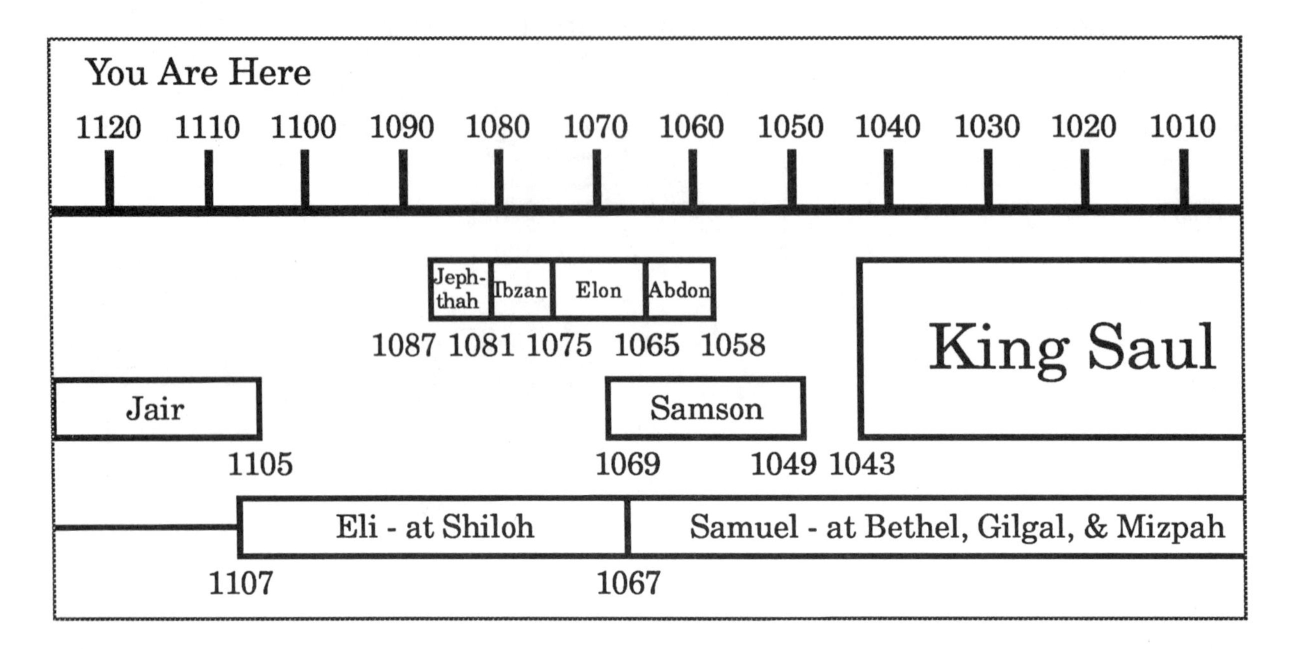

Lesson Goal: To understand that a necessary part of love is commitment.

Background Text: Ruth 1-4

Memory Verse: But God commendeth His love toward us, in that, while we were yet sinners, Christ died for us. Romans 5:8

How would you explain the meaning of love? This may not be easy because love sometimes deals with emotions which are hard to understand. Perhaps it would be better to ask, "Whom do you love?" We all have someone or something that we love and care for. We may love our family, friends, or even our pets. Receiving love and showing love to other people is a necessary part of our lives. However, we need to be careful to understand love so we can properly demonstrate it.

In the story of Boaz and Ruth, we have a beautiful illustration of love and compassion.

Oftentimes, love is misunderstood and confused with other emotions. True love is not a "fuzzy" feeling in our stomach, dizziness in our head, or holding someone's hand. Rather, true love is based upon a solid commitment to the person that we care for. The love which Boaz had for Ruth was based upon his commitment to her safety and well being. When Boaz met Ruth, he first provided for her immediate needs by feeding her. He later provided for her future needs by purchasing her inheritance and marrying her.

It is impossible to properly love someone without being committed to that person. Commitment means that we will take care of a person, doing whatever we possibly can to help. There is nothing wrong with sharing emotions and showing affection to someone. However, love that is based merely upon feelings will not last. True love is also founded upon a strong dedication to that person's overall well-being. This faithfulness then translates into actions of giving, providing, and caring for that person in a manner that harmonizes with God's Law.

Christ demonstrated true love to us by being committed through His suffering and death. His example of love gives us a pattern to follow when showing love to those around us. The love we give has as its foundation the love and commitment Christ gave to us.

<u>Questions</u>: Multiple choice -- circle the correct answer for each question.

1. Who was Naomi's husband? (Ruth 1:2)
   *Boaz
   *Elimelech
   *Mahlon
   *Chilion

2. What relationship was Ruth to Naomi? (Ruth 1:6)
   *Sister
   *Mother-in-law
   *Daughter-in-law
   *Daughter

3. What did Naomi's other daughter-in-law, Orpah, decide to do? (Ruth 1:15)
   *Return to her people and her gods
   *Go along with Naomi
   *Die in the desert
   *Help Ruth find a husband

4. To where did Naomi and Ruth return? (Ruth 1:22)
   *Jerusalem
   *Moab
   *Egypt
   *Bethlehem

5. What did Boaz say to the reapers? (Ruth 2:4)
   *Take a break for lunch
   *Get back to work
   *I am getting married
   *The Lord be with you

6. How much barley was Ruth able to glean after the first day because of Boaz's kindness? (Ruth 2:17)
   *A bushel of barley
   *Three cups of barley
   *Much barley
   *An ephah of barley

7. What did Ruth uncover? (Ruth 3:7)
   *Boaz's feet
   *The heap of grain
   *Her bed
   *Naomi's plan and purpose for Ruth

8. Why did Boaz go before the gate of the city? (Ruth 4:1-8)
   *To have a feast
   *To marry Ruth
   *To receive counsel from the elders as to whether or not he should purchase a new field for his barley crop next year.
   *To discuss among the elders and the kinsman the question: "Who will redeem the property of Naomi and marry Ruth?"

9. In Israel, how was the redeeming and changing of things confirmed? (Ruth 4:7)
   *They would shake hands
   *They would sign a contract
   *They would take off a shoe and give it to the other person
   *They would bow to each other and walk in a circle

10. What did the neighbors name Boaz and Ruth's child? (Ruth 4:17)
   *Jesse
   *Obed
   *David
   *Boaz Jr.

Thought Questions:

1. Define in your own words the meaning of love. ____________________

____

____

____

____

____

2. What can you do to show your love and commitment to your family and friends? ____________________

____

____

____

____

Lesson Review:

1. What are the four main points of the outline in the book of Ruth? (Ruth Background) ____________________

____

2. What will happen if we do not stay committed to God? (Lesson #41)

 ____

 ____

3. Explain how our lives are like a lump of clay before God. (Lesson #14) ____

 ____

Supplemental Exercise: Read Ruth 1-4 to complete the crossword.

– Across –

2. Who asked to be called "Mara"? (1:20)
3. Who went into the field to glean corn? (2:2)
4. Your God shall be my _______. (1:16)
8. What happened to Naomi's husband and two sons? (1:3-5)
9. Ruth was allowed to _______ among the sheaves. (2:15)
10. Boaz redeemed Naomi's land "to _______ up the name of the dead upon his inheritance." (4:5)

– Down –

1. What was the relationship between Boaz and Naomi's husband? (2:1)
3. "Now this was the manner in former time in Israel concerning _______ and concerning changing." (4:7)
5. Ruth told Boaz that she was thine _______. (3:9)
6. Boaz gave Ruth six _______ of barley. (3:15)
7. What kind of woman was Ruth? (3:11)
8. Orpah was Naomi's _______-in-law. (1:4-6)

1 3 5 6 7 8 9 2 4 10

Unit Test #3

Questions: Match the correct answer with the proper question.

1. ____ Who hid the two spies among the stalks of flax? (Joshua 2:3-6)
2. ____ What were the twelve men to take from the Jordan River? (Joshua 4:3)
3. ____ Where did the people camp after passing over the Jordan River? (Joshua 4:19)
4. ____ How many times did the people walk around Jericho on the seventh day? (Joshua 6:15)
5. ____ How many men first went up against Ai? (Joshua 7:4)
6. ____ What stood still when Joshua prayed? (Joshua 10:13)
7. ____ How many chariots of iron did Sisera have? (Judges 4:13)
8. ____ Who killed Sisera, the commander of the Canaanites? (Judges 4:21)
9. ____ How many men did Gideon take with him to tear down the altar? (Judges 6:27)
10. ____ Who went with Gideon down to the Midianite camp? (Judges 7:10)
11. ____ In Jotham's story, what eventually ruled over the trees? (Judges 9:14-15)
12. ____ Who came out of Jephthah's house to meet him? (Judges 11:34)
13. ____ What was the name of the woman that Samson loved? (Judges 16:4)
14. ____ To where did Naomi and Ruth return? (Ruth 1:22)
15. ____ What did Boaz and Ruth name their son? (Ruth 4:17)

a. Bethlehem
b. Rahab
c. Delilah
d. Seven
e. Gilgal
f. Nine hundred
g. Ten
h. Obed
i. Phurah
j. Sun and Moon
k. The bramble
l. Three thousand
m. Jephthah's daughter
n. Jael
o. Twelve stones

Definitions

Absolutes: Unchanging standards or laws which are used to govern one's life.

Altar: A structure where sacrifices are offered.

Accountable: The state of having to answer to someone regarding one's own thoughts and actions (Matthew 12:36).

Admonish: To warn, caution, or mildly rebuke.

Anarchy: A society without laws or government; disorder.

Archaeology: The scientific study of an old culture in order to learn about the people who lived there and their lifestyle.

Attitude: Inward feelings that affect the way we think and act.

Baal: A god of nature that was worshiped by the people who lived in Canaan.

Beguile: To mislead or deceive.

Blameless: Free from guilt or wrong doing; innocent.

Bondage: The state of being subjected to external control.

Calling: A job or responsibility which God assigns to someone.

Caution: Alertness or prudence in a dangerous situation.

Cherubim: Celestial beings distinguished by knowledge.

Chronological: Arranged in the order of time; from first to last.

Commitment: Given over to something or someone to insure all needs are met.

Compromise: To lower or readjust one's standards.

Condemnation: To declare judgment and sentence for punishment.

Conduct: Personal behavior; a way of acting.

Conformity: To be in agreement, harmony, or unity with something or someone.

Conscience: An internal recognition of what is right and wrong.

Consequences: The results of one's own actions.

Contentment: To be pleased or satisfied in one's circumstances.

Conversion: The act of changing one's beliefs and actions into conformity with a certain set of values.

Covenant: A promise or agreement.

Covetousness: To desire wrongly without regard to the rights of others.

Conviction: The state of being internally challenged; A strong belief.

Cubit: A measurement used during the Old Testament times; equal to approximately eighteen inches in length.

Deceiver: A person who misleads another by a false statement or action.

Demonic: Activity pertaining to demons and the forces of evil.

Depraved: Totally corrupt, wicked, and immoral.

Determination: The resolution and intention to accomplish a task.

Division: A separation of one group or object into multiple parts.

Doctrine: The truths or theological facts that a person believes.

Definitions

Enmity: A feeling of hostility or hatred.

Environment: One's surroundings, conditions, or influences.

Envy: A feeling of resentment or desire to possess something someone else possesses or has achieved.

Exclusion: The state of being left out or withdrawn from a group of people.

Exhort: To challenge, warn, give advice, or incite to action.

Evolution: The belief that the universe developed by chance, and was not created by God in a literal six day period.

Faith: The expression of trust in someone or something.

Faithfulness: Total, uncompromising commitment to someone or something.

Fear: A distressing emotion aroused by impending pain, danger, or evil.

Fellowship: A state of being in close communion with someone.

Figurative: Not literal; representing a figure of speech.

Fool: A person who lacks common sense; weak-minded or gullible; one who refuses to follow something he knows to be true.

Forfeit: Something to which the right is lost; to surrender.

Forgiveness: To grant full pardon from wrong actions.

Genealogy: An account of human ancestry from one generation to the next.

Gentile: Any nationality or race of people that is not Jewish.

Glory: Praise, worship, and magnification of someone or something.

Gospel: The message of salvation through belief in Jesus Christ.

Gratefulness: Warm or deep appreciation of kindness or benefits received.

Gullible: Easily deceived or cheated.

Holy: Godly in character; devoted to a pure life; obeying and serving God; completely righteous.

Humanist: A person who believes he can come to God on the basis of his own efforts and merits.

Idol: An image representing a false god.

Illustration: A picture used to tell a story or communicate an idea.

Immorality: A state characterized by evil, wickedness, and perversion. An act of living in sin.

Inheritance: Reception of a gift or blessing as a result of one's own position or relationship to another.

Jews (Jewish): The nation or tribe of people that has Abraham as its father. Also referred to as Hebrews and Israelites.

Justice: The moral principle of being righteous and obeying God's law.

Lapse: A failure or slight error.

Laver: A bowl or basin containing water in which to wash.

Literal: True to the fact; not exaggerated; not figurative.

Love: A strong commitment to another person or object; affection or compassion.

Mature: To grow in one's beliefs or values.

Meditate: To concentrate intently on something.

Definitions

Messiah: The expected Savior of the Jewish people; Jesus Christ.

Omer: A Hebrew unit of measurement equaling about two pints.

Oppress: To burden with cruel or unjust authority or restraints.

Pantheistic: The belief that God and nature are one; to worship nature is to worship God.

Persecution: Oppression or ridicule of a person or group of people.

Perseverance: A quality characterized by never giving up; always pressing on.

Perspective: A particular point of view.

Poetry: Literature written or spoken in verse or in figurative language.

Principle: A primary truth upon which one governs or rules his life.

Priority: Something that is of substantial importance.

Procrastination: To put off something until another day or time.

Prose: The ordinary form of written or spoken language without rhyme or meter.

Prosperity: To have good success.

Providence: The foreseeing care and guardianship of God over His creation.

Rebel: To actively rise up against an established authority.

Redemption: To buy back or purchase something that belonged to someone else; deliver; rescue.

Reincarnation: The belief that upon death, the soul moves to another body or form and does not go to heaven or hell.

Repentance: Regret and confession for a past sin, and resulting in a change of action.

Resist: To withstand, strive against, or oppose.

Responsibility: Answering or accounting for something or someone under one's own power and authority.

Restitution: Restoring something that was lost, damaged, or injured, either by payment or sacrifice.

Righteous: Morally pure and just; holy; obedient to God's laws.

Sacrifice: The offering of life (plant, animal, human) or some possession to a deity; to surrender or devote oneself to a Godly calling.

Salvation: Deliverance from the power and penalty of sin; redemption.

Selfless: Care and concern for someone or something greater than oneself.

Severe: Harsh; extreme; serious.

Shewbread: The bread placed every Sabbath before Jehovah on the table beside the altar of incense, and eaten at the end of the week by the priests.

Sin: Transgression or disobedience to God's Law. To fall short of God's standard.

Society: A body of human beings generally associated together as a community.

Sovereign: The supreme or independent power of authority.

Spiritual: Pertaining to sacred things; Godly.

Stewardship: Being righteously productive with the gifts God has given us.

Definitions

Submission: To surrender or obey; to humbly give oneself over to another.

Synagogue: A place where Jews assembled to worship.

Tabernacle: A tent used by the Israelites as a portable sanctuary before the building of the temple in Jerusalem.

Temptation: Prompting to do something that one should not do; an enticement to sin.

Testimony: The witness and explanation of something.

Theologians: Individuals who study and teach other people about God.

Tithe: The giving of one-tenth of one's income either in the form of money, produce, or agriculture to the Lord and His work.

Trial: A difficult situation in one's life.

Tribulation: A trial. A difficult time or circumstance in one's life.

Virtue: Moral excellence or goodness.

Vocation: An occupation, profession, or business; a trade or calling.

Vow: A solemn promise or pledge.

Wisdom: The application of knowledge to a given situation.

Appendix A

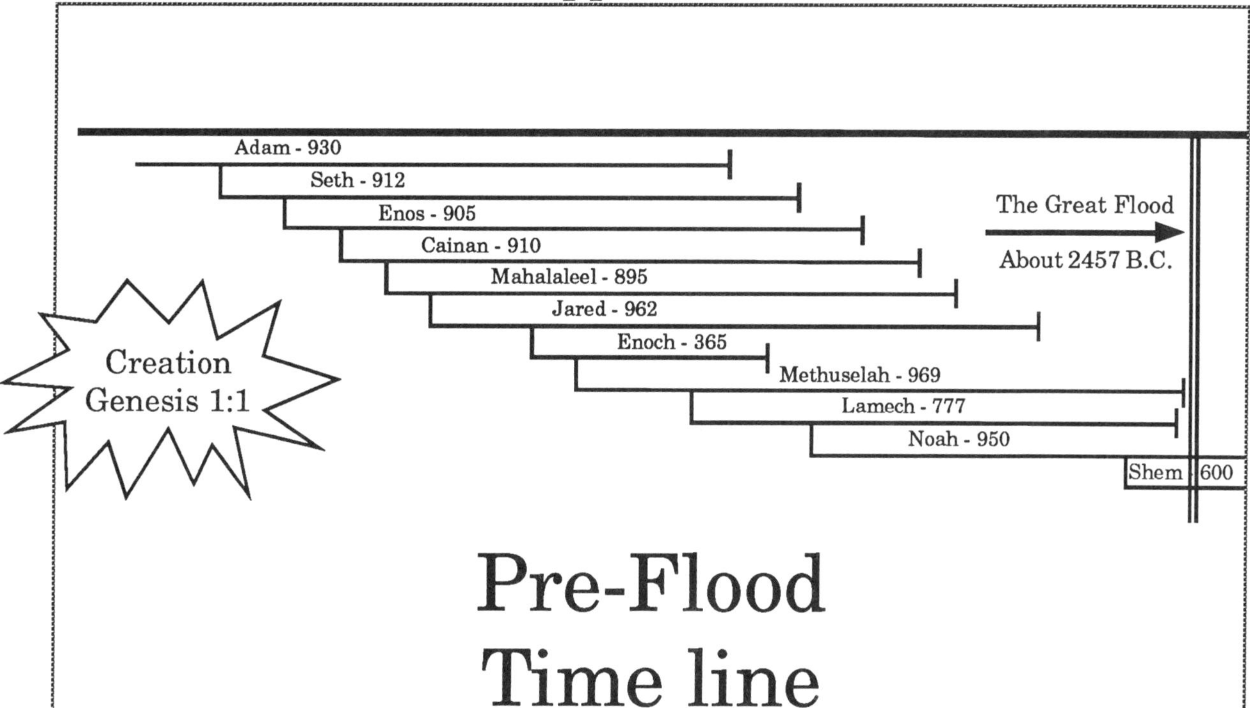

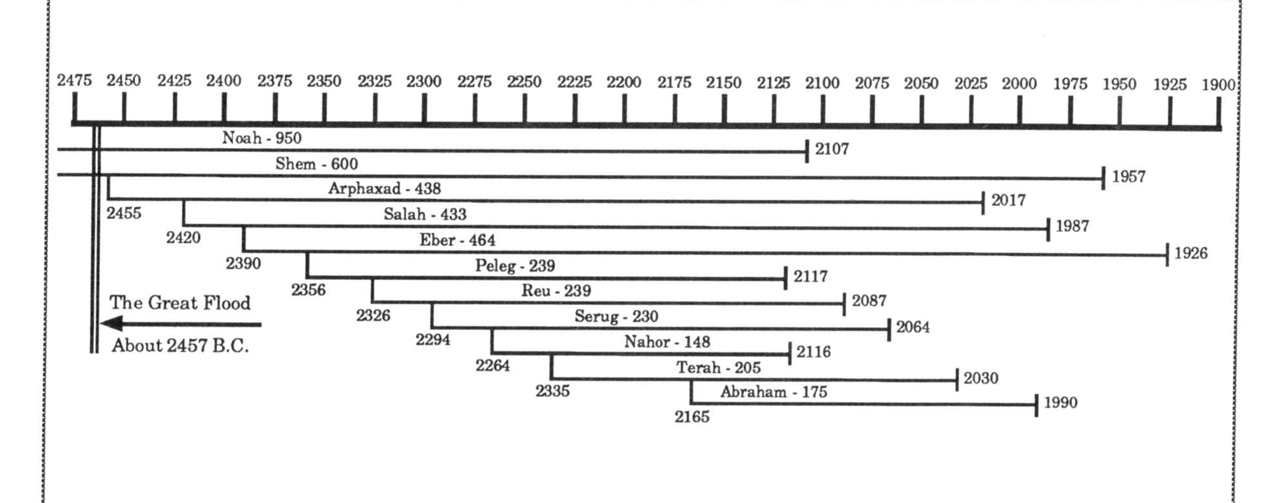

Post-Flood
Time line

Appendix A

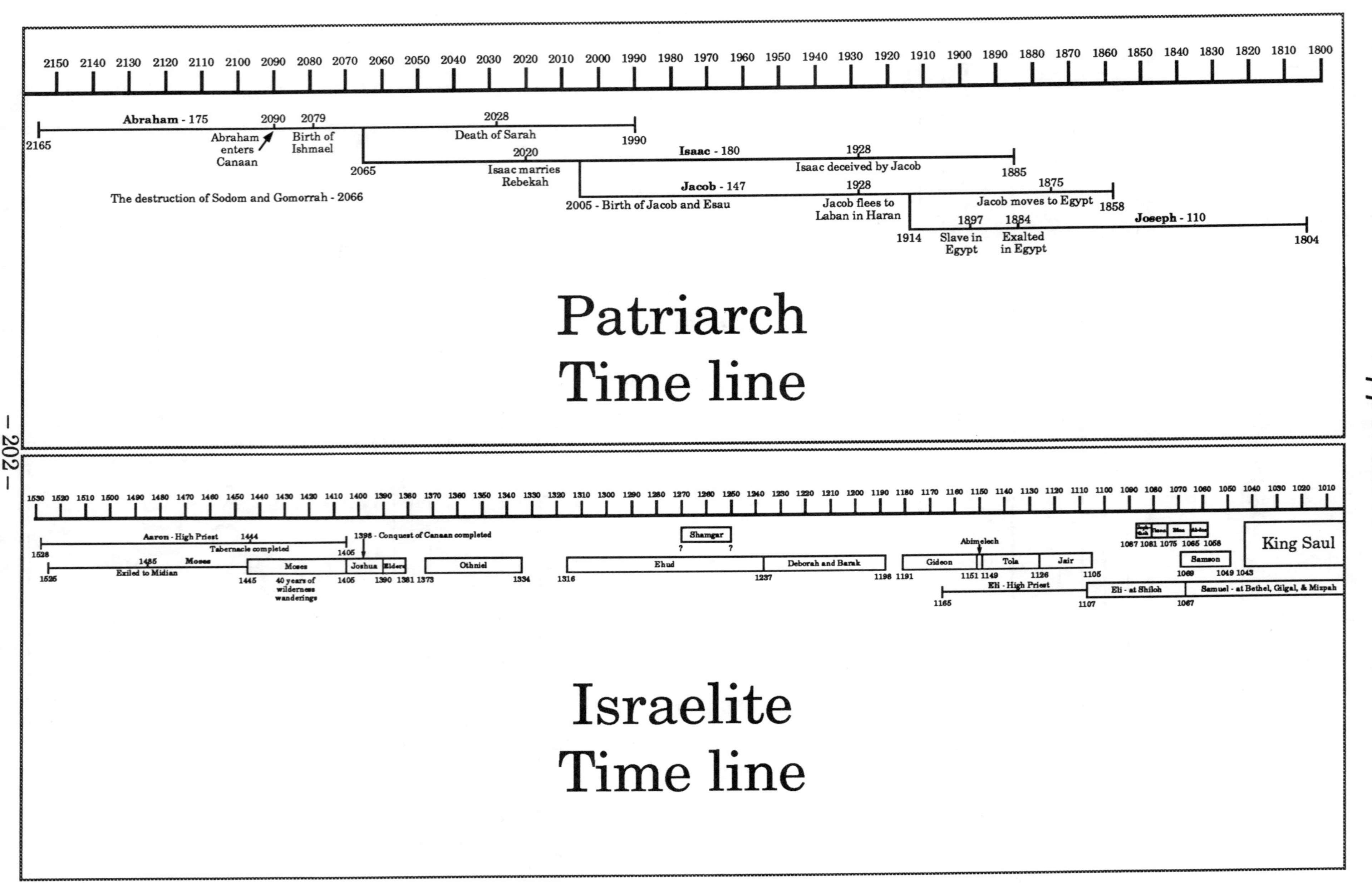

Patriarch Time line
Abraham - 175
2165
2090
Abraham enters Canaan
2079
Birth of Ishmael
2028
Death of Sarah
1990
The destruction of Sodom and Gomorrah - 2066
Isaac - 180
2065
2020
Isaac marries Rebekah
1928
Isaac deceived by Jacob
1885
Jacob - 147
2005 - Birth of Jacob and Esau
1928
Jacob flees to Laban in Haran
1875
Jacob moves to Egypt
1858
Joseph - 110
1914
1897
Slave in Egypt
1884
Exalted in Egypt
1804
Israelite Time line
Aaron - High Priest
1528
1444
Tabernacle completed
1406
1398 - Conquest of Canaan completed
1485
Moses
1525
Exiled to Midian
Moses
1445
40 years of wilderness wanderings
Joshua
Elders
1406
1390
1381
1373
Othniel
1334
Shamgar
?
?
Ehud
1316
Deborah and Barak
1237
1198
Gideon
1191
Abimelech
1151
1149
Tola
1126
Jair
1105
Eli - High Priest
1165
Eli - at Shiloh
1107
Samuel - at Bethel, Gilgal, & Mizpah
1067
1087 1081 1075 1065 1058
Samson
1069
1049 1043
King Saul

Appendix B

A =

B =

C =

D =

E =

F =

G =

H =

I =

J =

K =

L =

M =

N =

O =

P =

Q =

R =

S =

T =

U =

V =

W =

X =

Y =

Z =

The Topical Old Testament

HISTORY

Pentateuch

- Genesis
- Exodus
- Leviticus
- Numbers
- Deuteronomy

History

- Joshua
- Judges
- Ruth
- First Samuel
- Second Samuel
- First Kings
- Second Kings
- First Chronicles
- Second Chronicles

- Ezra
- Nehemiah
- Esther

EXPERIENCE

Poetry

- Job
- Psalms
- Proverbs
- Ecclesiastes
- Song of Solomon

Before Babylonian Exile

After Babylonian Exile

PROPHECY

Major Prophets

- Isaiah
- Jeremiah
- Lamentations
- Ezekiel
- Daniel

Minor Prophets

- Hosea
- Joel
- Amos
- Obadiah
- Jonah
- Micah
- Nahum
- Habakkuk
- Zephaniah

- Haggai
- Zechariah
- Malachi

References

Barnes, Albert. Barne's Notes.
Grand Rapids, MI: Baker Book House, 1949.

Beers, V. Gilbert. The Victor Handbook of Bible Knowledge.
Wheaton, IL: Victory Books, 1981.

Bryant, T. Alton, ed. The New Compact Bible Dictionary.
Grand Rapids, MI: Zondervan Publishing House, 1967.

Calvin, John. Calvin's Commentaries.
Grand Rapids, MI: Baker Book House.

Davis, J.D. Illustrated Davis Dictionary of the Bible.
Nashville, TN: Royal Publishers, 1973.

DeGraaf, S.G. Promise and Deliverance, Vol. I.
Ontario, Canada: Paideia Press, 1977.

Douglas, J.D. The New Bible Dictionary.
Wheaton, IL: Tyndale Press, 1982.

Encyclopedia Britannica. 1898 edition.
The Werner Company, 1898.

Frank, Harry Thomas, ed. Hammond Atlas of the Bible Lands.
Maplewood, NJ: Hammond Inc., 1977.

Hall, Terry. Bible Panorama.
Wheaton, IL: Victory Books, 1983.

Halley, H.H. Halley Bible Handbook.
Chicago, IL: Halley, 1927.

Harrison, Everett F. & Pfeiffer, Charles F., ed. The Wycliffe Bible Commentary. Chicago, IL: Moody Press, 1976.

References

Hovey, Bill. New Testament Time Line.
Time Line Resource, 1974.

International Standard Bible Encyclopedia.
Grand Rapids, MI: Eerdmans Publishing Co., 1939.

Morris, William, ed. The American Heritage Dictionary of the English Language. Boston, MA: Houghton-Mifflin Company, 1980.

Ryrie, Charles. The Ryrie Study Bible.
Chicago, IL: Moody Press, 1976.

Scofield, C.I. New Scofield Reference Bible.
New York, NY: Oxford University Press, 1967.

Strong, James. Strong's Concordance.
Iowa Falls, IA: Riverside Book and Bible.

Vine, W.E. Vine's Expository Dictionary.
Old Tappan, NJ: Fleming H. Revell, 1981.

Wemp, C. Sumner. Teaching from the Tabernacle.
Chicago, IL: Moody Press, 1976.

Whitcomb, John C., Jr. Old Testament Patriarchs and Judges. 1965.

List of Illustrations

List of Illustrations